D0016237

EVERYTHING YOU WANTED TO KNOW ABOUT INDIANS BUT WERE AFRAID TO ASK

YOUNG READERS EDITION

ALSO BY ANTON TREUER

The Indian Wars:
Battles, Bloodshed, and the Fight for Freedom on the American Frontier

The Assassination of Hole in the Day

Warrior Nation:
A History of the Red Lake Ojibwe

Atlas of Indian Nations

The Language Warrior's Manifesto:
How to Keep Our Languages Alive No Matter the Odds

EVERYTHING YOU WANTED TO KNOW ABOUT INDIANS BUT WERE AFRAID TO ASK

YOUNG READERS EDITION

ANTON TREUER

LEVINE QUERIDO
MONTCLAIR • AMSTERDAM • NEW YORK

This is an Arthur A. Levine book

Published by Levine Querido

www.levinequerido.com • info@levinequerido.com

Levine Querido is distributed by Chronicle Books LLC

Based on the book *Everything You Wanted to Know About Indians But Were Afraid to Ask,* by Anton Treuer, published by the Minnesota Historical Society Press, 2012.

Library of Congress Control Number: 2020937517

ISBN 978-1-64614-045-9

Printed and bound in China

Published April 2021

First Printing

For my son, Evan—the navigator.
You are the one you've been looking for.
The world is your map and the compass is inside you.

CONTENTS

INTRODUCTION: AMBASSADOR 1

TERMINOLOGY **11**

What general terms are most appropriate for talking about North America's first people?
What terms are *not* appropriate for talking about North America's first people?
What terms are most appropriate for talking about each tribe?
How do I know how to spell all these complicated terms?
What term is most appropriate—*band, reservation, tribe,* or *nation*?
What does the word *powwow* mean?
How can I find out the meanings of the place names around me that come from Indigenous languages?

HISTORY **27**

How many Indigenous people were in North and South America before contact?
When did Natives really get to North America?
Why does it matter when Natives got here?
What do Natives say about their origins?

Who else made it here before Columbus?
Did Natives scalp?
Why did Natives scalp?
Were Natives more violent than Whites?
Did Indians practice polygamy? Do they now?
What were historic Native views about homosexuality?
How was gender configured in Native communities?
Do Indigenous people in Canada get treated more fairly by their government than those in the United States?
What is the real story of Columbus?
Why does getting the Columbus story right matter?
Why are some people trying to change Columbus Day to Indigenous Peoples' Day?
What is the real story of Thanksgiving?
What is the real story of Pocahontas?
Who was Ely Parker?
What did Pontiac do?
Why is Tecumseh such a famous Native?
When did the U.S. government stop making treaties with Indians and why?
Why do some people use the word *genocide* in discussing the treatment of Indians?
What is the Doctrine of Discovery?
What was the historic relationship between Christian missionaries and Native people?
Were Indians ever slaves?
Was the swastika an Indigenous symbol before the Nazis used it?
How was killing off the bison related to the Indian wars?
Did Indians ever keep slaves?

RELIGION, CULTURE, & IDENTITY 83

Why do Indians have long hair?
Do Indians live in tipis?
What is fasting and why do Indians do it?
What are clans and do all Indians have them?
Where are the real Indians?
What does *traditional* mean?
Aren't all Indians traditional?
Why is it called a *traditional Indian fry bread taco*?
What is Indian time?
What are Indian cars?
I thought that Indians have a strong sense of ecological stewardship, so why do I also see a lot of trash in some yards?
Are Natives at the front of environmental activism, or is that a stereotype?
If Indians respect the environment, how come the Makah hunt endangered whales?
Do Indians have a stronger sense of community than non-Indians?
How are different gender identities and roles viewed in Native communities today?
What is life like for LGBTQ Natives today?
What's your perspective on Christian missionaries today?
Are a lot of Natives Christian today?
Is it true that the Pueblo and some other tribes combine Christian and traditional Native practices?
What is Indian religion?
Why do Indians use tobacco for ceremonies?
What are kachinas?

It seems like Indians have a deeper spiritual connection than people in many religious traditions. Is that true?
What is meant by Native "ways of knowing"?
What are some of the customs related to dating and marriage?
What happens when a Native and a non-Native person date?
What are some of the customs related to pregnancy and childbirth?
What are naming ceremonies?
Can a non-Native person get an Indian name?
What are coming-of-age ceremonies?
How come everyone's laughing at a traditional Indian funeral?
Do Indians charge for participation in their ceremonies?
What is a sweat lodge?
Do Indians still get persecuted for their religious beliefs?
What sports are most popular for Natives today?
What music is most popular for Natives today?
Why do Indians have so many kids?

POWWOW 145

What is a powwow?
What do the different styles of dance mean?
Why are "49" songs sung in English?
How come there are prize purses at powwows?
Can non-Native people dance at powwows?
Do women sing at powwows?
What is the protocol for gifts at powwows?

TRIBAL LANGUAGES **161**

How many tribal languages are spoken in the Americas?
Which tribal languages have a chance to be here a hundred years from now?
Why are fluency rates higher in Canada?
It seems like tribal languages won't give Native people a leg up in the modern world. Why are they important to Indians?
Why should tribal languages be important to everyone else?
What are the challenges to successfully revitalizing tribal languages?
When were tribal languages first written down?
Many tribal languages were never written. Why are they written now?
Why is it funnier in Indian?
How do tribal languages encapsulate different worldviews?
Why don't tribes do more to support language and culture?

POLITICS **175**

What is sovereignty?
Why do Natives have reservations or First Nations?
Why isn't being American or Canadian enough? Why do Indians need reservations today?
If Natives in the United States and Canada have their own nations, how did they become United States or Canadian citizens?
What is a non-federally-recognized tribe?
What's it like for Natives who aren't part of a recognized tribe?
What is the status of Alaska Natives?

Why do Indians have treaty rights? What other rights do they have that differ from those of most people in the United States?
What is allotment?
What is clouded title?
Is something being done about clouded title?
If tribes had hereditary chiefs, how come there is a democratic process for selecting tribal leaders in most places today?
What's the Indian Reorganization Act?
Do Indians ever work together politically and economically?
Why do so many Indians live in urban areas today? What is relocation?
What is life like for urban Indians today?
What is termination?
Why do Indians have their own police and courts in some places?
Why does the FBI investigate murders on some reservations?
Why do state law enforcement agencies investigate murders on some reservations? What is Public Law 280?
Don't tribes ever investigate murders on Indian land themselves?
Should Leonard Peltier be freed?
Was the American Indian Movement good or bad?
What is the Indian Child Welfare Act?
What is blood quantum, what is tribal enrollment, and how are they related?
How has tribal enrollment affected you personally?
What's it like for Natives who don't look Native?
How come some tribes ban the use and sale of alcohol?
Do all Indians have drinking problems?
Is there a solution to substance abuse in Indian country?

Why did COVID-19 kill so many people at Navajo Nation and other reservations?
Why are Indian politics often such a vipers' pit?
I heard that a lot of Indians serve in the U.S. military. How do they reconcile their service with the fact that the U.S. Army killed so many of their people?
What's it like for Natives who serve in the U.S. military today?
How do Indians feel about the use of Geronimo as the code name for Osama bin Laden?
What do you think about some tribes trying to legalize marijuana?
Do Indians vote Democrat or Republican?
Are things getting better for tribes?

ECONOMICS **239**

Do Indians get a break on taxes and if so, why?
Do Indians get a break on license plates?
Why should Indians be eligible for welfare if they are not taxed the same way as everyone else?
Are Indians all living in extreme poverty?
Are Indians all rich from casinos?
How has casino gambling affected Indian communities?
How have per capita payments affected Indian communities?
What is the future of Indian gaming?
Are tribes affected by many states legalizing gaming in non-Native spaces?
What should tribes be doing to improve the economic condition of their citizens?

EDUCATION **255**

What were Native residential boarding schools?
How come 50 percent of Indians are flunking their state-mandated tests in English and math?
Is there anything that works in the effort to bridge the achievement gap for Native students?
How does education policy affect Indian country?
Do Indians all have a free ride to college?
What are some myths and stereotypes about Natives?
Is anyone getting it right in Indian education?

SOCIAL ACTIVISM **271**

Why was the Dakota Access Pipeline protest such a big deal?
Do Indians face racial profiling from law enforcement?
What do Natives think about the Black Lives Matter movement?
How are Natives building bridges with other groups to fight racism?
What do Natives think about social activism in Latinx and other non-White communities?
Do Natives in Canada, South America, and the United States ever work together or communicate about shared struggles?
What happened at the confrontation at the Lincoln Memorial in 2019 and why does it matter?
Why is there so much concern about mascots?
Why is there such a fuss about non-Native people wearing Indian costumes for Halloween?
How come the Johnny Depp cologne commercial made so many Natives so mad?

Why is there such a fuss about public art, statues, and place names now?
Why is there so much advocacy about missing and murdered Indigenous women?
Does being Native make you worry about your safety or the safety of your family?

PERSPECTIVES: COMING TO TERMS AND FUTURE DIRECTIONS 309

Why are Indians so often imagined rather than understood?
As a White person, I don't feel privileged. So what do Indians mean by that term?
What do you think about the #MeToo movement and its impact on Sherman Alexie's career?
Why don't tribes solve their own problems?
All these problems are not my fault. Why should I be asked to atone for the sins of my ancestors?
Is there anything wrong with saying that some of my best friends are Indians?
Is there something wrong with saying that my great-grandmother was a Cherokee princess?
I might have some Indian ancestry. How do I find out?
Are DNA tests changing how people connect to tribes?
What do Natives think about Elizabeth Warren's Native ancestry?
Why is that picture *End of the Trail* so popular in Indian country?
How do Canadian First Nations people feel about the Truth and Reconciliation Commission findings?
What do you think about land acknowledgments?

Regarding casinos and treaty rights, I'm not racist, but it doesn't seem fair to me. What's wrong with that line of thinking?
I'm not racist, but it all happened in the past. Why can't Indians just move on?
Why do Indian people often seem angry?
How are social media and smartphones affecting life in Indian country?
What are some good books to read about Indians?
What do Natives think about books by non-Natives that have Native content?
Are there any good Indian movies?
Have you ever been the object of direct racial discrimination?
You're a testament to your race. How did you turn out so good?
How can I learn more?

CONCLUSION:
FINDING WAYS TO MAKE A DIFFERENCE **341**

RECOMMENDED READING 352
NOTES 356
PHOTO CREDITS 365
ACKNOWLEDGMENTS 367
INDEX 369

INTRODUCTION

AMBASSADOR

No matter what they ever do to us, we must always act for the love of our people and the earth. We must not react out of hatred against those who have no sense.

—John Trudell

Indians. We are so often imagined, but so infrequently well understood.

I grew up in a borderland. My family moved a couple times, but we usually lived on or near the Leech Lake Reservation in northern Minnesota. I went to school in the nearby town of Bemidji with plenty of other Native kids and many more Whites. The town is more diverse now, but in the 1970s and 1980s, it was almost entirely Whites and Indians. The town is surrounded by the three largest reservations in Minnesota (in land size and number of people), but the Native and non-Native worlds rarely interacted. The school took kids on field trips to Minneapolis, 225 miles away, rather than to the neighboring Native communities. Many Whites were scared of Indians and few had a chance to learn about Native Americans, so White folk usually just stuck to their imaginings. Many Indians were scared of Whites too (I know I was), so the disconnection cut both ways.

That borderland I grew up in was more than an awkward mix of races and communities. It was a divided and confusing place politically, legally, intellectually, and culturally. The tribes maintained their own governments and rarely got involved in the American political process, especially at the local level. And no outsider ever felt like they had any authority to ask about, much less comment on or participate in, anything happening on the rez. The web of contradictory jurisdictions and agencies that dealt with criminal affairs and Indian land never made much sense to anyone of any race.

Native Americans hadn't written many books, and school districts and the general public were not open to Vine Deloria, Jr. and the few other "radical" Indians who had actually managed to get anything in print. Most of the elders on the rez had gone to government-run residential boarding schools. Their children (the parental generation of my youth) often did not trust the government or schools as a result. Educators and administrators resented the parents' absence from school conferences and the truancy of many Native students, but nobody talked about the bigger issues, which sat like a giant bear in the corner of the room every time the schools and Native families interacted. My family and every one of my uncles and aunts harvested wild rice, snared rabbits, and made maple syrup every year, but most of my non-Native peers did not.

As a young person, I had several painful experiences with overt racial discrimination, but I also made some great friends in high school. Many were White. I was truly inspired by my history teacher, Thomas Galarneault, whose lectures and support contributed to my lifelong interest in education and history. I was encouraged by Marlene Bergstrom in the guidance office. And I was a great student. But the borderland remained a bramble on every level. I was tired of the tension, the confusion, and the mean-spirited statements of my peers about "drunken Indians." I applied to Princeton University on a whim and surprised everyone, from my peers to my parents and especially myself, when I got in. I had found a way out—or so I thought.

At college, I was looking forward to a breath of fresh air and a break from the borderland of my youth as much as I was to the challenges of a new stage of life. And those years remain some of my most treasured. But I still had a profoundly well-educated Princetonian ask me, "Where is your tomahawk?" Another time, a woman approached me in the college gymnasium and exclaimed, "You have the most beautiful red skin." I was too shocked to respond. I took a friend to see *Dances with Wolves* and was told, "Your people have a beautiful culture." My people come from the Great Lakes rather than the Plains and from the modern age rather than the 1800s, but again, I had no response. I made many lifelong friends at college, and they supported but also challenged me with questions like "Why should Indians have reservations?"

By my junior year, I realized I had not escaped the borderland. No matter how far I traveled, the haze engulfed everyone I met. Indians were imagined, not understood. And there were few resources and opportunities to do anything about it. I wanted to come home.

Homesick though I was, I was *not* going to be another statistic by dropping out of school. I decided to finish college, but started a quest to learn more about myself. I didn't want to run from the borderland. I wanted to understand it better and do something to make it easier for others to traverse.

While at Princeton, I heard that a Comanche medicine woman named Barrett Eagle Bear was coming to New Jersey from Texas to run sweat lodge ceremonies. The Comanche are from Texas and Oklahoma, and it's a little strange for Natives to run ceremonies outside of their home region. I was just smart enough to know that this person could be an impostor, but I was too hungry for a taste of home to care. I drove out to the wooded area where she would conduct her ceremony and found, to my great surprise, over fifty naked White people standing among the trees, waiting. One man was holding a staff adorned with a pair of deer antlers and chicken feathers. Part of me wanted to laugh because there were fifty naked White people standing in the woods. Part of me wanted to run away. There were fifty naked people standing in the woods. And part of me was furious at what looked like a bunch of White people playing Indian. This was not real. I started to doubt whether Eagle Bear was even Indian for allowing the charade. I kept thinking, "Is this what they think we are all about?" Being naïve, I opened the car door. I was immediately folded into a tight embrace by one of these naked strangers, who was hugging me—hard—saying, "I am so sorry for what my people have done to your people." Awkward. Now the desire to laugh, run, or get mad only grew.

Throughout my life, if I have ever thought or said that I have seen it all, I am soon shown something new. I carefully separated myself from the embrace of this naked stranger and looked at her face. She was an elder and seemed to be filled with genuine remorse, on the verge of tears. Respect was a value deeply embedded in my being from my upbringing and cultural experience. Lines on her face showed the wisdom of age and experience. I couldn't laugh. And I couldn't just yell at her, or give her a mean look and drive away. In a flash, my running from the borderland and my desire to find a way for others to travel through it brought me an epiphany.

I was not just another Indian. No Indian really is. Because we are so often imagined and so infrequently understood, I was (both unfairly and rightly) an ambassador for my people. If the misunderstandings that made growing up Native so frustrating for me were ever to be remedied, I would have to do my part to shine some light on the brambles and try to clear a path for others. As that old woman looked up at me, I knew I was probably the first

Indian she had ever met, and, though it wasn't fair to anyone, my reaction would be a testament to the character of my entire race. So I didn't laugh. I didn't rise to anger. I didn't call her out or drive away. I very politely said, "Could you put some clothes on? I would love to talk to you about all of this."

She put some clothes on. And we talked. I explained that for ceremonies at home we usually covered up in the presence of others, especially with both men and women present. We discussed the ceremony, geography, custom, and practice. We talked about history. I explained my feeling that guilt for Whites and anger for Indians did nothing to make the world a better place, especially for the people stuck with such emotions, understandable though they are. The secret was to turn anger and guilt into positive action.

She really listened and she learned a few things. In a weird way too, I got an education—from a naked stranger in the New Jersey woods. I learned something about the borderland. A real conversation requires safe space, an opportunity for genuine connection, and authentic, reliable information. And I learned something about myself. I had a place in that confusing borderland as someone who could shape his own story and impact other people for the better. I was an ambassador in a troubled place with the potential to make meaningful change.

When I commit to something, I always go all the way. The decks on my house could withstand an earthquake measuring 6.0 on the Richter scale. I have nine children. I take my job as role model for my children and ambassador for my people seriously. I don't drink alcohol—not because I am a recovering addict (I have never inhaled anything, or blacked out or vomited from drink) but because I want to send a message to my own people and to others. I want to challenge stereotypes about what it means to be Native. Abstaining is also important to the people whom I now serve at ceremonies: they are looking for a clean, sober place to heal, relying upon the integrity of the people who help at those ceremonies to provide that environment.

I gave up on my early plans of becoming an investment banker or lawyer. I never would have been happy in those roles. Instead, I graduated from Princeton with plans to walk the earth, which I did successfully for several months before I had to take a job. And then I dedicated myself to the pursuit of my tribal language, culture, and history. I eventually went to graduate school and entered academia. Through it all, I maintained one foot in the wigwam and one in the ivory tower, but I still see the borderland every day out my bedroom window. It is always an education not just about the world we live in, but about myself.

This book is designed for young readers as a tool to help all of us navigate this borderland. I originally published *Everything* with the Minnesota Historical Society Press, and it sold better than any of us could have hoped. I have expanded the topics here, with a lot more information on social activism and current events, and I have framed everything as best I can for a younger audience. Readers can read straight through, check out sections of personal interest, or use the table of contents and index to find answers to specific questions. I want this work to provide a place for people to get answers. It offers a first step to dispel erroneous imaginings and develop deeper understandings. Although curriculum is constantly under revision in public schools, we still have a long way to go to make it easy for Native and non-Native peoples to learn about Indian history, culture, and current events. Eighty-seven percent of America's schools don't require instruction on anything about Native Americans after the year 1900.[1]

This book and its format first emerged as part of the question-and-answer sessions that followed the many lectures I've given across the continent, on a variety of subjects. Within these safe spaces, people raised a lot of questions. A friend of mine, Michael Meuers, eventually suggested the title of this book as the headline for some of my public lectures. Since then, the appeal of this subject has grown, bringing me all over the United States and Canada to conduct teacher trainings and give public speeches.

Before launching into the questions and answers that form the guts of this book, I want to make one disclaimer. Just as no White person can speak for all White people, I cannot speak for all Indians. It would be unfair to ask, "What do all White people think about abortion?" Of course, there is a diversity of opinion on that and every other subject. It is the same for Indians. I have a house full of Natives and I don't even know what they are thinking half the time. But my experiences have taught me what questions people have about Indians, and I am motivated to pull those questions together here and address them. I often write about the Ojibwe, because that is the tribal experience I know best, and in many cases you will gain specific rather than generic answers. But I also provide examples and information about many of the hundreds of other Indian nations that populate this continent.

Some of the current issues I engage—including identity, tribal citizenship, casinos, mascots, and cultural revitalization—evoke strong and differing responses from Native people. I openly share my opinions, and they are thoughtful, well informed, and based on rich and detailed experience. But they are opinions, and I have taken care to make the difference between fact and opinion clear to you. I do not claim to represent "the Native view" in this book. My responses reflect the views of one Native person, and they have to be read with this understanding. As you read deeper into this work, I hope that you will feel motivated to seek out different opinions from other Native people.

I have also been really heartened by the response this book has had in the Native community. I originally wrote it trying to help the rest of the world understand us. But all Natives get bombarded with the same questions, and we need answers too. All Native people can speak to their own experiences of growing up and living Native lives. But I was raised by a Native woman with a law degree who became a tribal judge, and, coming out of high school, I would have been hard-pressed to explain tribal sovereignty to you. I think a lot of us feel this way about our own history. We went to the same schools as everyone else and got the same sugarcoated version of Christopher Columbus and the first

Thanksgiving as everyone else. That this work has been helping Native people understand their own history, culture, and experience in new ways is very gratifying. The material in this Young Readers Edition is intentionally designed for both Native and non-Native kids to deepen their understanding and help build a better world for all of us.

Thank you for taking the time to read this book. I hope that it will make a contribution to breaking down barriers and advancing everyone's ability to understand themselves and one another.

TERMINOLOGY

When asked what Indians called North America before Columbus arrived, noted scholar Vine Deloria, Jr., simply replied, "Ours."

What general terms are most appropriate for talking about North America's first people?

In Canada, after a long, inclusive, national discussion, most Indigenous people there settled on the term *First Nation* to describe themselves. They stopped calling their communities *Reserves* and starting calling them *First Nations.* To clarify the distinct identities of the Inuit and Métis in Canada, *First Nation* was not applied to the Inuit or Métis, but only to those formerly officially called *Indian* in Canada. Indigenous people stopped referring to themselves as *Aboriginal* or *Indian* and started calling themselves *First Nations people.* The Canadian government made it official policy and the change is universally accepted. The confusion and controversy are gone. Personally, I really like this. The decision-making process involved everyone, and even though there were a lot of different opinions, they arrived at a term everyone could get behind and use. Furthermore, the federal and provincial governments in Canada formally accepted the change in terminology and it was applied across the country. The process and the term itself are inclusive. The term speaks to the indigeneity of the first people of the land and their sovereignty as nations, and the process of having First Nations people come up with the term was empowering.

I'd love to see us do something like that in the United States as well—maybe *Native Nation* instead of *First Nation,* just to distinguish the American label from the Canadian one. The problem in the United States is that there is no established inclusive process for making such a decision. Some organizations, like the Native American Rights Fund, have doubled down on *Native American,* and the term *Native American* or simply *Native* is politically correct—unlikely to be directly challenged. But *Native* can be unclear. If I say "a Milwaukee native," it's not clear if I'm talking about a Native American person from Milwaukee or someone of any race who was born and raised there. Native American is usually less ambiguous than Native, but not for everyone. And the term itself is more recent and is not for everyone. *Indigenous* has been used by a lot of Natives lately, and it's nice because it's inclusive of Indigenous people all over the planet—and there is affinity between different Indigenous groups. But it also lacks specificity. So, we end up being forced to use a lot of syllables again by saying "North American Indigenous person." In written forms, we have begun to capitalize *Native* or *Indigenous,* and that is the trend now, to distinguish this group of people from broader categories, but that still doesn't solve the problem when we are talking. Other groups, like the American Indian Movement and the National Congress of American Indians, have doubled down on *American Indian.*

The word *Indian* comes from a mistake: on his first voyage to the Americas, Columbus thought the Caribbean was the Indian Ocean and the people there were Indians. Columbus's use of the word and his assumptions about it are well documented in his writings and those of other Spanish officials who accompanied him on the voyage and corresponded with him. People as varied as Russell Means, Peter Matthiessen, George Carlin, and a few others have claimed that the word *Indian* is actually derived from the Spanish phrase *una gente in Dios* (people of God). But Columbus never used that phrase in reference to any people in the Americas.[2] Use of the word *Indian* had nothing to do with the words *in Dios*. It was a mislabeling based on Columbus's confusion about where he was when he first arrived in the Americas—and it stuck, even after the mistake was well known in Europe.

I use the terms *Indian, Native, Native American,* and *Indigenous* in this book intentionally and with full knowledge of their shortcomings and the risk that some of them are confusing or even give some people offense. There is no way to solve the terminology debates to everyone's satisfaction right now, and it is even more important to make safe space for everyone to start asking questions. I also find Sherman Alexie's remark resonant: "The White man tried to take our land, our sovereignty, and our languages. And he gave us the word 'Indian.' Now he wants to take the word 'Indian' away from us too. Well, he can't have it."[3] I have more on Sherman Alexie himself later in the book.

Because terminology is not settled—even Natives can't agree on a word to use—I also recommend that young people initiate discussion with their peers and schools about appropriate labels, especially if you have Indigenous friends and classmates. Remember that Indigenous people may look brown, White, or Black, because so many of us are racially mixed. Many schools have a Native American Parent Committee, for example, and they really appreciate student input.

That's a great place to talk about this subject. I have seen high school students petition for terminology decisions at their schools and even for changing the names of towns and lakes. They have made meaningful and permanent changes to adult discussions and the maps we all use. Such efforts can be very empowering and helpful. They are especially effective if you directly engage Native people around you, rather than letting other people decide things for them. If you do this, you can always tell anyone who ever gives you a hard time about the terms you use, "We are following the advice of Native people in our community on terminology." That way you don't have to tell someone they are wrong and you can know your Native community has your back.

As much as possible, we should all use the terms each tribe uses for self-reference: they are authentic and loaded with empowered meaning. You can always call Dakota people Dakota and Oneida people Oneida. (Tribes may also have terms to refer to other individual tribes, or more than one tribal group in general, but using a different tribe's word for another group can sound ethnocentric to members of other tribes, since each tribe has their own language and words.) Regardless of all decisions about labels, however, it is most critically important that we respect one another and create an environment in which it is safe to ask any thoughtful question without fear. The only way to arrive at a deeper understanding is to make it acceptable to ask anything you wanted to know about Indians, but were afraid to ask, and get a meaningful answer rather than an angry admonition.

What terms are *not* appropriate for talking about North America's first people?

It's important that fear of sounding ignorant or racist not paralyze communication about Indians. Knowing what terms to use and which to avoid can help ease that fear. Most Native people frown on use of the words *squaw, brave, redskin,* and *papoose.* These words create distance, employ hurtful clichés to point out difference, and say clearly that "those people" are not normal.

Squaw is considered particularly offensive. The true origins of the word are a subject of some debate. Some Indian activists have asserted that it is a corruption of a Mohawk word for female genitalia, although that theory has been debunked by linguist Ives Goddard and others.[4] Others assert that it is derived from the Cree word for woman, *iskwe,* or its Ojibwe variant, *ikwe.* Considering the word was first used by the French (who had a lot of interaction with the Cree, Ojibwe, and other tribes from the Algonquian language family), this seems more likely. The words in Massachusett and other Algonquian languages on the Atlantic Seaboard are quite similar to Cree and may also be the more likely origins of the word's transfer to English. Regardless of origin, *squaw* has often been used as a negatively value-laden term, and most Native people find it insulting. Sexual assault rates in America for women in general are 25 percent, but they are 50 percent for Native women.[5] Most crime in America is White-on-White, Black-on-Black, and so forth, but crimes of sexual violence directed at Native women are mainly perpetrated by White men.[6] So the derogatory term and being "treated like a squaw" are intensely personal and painful to a majority of Native people. Most special terms for minority women (Negress, Jewess) have similar perceptions. There is ongoing work to change many place names (Squaw Valley, Squaw Lake, etc.) into something less offensive, but those efforts are often met with resistance.

It used to be easy for non-Native people to ignore Indigenous views. We are a small percentage of the population and don't occupy a lot of positions of power in the media or politics outside of our tribes. But social media has completely changed the way we communicate and its impacts. A few years ago, my brother moved to California and was shopping when he ran across a loaf of bread for sale named "Squaw Bread." This is actually a thing in the American West, but we had never seen it in Minnesota. He thought, "What the heck?" He took a picture and texted it to me. I thought, "What the heck?" And I posted it to Facebook. I am maxed out on Facebook friends at 5,000-plus followers. They said, "What the heck?" And my Facebook feed started to blow up.

I realized that the maker of the bread, Old Town Baking Company, had a Facebook page of their own, so I tagged them in the post. The conversation quickly moved to their Facebook page, and it made them very uncomfortable. They really should have responded by saying,

"We are sorry. We had no idea this caused offense. We will reevaluate the label at our next meeting." But they didn't. They started cleaning their Facebook page—deleting criticism and leaving all defensive posts about their bread. So, I created a new Facebook page called "Old Town Baking Company: Squaw Bread Needs a New Name." The conversation moved there. Within a couple of days, the owners were on the local television station, in the newspaper, and online saying what they should have said in the first place: "We are sorry. We had no idea this caused offense. Please send us your recommendations so we can change the name of our bread."

We still get ignored. We still get imagined. We still get resistance. But the world is changing quickly. And there is increasingly a price to pay for those who insist on being on the wrong side of history.

What terms are most appropriate for talking about each tribe?

Each tribe has its own terms of self-reference. Finding the appropriate labels can be confusing because the tribal terms of self-reference are not necessarily those employed by the U.S. or Canadian governments. Sometimes they are not even the same as the terms used by tribal governments. And the preferences of Indigenous people vary from person to person as much as they do for anyone else.

The Ojibwe are a good example of this. The word *Chippewa,* frequently used in reference to the Ojibwe, is actually a corruption of *Ojibwe.* Europeans frequently missed subtleties of Ojibwe pronunciation, hardening sounds and omitting letters. The soft *j* was written down as *ch,* and the soft *b* was written as *p.* The *o* was not even written, and the *e* was written as a short *a.* There have been many spellings. But the term *Chippewa* was used by the U.S. government and never changed. Even today, the Bureau of Indian Affairs (the agency that deals with Indians) uses *Chippewa.* Furthermore, the term was used in the constitutions of all Ojibwe reservations in America because those documents were drafted by the U.S. government, rather than by tribal people.

Tribal advocacy for the word *Ojibwe* is slowly winning out now, however, as many reservations officially use it for their tribal names and revised constitutions. (Constitutional reform is touchy for all governments—tribal, state, and federal—because of issues like tribal enrollment, so even when tribal people support terminology change, making the change is harder than it should be.) To compound things further, though, Ojibwe people today use the term *Ojibwe* as a tribally specific term for self-reference (Ojibwe only) but also use *Anishinaabe* to refer to all Indians—Ojibwe, Dakota, and others. The word *Anishinaabe* is used as commonly as *Ojibwe* by tribal members in everyday conversation, which has led to some confusion about their distinctions, but *Ojibwe* is tribally specific and *Anishinaabe* includes all tribes.

For most tribes, there is one tribal term of self-reference and one other term, either corrupted from the original or entirely foreign. Sometimes those corrupted terms are more common than the more accurate ones tribes and tribal people use. Such is the case for the people the Spanish called *Navajo* but who call themselves *Diné.* Early European explorers named the tribal groups they saw, often ignoring the people's own names for themselves. This happened for the Ho-Chunk, whom the Ojibwe called *Wiinibiigoog* (meaning "people of the muddy water"), which the French corrupted into *Winnebago.*

Dialect differences within a tribal group sometimes cause confusion as well. The people called *Sioux* really comprise three major language groupings—Dakota, Nakota, and Lakota—who formed an alliance known as the *Oceti Sakowin* (Seven Council Fires). But the Dakota are not the Lakota; calling them Sioux or Oceti Sakowin still leaves outsiders unsure of which group is being discussed because this name applies to seven different Dakota, Nakota, and Lakota groups (and the Lakota further diversified into seven more bands). Additionally, the word *Sioux* itself is a French corruption of the Ojibwe term *Naadowesiwag* (a species of snake), which was a code word for "enemy" and often frowned upon by Dakota tribal members. But sometimes scholars and even tribal members use the term *Sioux* as an easy one-syllable way to speak about the entire grouping in spite of the issues with the term.

How do I know how to spell all these complicated terms?

It is usually best to use the preferred spelling of each reservation's tribal governments (*Potawatomi, Menominee, Ottawa, Assiniboine,* and *Ho-Chunk,* for example).[7] Sometimes tribal government spellings do not reflect the preferred spellings of tribal members or linguists, but they are still your safest bet. Tribal governments are elected by the tribal membership, and even though they sometimes move slowly in making decisions, they usually reflect the will of the people on matters like this. Most tribes now keep up-to-date websites that list preferred names and spellings.

What term is most appropriate—*band, reservation, tribe,* or *nation*?

Before Europeans tried to colonize Indians, none of these labels were used by Indians to describe themselves. Those words meant something to Europeans, not to Natives. But that changed over time. There was a lot of diversity in North America when Europeans first arrived. There still is. The Aztec Empire had massive cities and 10 million citizens. Their society was highly structured and perhaps the closest thing to what Europeans called a *nation* or *empire*. But the majority of tribes in the Americas were smaller and simply called themselves *the people*. Most lived in villages, and the village was the primary social and political unit in their lives. Even populous tribes like the Ojibwe, who occupied millions of acres of territory, did not function as a single political group. Each village was independent. Today there are over 200 Ojibwe villages (over half of them in Canada and the rest in the United States), but there were even more during the treaty period (in the 1800s). And the Ojibwe were one of around 500 Indian tribes in North America. The

Lakota, Cree, Navajo, and many other tribes had similar dynamics.

Colonial powers, especially the British and Americans, wanted to simplify the politics so they could get Indian land faster. That process started with the construction of new labels for Native communities that in turn drove the evolution of new Indian political structures. Instead of making hundreds of treaties with each and every Ojibwe village, the U.S. government summoned numerous chiefs from many villages in a region to a treaty conference and called them the chiefs of a certain *band*. The concept of band was as new as the label to the Ojibwe, but once the political process began, the label and the concept stuck.

Even today, the tribal citizenship cards of most Ojibwe people in Minnesota note the person's band—Mississippi, Pillager, Lake Superior, or Pembina, for example. The U.S. government also put the word *band* into the constitutions for many tribes. Sometimes there are two to four bands represented on one reservation. In Washington and Oregon there are sometimes many bands and even many tribes that are confederated together on the same reservation. The concept of band meant a lot at treaty time, and it sometimes matters in land claims cases today, but the label and concept mean little else to most tribal people. The term is not offensive, but it can be confusing.

The word *reservation* was used to talk about the lands that were reserved or set aside for various groups of Indians at treaty time. A reservation is the place that many Native people call home today, and even those who live elsewhere associate strongly with their home reservations. These are the places where most cultural and community events are held and where tribes spend their resources trying to strengthen their communities and prepare for the future.

The word *tribe* gets used two ways: as a label for all people of the same shared cultural group (as for the Blackfeet, who have communities in many places in both the United States and Canada) and also as a word for each reservation's government (as in the Blackfeet Nation, located on the Blackfeet Indian Reservation in Montana). Tribes, or tribal governments, are not just cultural groups. They are governments, and complex laws define their power.

Tribes are in fact *nations.* They make laws, hold elections, administer funds, and interact with other governments. Because tribes are nations, tribal leaders and citizens often emphasize and reinforce their status by use of the word *nation,* and that term is preferred by some tribal people. The words *band, reservation, tribe,* or *nation* are sometimes used interchangeably, and none cause offense, but they all speak to the complicated history and politics in Indian country.

What does the word *powwow* mean?

A Google search will reveal hundreds of thousands of results for *powwow,* but the definitions you find are not the same. The first usage of the term in English occurred in 1624. Most scholars agree that *powwow* is derived from a word in the languages of eastern Algonquian tribes (usually Narragansett or Massachusett) for "spiritual leader." It was later incorrectly used for many types of ceremonial and secular events that involved dancing, and it has been spelled several different ways. There is a lot more on powwows later in this book.

How can I find out the meanings of the place names around me that come from Indigenous languages?

All languages are composed of roots, and those roots are loaded with meaning. In English, most roots come from the language's Latin, Greek, Celtic, and Germanic underpinnings, usually unknown to everyday speakers. But for most people whose first language is their tribal language, the roots of words and their deeper meanings are often known.

For example, the city of Bemidji, Minnesota (my hometown), gets its name from an Ojibwe word, *Bemijigamaag*, meaning "the place where the current cuts across" or "a river runs through it." That word describes the unique geography of the place. Four major watersheds form a continental divide in Bemidji. The Red River watershed flows west and north toward Winnipeg. The Rainy River watershed flows north through the Big Fork River into Rainy River. The Lake Superior watershed flows east. And the Mississippi watershed begins by flowing northwest, pulled toward the Red River watershed, and then north, toward the Rainy River watershed. It then flows east, toward the Lake Superior watershed, before charting its own course southward to the Gulf of Mexico. Bemidji is located on the northernmost point of the Mississippi River. Prior to the building of the power dam on the Mississippi, Lake Bemidji was actually two separate lakes, connected by a shallow stretch of water off of Diamond Point. The Mississippi River did not flow through those two lakes; it simply cut across the corner of the larger one—a very rare geographic feature. The Indigenous population that lived in Bemidji knew all of this, and their understanding is reflected in the name they chose.

Most Indigenous place names have similar deep meanings. Europeans liked to name a lake or village after a person or another place—Georgetown (after George Washington) or New York (after York in England), but they used a lot of Indigenous place names as well. They usually messed something up when writing Indigenous names down, so the spellings and pronunciations are not always perfect matches with the words in tribal languages. To find the deeper meanings of the Indian names for the places in which you live, it is often necessary to do a little research. Fortunately, some great books, like Virgil J. Vogel's *Indian Names in Michigan* and Warren Upham's *Minnesota Place Names,* have done a lot of groundwork to help you understand places in the Great Lakes region. Also, the writings of early explorers, such as Henry Schoolcraft and Frederic Baraga, contain a wealth of information. There are similar books for other parts of the country—ask your local librarian for advice.

HISTORY

The settlement of the North American continent is just as little the consequence of any claim of right in any democratic or international sense; it was the consequence of a consciousness of right, which was rooted solely in the conviction of the superiority and therefore the right of the white race.

—Adolf Hitler, Speech to the Industrie-Klub of Düsseldorf (January 27, 1932)

How many Indigenous people were in North and South America before contact?

Nobody knows the exact number, but most scholars agree that it was at least 90 million.[8] New genetic and archaeological research is giving us more accurate information about how many people there were and the size of the communities and cities in which they lived. Any books published over ten years ago are probably out of date, and anything published before the year 2000 is probably just plain wrong about the size of Native populations pre-contact.

Europeans brought diseases to which Indians had little natural immunity, and those diseases, traveling far faster than Europeans, rapidly depleted the Native population in many places. By the time Europeans were trying to explore the continental United States, the diseases they had brought to the East Coast had already ravaged local tribes. Bartolomé de Las Casas estimated that the Indigenous population of Española, now known as the island of Haiti and the Dominican Republic, was 2 million people. Other Spanish chroniclers during Columbus's first four trips affirm that estimate—all for just one island in the Caribbean. The Spanish also estimated that the Indigenous population within the Aztec Empire was more than 10 million people. Archaeological evidence and early Spanish observations confirm that the capital city of the Aztec Empire was three times larger than the largest city in all of Western Europe at the time (London).

Las Casas believed that the Spanish Empire killed between 40 and 50 million people in Mesoamerica alone.

The East and West coasts of North and South America were very densely populated before contact with Europeans, more so than Western Europe. People in desert regions and the Great Plains were spread out. Conservative estimates of the Indigenous population of the Americas are around 75 million people. Others put the figure over 100 million. I found Charles Mann's book *1491: New Revelations of the Americas Before Columbus* especially convincing.

The higher population estimates are being validated more and more as archaeologists do more work. European settlers chose many of the same sites as did Indians for their major settlements (Green Bay, Toronto, Ottawa, St. Paul, New Orleans, Vancouver, Seattle, San Francisco, Chicago, Milwaukee, New York, Mexico City), making archaeological research in these places more difficult. But new technologies and methods continue to develop, and we will have more and even better answers to this question in years to come.

There were a lot of humans in the Americas before contact with Europe. The idea that the Americas were populated by a few scattered bands of roaming nomads is simply a myth designed to alleviate White guilt about the genocide and theft required to take the land.

When did Natives really get to North America?

Between 45,000 and 11,000 years ago, the buildup of continental ice sheets lowered sea levels and exposed a shelf of land between Alaska and Siberia.[9] Most archaeologists used to believe this was how people came to the Americas, and many still do. But the dates have changed and scholars have a lot of very different ideas about how people made the trip. Many books assert that Indians became the first Native Americans when they arrived here by crossing this land bridge and moving down an "ice-free corridor" into the modern-day United States. Those books point to an archaeological site in Clovis, New Mexico, containing human-made tools used to kill large mammals, as the oldest evidence of humans here around 11,000 years ago.

This theory of human origin in the Americas (usually called the Clovis First Theory) is now being challenged in the scientific community.[10] Research on the Clovis site by Michael Waters, Thomas Stafford, and others has confirmed evidence of humans there between 10,900 and 11,050 years ago. But at Monte Verde in Chile, Mario Pino and Thomas Dillehay found human tool marks on mastodon bones and evidence of human-made structures dating back 13,800 to 14,800 years. At the Meadowcroft Rockshelter in Pennsylvania, James M. Adovasio and other archaeologists have found tools, ceramics, knives, and spear points that are 16,000 to 19,000 years old.

At least fifty other major archaeological sites point to human existence in the Americas between 19,000 to 50,000 years ago. Some sites show evidence of human beings in the Americas *before* the last land bridge connected the continents. Archaeologists are still arguing about the dates and the validity of many sites, but increasingly the scientific community is saying that the Clovis First model of human migration to the Americas is simply wrong. Most scientists now favor the theory that people came to the Americas either by land or by traveling along the Pacific Coast in boats long before the Clovis dates.

Why does it matter when Natives got here?

What those books do not always say, but do imply, is that "we are all immigrants here." That thought has sometimes been used to defend or justify the dispossession and genocide of Natives. Most of the ancient societies we credit for starting "civilization" (Egypt, Phoenicia, Greece, China) are 4,000 to 5,000 years old. There weren't even human beings anywhere in the British Isles 12,000 years ago (the entire area was covered with ice). But there were Indians in the Americas then. No matter how you look at it, Native Americans are not immigrants. They are indigenous to the Americas.

What do Natives say about their origins?

There are Dakota people who know that Indians came from Spirit Lake. There are Hopi people who know that Indians emerged from the center of the earth in Arizona. There are Christians who know that the story printed in the Bible is an accurate description of mankind's arrival in the world. Some of those Christians are Indian, including a Pueblo man who told me that Jesus Christ traveled

North America 2,000 years ago; he was just known by a different name in Pueblo country. I do not point out these differences of belief to deride any of them. It is important to realize how divergent some of the origin beliefs held by Natives are; and it is also critical to know just how strongly they are held.

There are big differences between the origin beliefs of various tribes, but some commonalities too. All North American tribal origin legends describe a spiritual creation. Most say that the place where humans were put on earth by the Great Spirit is in North America, even though different tribes say it happened in different parts of the continent.

In addition to the religion versus science debate, many Indians get upset that their own stories are so easily dismissed by the rest of the world. Tribal wisdom-keepers, elders, spiritual leaders, and ways of knowing are still highly valued and also very valid.

Who else made it here before Columbus?

Seafaring Polynesians definitely made it to South America. The sweet potato, indigenous to the Americas, proliferated throughout Polynesia before Columbus. Words from South American tribal languages traveled to Polynesia, and Polynesian peoples shared boat designs with Indians in Chile. The Vikings also made it to eastern Canada about 500 years before Columbus. Archaeological excavation offers evidence of their visits. The Inuit (Eskimo), Inupiat, Yupik, and Chukchi people are genetically different from other Native Americans. That population spans across the Arctic of North America and Asia, and the genetic and linguistic evidence we have suggests that they arrived much more recently than the rest of the Native American population, though long before Columbus. This is a statement about chronology, not legitimacy. The Indigenous people of the North American Arctic are still indigenous to this continent.

Did Natives scalp?

Yes. Some people think that Europeans introduced scalping in North America as a form of bounty hunting. There isn't a lot of archaeological evidence of scalping before contact with Europeans. However, many historians do not agree. If scalping started in Europe, why was it primarily done in North America? Also, when the French first entered the Great Lakes area, they saw Indians scalping their Indian enemies. Samuel de Champlain, for example, reported meeting the Algonquians at Tadoussac in 1603 when they were celebrating a victory over the Haudenosaunee (Iroquois) and dancing with about a hundred scalps. It's more likely that Europeans knew Indians practiced scalping and tried to change the custom into a bounty system during the French and Indian War, and other conflicts, as a way to encourage Indians to kill one another and to offer proof before being paid. Regardless, we know definitely that Indians did scalp one another from first contact through the middle of the 1800s in some places.[11]

Why did Natives scalp?

In the Great Plains and Great Lakes, where scalping was practiced, Indians did not scalp simply to mutilate their enemies or for bounty until Europeans came. They scalped for different reasons. When someone was killed in war or a raid, it was widely believed that their soul was offended. That offense could get in the way of a dead person's soul traveling to the spirit world. Although each tribe had a different peaceful ceremony to remove the "offense" so their loved ones could go on to the next world when they died, there was another way—by killing an enemy. When an enemy was killed for this purpose, they were typically scalped so that family members could attend a scalp dance and pray their successful warriors had removed the "offense" on their loved ones. They often mourned not just for their family members but for the enemy who was killed. Europeans had a hard time understanding this belief, and in their wars with Native Americans and their wars with one another where they asked Indians for military allegiance, they encouraged scalping as a form of bounty hunting. This started to change the reasons for scalping and made the practice more widespread for a time. It also caused confusion about who started the practice in the first place.

Were Natives more violent than Whites?

No. All humans have a violent past. Everyone has someone somewhere in their family tree who clunked someone over the head and stole their food. But there is no evidence that Native Americans were more warlike or more likely to hurt one another inside their tribes, villages, and families. In fact, while all humans on the planet sometimes fought over territory, resources, or ethnicity, violence did not grow in scale or viciousness until the agricultural age (starting around 10,000 years ago). When it did, the large population centers that grew in the Middle East and Europe saw the largest change. In *Guns, Germs, and Steel,* Jared Diamond describes how these developments in this part of the world led Europeans in particular to conduct a new kind of violence. Instead of just killing people for territory or resources, Europeans started killing people because of their religion and race. Religion and race were not grounds for conflict before the agricultural age. Race was a new concept to humans at that time. And racial and religious divisions of societies were new too. This evolution in Europe set up Europeans to commit the greatest violence in human history. It enabled them to colonize the rest of the world.

Did Indians practice polygamy? Do they now?

Polyandry (a woman having more than one husband at the same time) was rare, but polygyny (a man having more than one wife) was a common practice among many tribes, a custom born of necessity. Men went off to war, traveled under dangerous conditions, went fishing on thin ice, and died younger than did women. As a result, there were significantly fewer men than women in many Native communities. Women had an immense work burden: raising crops, gathering and preserving foods, tanning hides, making clothing, and caring for small children. As a result, in many tribes, men could have multiple wives, but women could have only one husband. Today, we think marriage is about falling in love with the right person, but for most cultures for most of human history, marriage was mainly an economic arrangement. If there were more women than men and women were safer and had an easier time providing for their children by being married, polygamy (the polygyny kind) made sense.

Although Native American polygamy evolved because of work and death dynamics rather than sexual power, the concept became culturally ingrained in many Native communities before contact and persisted long after the start of the treaty period, in the 1800s, when the need for it disappeared. It was more common for a man to marry two or three sisters rather than women from different families.[12] Polygamy started because there were more women than men, but some people, like Ojibwe Chief Hole in the Day, used marriage into different families as a way to gain political power (even though this was the exception rather than the rule). As mortality rates shifted and missionaries began to gain converts, the practice of polygamy was eventually abandoned by most tribes. A few tribes in South America still practice polygamy. Observing the dating habits of Native teenagers, some North American tribal elders joke that some young people didn't get the message that the practice has ended.

What were historic Native views about homosexuality?

Native American views on homosexuality were as varied and intense as those of the general population at the time of contact and remain so today. Today homophobia is just as big a problem in Indian country as it is anywhere else. But the record shows there was a respected and empowered place for homosexual men and lesbian women in historic Indian communities.[13]

Identity can be very complicated. In historic Native communities, sexual identity was perceived as having much less to do with who was having sex with whom and much more to do with how people presented themselves and their

Osh-Tisch (left), a Crow *baté*, or person assigned male at birth who is a woman, and able to take on both traditionally female and male roles.

gender to the world. In many Indian communities, the most common identities other than heterosexual, cis men and women were men who functioned as women in the traditional gendered division of labor and had male sexual partners, and women who functioned as men in all realms of the accepted gender role. The divisions of labor and social duty along gender lines usually left two primary groupings—male and female. A man who functioned as a woman in society usually adopted the customary clothing of women and performed the same duties and work as women. The same was true for women who wore the customary clothing and accepted the work and war duties traditionally reserved for men. Socially and even academically people have sometimes used the label *two-spirit* as a broad category for all nonheterosexual and non-cis-gender identities, even though there is a lot of variation in those identities historically and today.

How was gender configured in Native communities?

Each tribe had its own customs concerning gender, and they varied significantly. Many tribes had a strict gendered division of labor.[14] Women and men each had specific duties and rights. They even wore different types of snowshoes in some tribes.

Indian thinking about gender developed differently than in Europe, where different duties often meant unfair treatment of women. When asked why men and women sat on opposite sides of a ceremonial lodge, Mary Roberts, an elderly Ojibwe woman, explained that it was "to remind us that women and men each own half the lodge."[15] Usually, Indigenous gender roles hinged on balance rather than equality. Often Native women owned the home and had much greater power in marriage and divorce than did women in European societies. But no people on the planet had it perfectly fair. No culture should be romanticized or denigrated; like all others, Indians should be understood and evaluated on their own terms.

Do Indigenous people in Canada get treated more fairly by their government than those in the United States?

Canadian First Nations people have not fared much better than Native Americans. Political and social developments for Natives of both countries have been similar but not the same. The U.S. and Canadian governments both attempted to diminish the status of tribal communities as sovereign nations. Both countries tried to assimilate the Indigenous population. Both countries removed Natives to reservations and sent their children to residential boarding schools (I will say more about these later). Natives in both the United States and Canada are not as safe as non-Natives. Widespread issues of substance abuse and educational disparities plague Native communities on both sides of the border.[16]

There are some differences. Canada is part of the British Commonwealth, and its independence was obtained peacefully rather than by revolution. For Canadian First Nations people, this meant suffering through the colonial regimes of the French and British. Indigenous people in the United States had to suffer through—depending on the place—the colonial regimes of the Russian, Spanish, Dutch, French, British, and, most important, U.S. governments. There were many ugly chapters in each of those colonial regimes, but some of the most intense physical violence was directed by the U.S. government and also state and local militias in the early American frontier age—the famous massacres often portrayed in movies.

Also, the U.S. population is much larger than that of Canada, and 80 percent of Canadians live within fifty miles of the U.S. border. As a result, there are many parts of Canada where the Indigenous population was and still is a regional majority. Some tribal communities in Canada are isolated, requiring a plane or boat for access. This separation has enabled some of these communities to maintain higher rates of fluency in their tribal languages and to rely more upon traditional lifeways, such as hunting, fishing, and trapping, to sustain themselves.

The legal structure of tribal sovereignty is also different in the United States and Canada. In the United States, the status of tribes as independent nations is verified and affirmed in treaty relationships and many court cases, leaving American Indians with a legally recognized and retained sovereignty. Canadian Natives have struggled to have their status as sovereign nations viewed that way or declared legally in provincial or federal courts. Ongoing efforts to affirm the sovereignty of First Nations in Canada have largely focused on political process and constitutional reform. In the United

States, most of those battles have been in the courts and focused on interpreting Native status and rights in the U.S. Constitution, creating another big difference between the statuses of tribes in both countries.

In both the United States and Canada, there are many Indigenous people who are not recognized as Indigenous by their respective national or tribal governments. Some cannot prove a percentage of Indigenous blood for tribal enrollment. In Canada, a distinct status is conferred to the Métis community as well. Most Métis have Indigenous and French blood although a culture that is distinct from both. Some of the Métis feel like they are second-class citizens in the eyes of the national government and the First Nations.

In recent years, Canada has engaged in a national conversation about its treatment of First Nations people and established a Truth and Reconciliation Commission. Through the Commission, Canada determined that they engaged in cultural genocide. There have been some efforts to explore restorative justice since. There is more on the Truth and Reconciliation Commission later in this book. America has yet to even start a conversation like this.

Canadian Natives fared differently, not better. The most essential things that define Indigenous people as distinct groups—language, cultural practice, and belief—are threatened in both places. Many tribes, such as the Blackfeet and Ojibwe, have tribal communities on both sides of the border. Common geography, unifying cultural movements such as the powwow, and similar struggles serve to unify Indigenous people in both places despite the differences in their histories.

What is the real story of Columbus?

The story of Christopher Columbus is one of the best known in history but also one of the most misunderstood. I will try to separate fact from fiction and provide a different perspective on this deservedly famous historic figure.

In order to discuss the importance of Columbus in Indian history, we first have to lay out some background information in European history. In 1492, Spain was in the midst of a longtime trade feud with Portugal, and Portugal was winning. In 1486, the Portuguese explorer Bartolomeu Dias had rounded the Cape of Good Hope. Previously, the only way any European dared travel to India or China was through the Mediterranean and Middle East. In the Mediterranean were numerous pirates and middlemen, whose activities raised prices on trade goods. Once Portuguese traders figured out how to get to Asia by going around the southern end of Africa, they could bring their goods to market at far less expense.

As was customary, the first European country to "discover" a trade route or arrive in a certain "primitive" place claimed possession of that place, that route, and all human inhabitants of the "new" lands. The Portuguese laid claim to traveling around the south end of Africa. By 1498, several years after Columbus's first trip to the Americas, Vasco da Gama made it all the way to India via this route around

Africa, and claimed that the whole route was exclusively Portuguese. At the time, France's and England's navies were both quite weak compared to those of Spain and Portugal.

Spain was also running out of money, the result of staging an inquisition from 1480 to 1492. The depleted Spanish treasury would have a big impact on Columbus and on Indians. In addition, Spain had been busy conquering Muslim towns in the southern Iberian Peninsula. Much of that area had been colonized by powerful nations from northern Africa between 711 and 718. However, by 1492, Spain had finally vanquished its foes and united the peninsula under Spanish rule (except for Portugal). Columbus was funded by the Spanish monarchy mainly because their small investment in his expedition was worth the risk in case Columbus was successful.

Christopher Columbus, as he is known by the Latin spelling of his name, was actually born Cristoforo Colombo, the son of a middle-class Genoese weaver. Although it is widely believed that Columbus was a genius for figuring out that the world was round, this information was common knowledge for all educated Europeans of the day. Understanding of latitude had been developed by Eratosthenes in the year 300 B.C. Eratosthenes also made the first estimate of the circumference of the globe and was accurate to within 2 percent. Knowledge of longitude was developed by Ptolemy in the year A.D. 280. By the year 1000, most educated Europeans knew the earth was round.

Columbus asked the Spanish monarchy to pay for his voyage, make him a Spanish noble, and give him one-tenth of the gold brought back on any trade route he might discover. Amazingly, all of those requests were granted.

He was also lucky. Columbus was trying to travel to India by sailing west and just didn't know that the Americas were between Europe and Asia when going in that direction. The Portuguese and the Spanish staged voyages from different locations—if Columbus had sailed for any country other than Spain, he would probably not have been successful. Spain began most of its exploratory expeditions from the Canary Islands. This departure point enabled Columbus to avoid the westerly trade winds and make it to the Americas. And, while sailors were typically uncomfortable sailing without sight of land for many days, there was no mutiny on Columbus's first voyage.

All of Columbus's original journals, notes, and letters survive today in various archives. We know a lot about what he thought and said. In his first writing for the Spanish monarchs after arriving in the "new world," he wrote, "Should your Majesty command it, all the inhabitants could be taken away to Castile, or made slaves on the island. With 50 men we could subjugate them all and make them do whatever we want."[17]

Columbus first arrived in the Bahamas. He then traveled to Española, what the Spanish called the present-day island of Haiti and the Dominican Republic, where he spent most of his time. As noted earlier, the Spanish estimated the Indigenous population of Española to be around 2 million people. Tribal people there accepted the Spanish as visitors and friends. Communication must have been extremely difficult since the Indians and the Spanish didn't know the same languages, and there were many misunderstandings, including an exchange between Columbus and the principal Taino chief, Guacanagari. Columbus gave the chief a red cape and the chief gave him a tiara. The chief saw this as a fair exchange to cement friendly trade, but Columbus interpreted the gesture as one of submission—that the chief was surrendering his kingdom to the Spanish.

One of Columbus's three ships was damaged and had to be scuttled. As a result, he had to leave thirty-nine sailors behind when he returned to Europe. He brought back with him small gold trinkets, food, and a few Indians. The Indians were captured in secret—they did not come willingly.

Upon reaching Spain, Columbus was received with incredible fanfare. He was granted all the primary requests he'd made before his voyage. He did not acquire large quantities of gold in the Americas. In fact, most of the gold he collected the Taino (Arawak) Indians had traded for with tribes from Mexico. However, Columbus was sure to point out that there were vast quantities of gold to be had at Española and large quantities of resin, spices, and other valuable trade goods.

On Columbus's second voyage to North America, Spain sent a military force, scribes, and other officials. The Spanish were surprised when they arrived at Española. The thirty-nine sailors left behind had all been killed. From their writings, it soon became clear what had happened. They had no food, provisions, or means of subsistence and survived only by the good graces of their Indian hosts. The Spaniards took numerous Indians as enslaved persons, using them to get food, provide shelter, and for sex. Eventually, the Natives grew tired of their maltreatment and killed all thirty-nine. The returning Spanish force, however, saw the killing of their countrymen as unprovoked. The Indians had to be punished.

The Spanish government at Española required all Natives to bring one hawk's bell—about a quarter teaspoon—of gold dust to them four times every year. Chiefs were required to bring ten times that amount. This demand could not be met, however, because of the lack of large, readily available supplies of gold on Española. For failing to meet the gold dust tribute, Indians had their hands chopped off—literally tens of thousands of Indians were killed this way. The Spanish immediately sent their army to round up "renegade" Natives and punish them. The cruelties enacted upon Native people were so severe that many committed suicide by drinking cassava poison rather than submit to maltreatment at the hands of the Spanish.

An image from a curriculum developed by Lifetime Learning Systems, Inc., and employed in the Milwaukee Public Schools system in the 1990s.

Bartolomé de Las Casas, a Jesuit priest and later bishop in the Catholic Church, wrote several books about the "new world." In one of those books he wrote, "The Spanish are treating the Indians not as beasts, for beasts are treated properly at times, but like the excrement in a public square . . . Columbus was at the beginning of the ill usage inflicted upon them."[18]

Las Casas went on to write:

> The Spaniards made bets as to who would split a man in two, or cut off his head at one blow; or they opened up his bowels. They tore babies from their mother's breast by their feet and dashed their

A 16th-century engraving by Theodore de Bry, based on firsthand accounts, of some of the first Spanish voyagers throwing Indians to the dogs.

> heads against the rocks. They speared the bodies of other babes, together with their mothers and all who were before them, on their swords . . . They hanged Indians, and by thirteens, in honor and reverence for our Redeemer and the 12 apostles, and, with fire, they burned the Indians alive . . . I saw all the above things . . . All these did my own eyes witness.[19]

Why does getting the Columbus story right matter?

I have always been amazed that we know so much about Columbus but say so little about the dark side of his story. Columbus kept numerous notes and journals. Las Casas wrote books that detailed Columbus's voyages to the Americas. In spite of all we know, the version of events that we often teach our children is very different from what actually happened. This is starting to change: there are more and more revisions to curricula and better resources available to those who teach it. However, we still have a long way to go to remedy the difference between fact and mythology in our education around Columbus. And we have an even longer way to go in informing our society and changing our politics around the subject. Columbus is seen by many as a hero. There are more places named after Christopher Columbus in the United States of America than anyone else in history except George Washington. And no wonder he is mythologized as a hero, given what we are teaching our children.

Grade school curricula often show an Indian welcoming Columbus and Columbus ready to hug the Indian, with the caption "In 1492, Columbus sailed the ocean blue." And frequently, the words *celebrate* and *new world* are emphasized in this narrative. How can you discover a place when there are already people there? Obviously, Columbus did not discover America. It was a new world to Spaniards, but it was not a new world to Indians.

But let's be fair. Columbus's mission established sustained permanent contact and communication between the Americas and the rest of the world. Neither the Vikings nor the Polynesians accomplished that. It was the culture of Spain and the rest of Europe during that time to make claims of discovery and possession. Columbus was, after all, a man of his times.

But consider this line of thinking. As I traveled in Europe some years ago, I wanted to see concentration camps. Outside Munich, Germany, I looked for Dachau. However, there were no road signs until I was only one kilometer away. It seemed like the Germans were hiding that camp, like they were ashamed of it. I then went to Austria and looked for Mauthausen. I found it, but there as well, I only found road signs about two kilometers away. Austria had joined Germany with the Anschluss and was part of the Final Solution—they had something to be ashamed of, too. But if you go to Auschwitz, in Poland, you will see signs 200 kilometers away, 150 kilometers away, 100 kilometers away, 50, 25, 10. You can't miss it. It's like they are saying, "Look what the Nazis did to us."

All human beings have dark chapters in their personal histories. And all nations have dark chapters in theirs. Nobody should be stuck in shame. However, it is important for all countries and all individuals to examine dark chapters in order to learn from them and prevent them from reoccurring. Germany mandated instruction about the Holocaust, issued formal apologies, and made reparations to Holocaust survivors. These steps and actions in no way made up for everything that happened during the Holocaust. However, they did make it possible to have a conversation about healing and helped lessen the chance of a holocaust ever happening there again.

Here in the United States, very little effort has been made to voice formal apologies, make reparations, or pass political mandates about education.[20] Yet this country was founded in part by genocidal policies directed at Native Americans and the enslavement of Black people. Both of those things are morally repugnant. Still, I love my country. In fact, it is because I love my country that I want to make sure the mistakes of our past do not get repeated. We cannot afford to cover over the dark chapters of our history, as we have for decades upon decades. It is time for that to stop.

In 1992, on the 500th anniversary of Columbus's first voyage, we had an opportunity to set the record straight and to strive for healing. The stories about Columbus were not hiding; people were hiding the stories. But in 1992, instead of saying, "Let's make the next 500 years different," the U.S. government simply established the Quincentenary Jubilee Commission. It is hard for many people to see how much damage is done by pretending there were no ugly chapters in American history.

Then-president George Bush, Sr., received a first-class education in the United States. However, no American president has written his own speeches since Abraham Lincoln. Each has a staff of smart and educated people with a huge amount of resources to craft policy and speech. Bush and his staff could have done so much better. But at the time I highlighted the words that jumped out at me from his statement about the Quincentenary Jubilee: "We are approaching a *momentous* year in history, a year that will mark the five hundredth anniversary of one of the *greatest achievements* of human endeavor: Christopher Columbus' *discovery* of the *New World* . . . Christopher Columbus not only opened the door to a New World, but also *set an example for us all* by showing what *monumental feats* can be accomplished through perseverance and *faith*. I strongly encourage every American to support the Quincentenary, and to discover the significance that this milestone in history has in his or her own life." His example was followed, but it is not one I would like my children to follow.

Like Christopher Columbus, George Bush, Sr. was a man of his time. However, it is important that we hold our leaders accountable for their words. We have enough information and resources to get this story right. We do not have to sugarcoat our history. On the contrary, we owe it to those who died and suffered, and we owe it to future generations, not to lie to them. When one is teaching high schoolers, it is easy to look at the writings of someone like Las Casas and talk about different perspectives on Columbus. At many schools, Columbus is put on trial and students argue multiple perspectives—a hero or a villain—but also that he was a man of his time and needs to be understood as such. No matter the conclusions, this activity certainly provides a more well-rounded discussion and understanding of the explorer. As a student, you have likely been exposed to plenty of one-sided history already. It's not just refreshing, but empowering, to get a real and nuanced perspective. You deserve that.

Native Americans changed the world with the introduction of many types of food, medicine, obsidian scalpels still used in surgery today—all kinds of things—and the rest of the world changed Indians, sometimes in positive ways. Examining these gifts is a better entry point for this part of the historical narrative than glorifying the beginning of a colonial regime that killed millions. And make no mistake about it—there is glorification of this conquest.

Depicted on the great seal of the Territory of Wisconsin is an image of an Indian facing west, apparently boarding a steamship. The Natives of that state, the Ho-Chunk (or Winnebago), were subjected to nine separate removal orders. Some were forcibly relocated from the region by being boarded onto steamships and sent to Santee, Nebraska. On the seal is also a White farmer industriously plowing up the land, plus the emergence of the state capitol building in the background. And the Latin caption says it all: "Civilization Succeeds Barbarism." There is no way to interpret this seal other than as a glorification of the forcible removal of Indian people from Wisconsin and the land being turned over to Whites.[21] We often celebrate even

the ugliest chapters of our history. We need to think hard about why we do that and what message it sends.

There are some excellent resources available for you. The book *Rethinking Columbus* has a lot of great information for young readers. There is a lot of discussion about the Columbian Exchange—the transfer of ideas, technologies, and raw materials between Indians and the rest of the world—Columbus himself, the early Spanish conquest of the Americas, and many other topics in Native history. I also recommend *Columbus: His Enterprise* by Hans Koning, which is user-friendly and informative.

Why are some people trying to change Columbus Day to Indigenous Peoples' Day?

There are a lot of ways to reframe our approach to history. Over 130 cities have already changed Columbus Day to Indigenous Peoples' Day. Minnesota, North Carolina, Alaska, Maine, South Dakota, and Oregon have done the same at the state level. Other states are considering the change too. I think it's likely that this will happen at the national level someday. I support the change. It is not about erasing Columbus from history. It is an effort to reframe our marking of history from the celebration of an important but controversial person who orchestrated genocide to the celebration of Indigenous people who survived that genocide. Columbus should be studied—honestly studied. Reframing the commemoration of European contact with Indigenous people in the Americas, with a focus on the Indigenous experience rather than on mythologizing or celebrating Columbus, makes sense to me. That way we can focus on healing for everyone instead of rubbing salt in old wounds.

What is the real story of Thanksgiving?

Some of the things we often hear about Thanksgiving are correct, but some are exaggerated or just plain wrong. Chief Massasoit of the Wampanoag did forge a peaceful relationship with the Pilgrims when they first arrived. A Patuxet Indian named Tisquantum (sometimes called Squanto), who had briefly been a captive in England, lived with the Wampanoag in the early 1600s, when this relationship developed. Massasoit, Squanto, and many Wampanoag did teach the Pilgrims how to farm corn, beans, and squash; rotate crops; maintain soil fertility; and survive in the harsh New England climate. This first part of the Thanksgiving myth bears some truth.

However, there is no evidence of a tribal-White harvest celebration during the first Pilgrim winter in America, in 1620–21. Although the Wampanoag, Pequot, and other Indians in the region routinely celebrated their fall harvest, the first evidence of a White-tribal harvest celebration appears in 1637—sixteen years after the first Pilgrims arrived. Also, the idea that the Indian-White relationship was all peace, hugs, and good eating is just a myth. Metacom (called King Philip by the British) was one of Massasoit's sons. In 1675, a chain of events led to a massive conflict sometimes called King Philip's War. Around 5 percent of the White population and 40 percent of the Native population in the region were killed. Metacom's wife and children were sold as slaves in the West Indies, and the chief himself was killed by the Puritans. His head was placed on a pike and displayed in the village of Plymouth for more than twenty years.

The real Thanksgiving—it was complicated. Thanksgiving wasn't established as an American holiday until the Civil War era and didn't become a formal federal holiday until 1941.

What is the real story of Pocahontas?

Soon after the British established Jamestown, in 1607, Captain John Smith was captured by Opechancanough, half brother of Wahunsenacawh (principal chief of the Powhatan Confederacy).[22] Wahunsenacawh's daughter, Pocahontas, helped Smith escape. Smith wrote about his captivity in 1608, 1612, and 1624, but only his last account mentioned that he was going to be executed before Pocahontas intervened, a clear embellishment.

In 1609, Captain John Ratcliffe demanded that the Powhatan provide food for the British settlers. When the Indians said no, he declared war and attacked their villages repeatedly from 1610 to 1614. Pocahontas was captured by the English in 1614 and ransomed to her father. The chief agreed to peace in exchange for her return, but the English continued to hold her to manipulate him. Pocahontas, still a teenager, was baptized and married to English planter John Rolfe (not John Smith), in spite of the fact that she was already in a relationship with a Powhatan man. Though she was never free to choose her relationship, she still wrestled with divided loyalties. She went with Rolfe to England, where her beauty brought her a great deal of attention, but she died, at age twenty-two, before she could return to America. Her son, Thomas Rolfe, survived and settled in Virginia, where some of his proven descendants still live today.

Who was Ely Parker?

Natives made America as much as people from any other group, even though Americans today are taught that Indians are something that happened in the past. One really important maker of American history was Ely Parker (1828–1895). Parker descended from a long line of Seneca chiefs that included Red Jacket, who was especially famous for negotiating the first treaties his people signed with the U.S. government. Parker was a chief (sachem), but also an accomplished engineer, lawyer, and U.S. public servant. While he served his home community, he also completed law school. Officials in New York refused to let him take the bar exam after he finished, though, simply because he was a Seneca Indian. Parker

refused to give up, so he went back to school and earned an engineering degree. When the U.S. Civil War started, Parker used his status as a chief to organize Seneca warriors to fight for the Union in a racially segregated unit. In spite of his loyalty to the American cause, the U.S. government did not let him enlist his Seneca warriors as U.S. soldiers, again simply because they were Native.

After that, Parker applied for a position as an engineer in the Union Army. He was denied again because of his race.

He kept writing letters and petitioning for the right to fight until General Ulysses S. Grant, realizing that most of his engineers had died at the siege of Vicksburg, gave Parker a commission in the Union Army. Grant was so impressed with Parker's field record that he promoted Parker and asked him to serve as his adjutant. Parker wrote most of Grant's personal letters and military orders for the rest of the war and drafted the Confederate terms of surrender for the Union. After the Civil War, President Grant appointed Parker as Commissioner of Indian Affairs. Parker was the first Native to be put in charge of the U.S. government office that oversaw relations with all the tribes in America. In spite of his accomplishments and service record, nobody in the U.S. government would hire him after Grant left office. Ely Parker lived in poverty for the last twenty years of his life, but he still left a proud legacy of service to both the U.S. and Seneca nations.

What did Pontiac do?

Pontiac (1720–1769) was an Ottawa Indian who was most famous for uniting many different tribes in a common struggle against the British in 1763. His forces staged a lacrosse game in front of the British fort at Michilimackinac (Michigan) with hundreds of players on each side. When the game got close to the fort, British soldiers lined the walls to watch. One of the players threw the ball over the wall, and they demanded the British open the gate. When the gate was opened, the players charged in, took out concealed weapons, and seized the fort. Pontiac's warriors took over nine out of the eleven British forts in the Great Lakes that year and put the other two under siege. His hopes for French reinforcements were never met and he eventually abandoned the sieges, but the British changed the way they treated Natives in the Great Lakes after that. More important, his successes showed Indigenous people the power they had when they combined their forces and led to more successful Native resistance movements.

Why is Tecumseh such a famous Native?

Tecumseh was a Shawnee chief who united Natives from many tribes to fight for their freedom and way of life. He was a one-of-a-kind politician and built several villages. He was also a military genius, whose tactics and military psychology are still studied at war colleges in many countries. Tecumseh lived from 1768 to 1813 and was one of the most celebrated Indian leaders of all time, inside and outside Native communities. Even White men like William Tecumseh Sherman, who ironically led some of America's genocidal attacks on the Plains Indians, were named after him. Tecumseh brought together tribes from the southern Great Lakes to build new villages and alliances, but ultimately they were pulled into the British-American War of 1812.

Tecumseh spoke several tribal languages and traveled tirelessly all over the eastern United States. His own people, the Shawnee, suffered terribly in the first years of the American republic. His father was killed in 1774, at the Battle of Point Pleasant. In 1779, Kentucky militia burned his childhood village. In 1780, his family moved to another village, but the Americans burned that down too. In 1782, he had to rebuild again, this time in Bellefontaine, Ohio. Many of his relatives, including small children, were killed by American settlers and militia, even though his tribe was not at war with the United States. Tecumseh fought in the Old Northwest War, including the Battle of Fallen Timbers, but what he really wanted was to find a way for his people to live in safety and peace.

In 1808, Tecumseh built a new village called Prophetstown in what is now Indiana. In 1811, he left his brother Tenskwatawa in charge of Prophetstown while he visited other tribes. The Americans attacked Prophetstown with 1,000 militiamen. They burned the village and destroyed all their crops. The War of 1812 started soon after, and Tecumseh agreed to help the British. At the Battle of Brownstown, Tecumseh fearlessly set an ambush with only 24 warriors, killing 18 soldiers, wounding 12, and routing the entire force of 200 soldiers. American troops were so scared by the sudden hand-to-hand combat and war whoops that more than 70 ran away from the fight.

Tecumseh again amazed the British and Americans during the Siege of Detroit in 1812. He told British Major General Isaac Brock to pull his force away from the American fort, but not to retreat. Then Tecumseh led 600 warriors through the woods to the field in front of the fort. As soon as they had marched to the top of the hill, they snuck back into the woods. He had them do this all day long. The Americans were sure that Tecumseh had an overwhelming force, and Brigadier General William Hull, the American general, surrendered without contest. Tecumseh took 2,500 Americans captive with only 600 warriors. The British offered him an appointment as brigadier general in the British Army, but he refused. Tecumseh also distinguished himself later at the Siege of Fort Meigs in 1813.

At the Battle of the Thames, William Henry Harrison led the 3,500-strong U.S. force against 800 British troops and 500 warriors under Tecumseh. The British general retreated and left Tecumseh in a bad position. The chief was mortally wounded in the American assault. Over the next few decades, the Americans attacked and displaced the tribes from Tecumseh's confederacy, moving many to Oklahoma or Kansas. Others retreated to Canada.

When did the U.S. government stop making treaties with Indians and why?

In 1789, the U.S. Constitution established the right of the United States to make treaties with foreign countries. Indian tribes were foreign countries in American law. In law and practice, treaties with Indians were the same as treaties with any other nation. But in 1871, there was a power struggle between the U.S. House of Representatives and the U.S. Senate.[23] The House was in charge of money for dealing with Indian affairs. Only the Senate ratified treaties. Congressmen wanted to have more say over treaties with Indians. The Senate refused to change the Constitution or involve the House of Representatives in the treaty process. In response, the House terminated the right to treat with tribes when they passed the budget that year.

After that, new treaties could no longer be made. It seems strange that the United States would stop making treaties with Indians when they were still trying to get Indians to sell their land and relocate. But the government found new ways to make that happen after the end of treaty-making. Usually they used congressional acts and executive orders—which were occasionally negotiated.

Why do some people use the word *genocide* in discussing the treatment of Indians?

The dictionary defines *genocide* as "the systematic killing of all the people from a national, ethnic, or religious group, or

John Gast captured the concept of "Manifest Destiny" perfectly in this painting, *American Progress*, which shows Indians and wild animals retreating ahead of white settlement.

an attempt to do this."[24] The legal definition of genocide developed by the United Nations in 1948 is "any of the following acts committed with intent to destroy, in whole or in part, a national, ethnical, racial, or religious group, as such: killing members of the group; causing serious bodily or mental harm to members of the group; deliberately inflicting on the group conditions of life calculated to bring about its physical destruction in whole or in part; imposing measures intended to prevent births within the group; forcibly transferring children of the group to another group."[25]

MONEY FOR INDIAN SCALPS.

ARIZONA AND NEW-MEXICO SETTLERS PROPOSE TO DESTROY THE SAVAGES.

DEMING, New-Mexico, Oct. 11.—It has been recently telegraphed that the pioneer settlers in the border counties of Arizona have brought to light an old law in several counties offering a reward of $250 each for Indian scalps. Under this law, which is nothing more than an order made by the County Commissioners, the ranchmen and cowboys in Cochise, Pima, and Yavapai Counties are organizing in armed bodies for the purpose of going on a real old-fashioned Indian hunt, and they propose to bring back the scalps and obtain the reward. Word now comes from Tombstone, the county seat of Cochise County, that the reward in that county has been increased to $500 for a buck Indian's scalp. The authorities of Pima and Yavapai Counties have taken steps to increase the reward to $500, and it is said Yuma, Apache, and Maricopa Counties will follow suit.

This reward system, while it may seem savage and brutal to the Northern and Eastern sentimentalist, is looked upon in this section as the only means possible of ridding Arizona of the murderous Apaches. The settlers of New-Mexico and Arizona are aroused on this question, and propose to act henceforth independent of the military authorities. From time immemorial all border countries have offered rewards for bear and wolf scalps and other animals that destroyed the pioneer's stock or molested his family. Why, therefore, asks the Arizona settler, should not the authorities place a reward upon the head of the terrible Apache, who murders the white man's family and steals his stock like the wolves? "Extermination" is the battle cry now, and the coming Winter will witness bloody work in this section.

Public sentiment in this part of New-Mexico and Arizona is strongly in favor of the immediate removal of Gen. Crook, who, it is declared, has always been overrated as an Indian fighter. It is the general belief here among old white scouts that Gen. Crook has been duped by his Indian scouts, and that the latter have always had secret understandings with Geronimo, and have repeatedly sent him word of movements of troops.

The New York Times

A 1885 article in the *New York Times*.

The reason that some people use the word *genocide* in discussing the treatment of Indians is that every single part of the dictionary and legal definitions of the word can be used to describe the historical treatment of Indians.

France attempted genocide on the Fox Indians in the 1730s, even refusing to allow women and children to surrender and issuing an official genocidal order to back up their actions. During the French and Indian War, the British sent blankets infested with smallpox to enemy tribes. Commander Lord Jefferey Amherst instructed his subordinates to "inocculate the Indians by means of Blanketts, as well as to try Every other method that can serve to Extirpate this Execrable Race"; a recent outbreak had made blankets available, and by the next spring, tribes in the area were suffering from the disease.[26] The Russian, Spanish, and American colonial regimes all engaged in genocide toward the Indigenous peoples of the Americas. In the United States, attempts to eradicate entire tribes had the greatest success in California, but other genocidal efforts were carried out across the country against the Apache, Lakota, and numerous other Native nations. After the Dakota War of 1862, the tribal population in southern Minnesota was systematically hunted down, harried, relocated, and disrupted to the point where the state was almost completely depopulated of Dakota Indians. The present Dakota communities there have never fully recovered. The governor of Minnesota at the time, Alexander Ramsey, said, "The Sioux Indians of Minnesota must be exterminated or driven forever beyond the borders of the state."[27]

Even more recently, Indians have endured policies that fit the legal description of genocide, including the residential boarding school programs of the United States and Canada, the systematic removal of Indian children from their homes by social service agencies, the ongoing disregard for extreme poverty and homelessness in parts of Indian country, and the involuntary sterilization of Indian women by the U.S. Department of Health. (The U.S. government sterilized 25,000 Indian women by tubal ligation without their consent in the 1960s and 1970s.)[28] Similar practices were documented in Canada. *Genocide* might be the most honest word we have to describe these events.

What is the Doctrine of Discovery?

For most of human history, people of all races and cultures were communal. From the Celts who settled the British Isles to the Mongols of the Asian steppe, from the Zulus in southern Africa to the Inuit of the Arctic, people harvested food together and combined both their efforts and the food they harvested to create a common food supply. When people were hungry, they took what they needed from that source. This is what Karl Marx called "primitive communism"—from each according to his or her ability, to each according to his or her need. Throughout this history people sometimes killed one another over territory and resources. But the fundamental structure of human societies was communal.

Around 11,000 years ago, the last ice age ended. Huge glaciers that covered most of the Great Lakes melted. A massive ice dam on Hudson Bay gave way and ocean levels rose nine feet. Most cultures of the world have a story about a massive flood (Noah's Ark, the Great Flood story of the Ojibwe, and more) because there actually was a massive flood. The end of the ice age and the flood changed the weather systems of the planet and eventually helped give birth to the agricultural age. Before this, people hunted, fished, and gathered. Now they started to farm. And farming increased human food production dramatically. We had more babies and the babies didn't die as often in infancy. The human population grew. We got more efficient at making food and had more time for other things, like music, art, and war. In nine different parts of the planet, simultaneously, people figured out how to farm. From Japan to Polynesia, South America to the Middle East, our lives transformed.

In an area sometimes called the Fertile Crescent in the Middle East, farming flourished.[29] Today that area is largely desert, but 10,000 years ago it was some of the best farmland on the planet. And that's where people also figured out how to lock up the food. At first, that meant someone literally put a lock on the food cache from everyone's harvest. And whoever held the key could say, "I need everyone to work an extra thirty minutes today in the fields; and I am taking the day off." This practice made room for a kind of unfairness we had not experienced very much before then. Eventually, instead of an actual key, humans in the Middle East developed an economy that used money, and the "key" was monetized. If you held the money, you held the key, and people who wanted food couldn't just take what they needed from a common food supply. They had to get money. Eventually societies got more and more hierarchical.

It's not an accident that the three largest religions of the world—Christianity, Islam, and Judaism (collectively called the Abrahamic religions)—all came from a part of the Middle East called the Fertile Crescent. Those religions were exported from there to Europe and from there to the rest of the world eventually as part of a new kind of violence—colonialism. Although people have always waged war and been mean to one another, the kind of hierarchy that emerged in the Middle East and Europe encouraged colonial violence. Instead of killing other people to take their land and resources, the invaders started to tell people that they could worship God only the way the colonizers did, speak only the language the colonizers spoke, and do things only the way the colonizers did. In other words, the new cultures emerging in the Middle East and Europe required all others to assimilate or die. They were the first in the world to make such ideas the center of their value systems and ways of dealing with one another.

People have probably often thought that their religions were better than others throughout human history, but this belief grew and dominated Judaism, Islam, and Christianity. People from the Middle East and Europe soon believed that some people were preordained by God to rule and all others to serve. Increasingly, it was not just the rulers who believed this—the people being ruled believed it too. As Judaism, Islam, and Christianity controlled the lives of people in the Middle East and Europe, humans clashed with one another and with the natural world in new ways. The resources of the land and people were increasingly bent to the service of elites instead of the greater good. The people even waged wars on animals that might "compete" for resources humans could use. The kings of Europe especially fought one another for control of the land and resources and people. Just think of the English and French and their many wars throughout history.

Eventually, the Pope tried to intervene. The Pope wasn't just a religious figure then as he is today. He was a political force. He wanted the Christian kings of Europe to quit killing one another and get busy killing Muslims by going on crusades—colonizing other people and converting them to Christianity. Now the language of hierarchy and colonization changed. Instead of "the divine right of kings" (God made some to rule and others to serve), the Pope declared the divine right of *Christian* kings.

To reduce the conflict between Christian kingdoms, the Pope issued a series of edicts, often called *papal bulls* (in reference to the *bulla,* or wax seal, on papal documents). These edicts declared that only Christian kings could rule and all others had to serve. They also said that if a Christian king sent his vassals, armies, or people to a country, continent, or place that was controlled by non-Christian people, the non-Christian people had no authority to rule themselves. The Pope said any Christian kingdom that "discovered" other places or people could claim ownership of all the people there and all of their lands.

The Pope issued this series of papal bulls in the 1490s, the time that gave birth to the age of discovery. Collectively, the messages in the papal bulls are called the Doctrine of Discovery. Columbus went on his famous voyage within two years of the first of these edicts. Europeans were Christian by this time. Muslims had retaken much of the Middle East. So, the Christian kings of Europe sent their armies out to discover, claim, and colonize the rest of the world. Columbus did not create the age of discovery. The Doctrine of Discovery created Christopher Columbus.

The Doctrine of Discovery enabled the slavery and genocide that followed. When England broke away from the Catholic Church, they still carried the Doctrine of Discovery as part of British law. When America had its Revolution and broke away from England, they still referred to the Doctrine of Discovery in American law, including rulings of the U.S. Supreme Court. It seems strange that the U.S. Supreme Court would refer to Catholic Church documents since the U.S. Constitution prohibits the establishment of a state religion. But the Doctrine of Discovery was too important to the idea of colonization to be abandoned in spite of its conflicts with the Constitution.

By the time Henry Rice was negotiating a treaty with the Ojibwe in Minnesota in 1855, for example, America was free from the British and seemed to have nothing to do with the Catholic Church. But Rice told the Indians they had no ownership of the land because the President of the United States had bought it from France in the Louisiana Purchase of 1803, even though no Indian had ever sold the land or given permission to France or the United States. He said that the Indians had never owned the land; they had only an aboriginal occupancy because they were not Christians. The entire taking of Native land and killing of Native people was enabled by and received impetus from a decree by the Pope—a decree that is still part of America's legal structure.

In the 21st century, some churches have formally repudiated the Doctrine of Discovery, saying that the doctrine and everything it enabled are not moral, ethical, or aligned with their religious teachings. Those churches include the national Lutheran and Episcopal churches in the United States, which have large followings. Others, like the Catholic Church, have refused to repudiate or retract the doctrine.

What was the historic relationship between Christian missionaries and Native people?

Complicated. When Europeans came to the Americas, they were never content to let Natives be who they wanted to be. They expected to eradicate them one way or another—by killing them off (genocide), relocating them (removal), or forcing their assimilation to colonial culture (converting them to Christianity, making them speak European languages, and crushing tribal cultures). Missionaries were not simply evangelizing their faiths—they were part of the colonial apparatus. As such they didn't just want to share their ways—they wanted Indians to abandon their own.

Because missionaries wanted Indigenous peoples to discard their pre-contact religious beliefs and traditions, many Natives resented them, and many still do today. In a way, even though missionaries saw their actions as well intentioned, many Natives received their attentions either as attacks on tribal culture or at least as forms of conditional love. In other words, many Indians believed that missionaries cared about them only if they quit being Native in terms of religion.

At the same time that there was and remains a real tension with missionaries because they sought to eradicate tribal religious beliefs and practices, many Natives did convert to Christianity. Even today there is a diversity of faith traditions in Indian country. In Oklahoma, most of the tribal population is Baptist or Methodist. In many tribal communities in the Great Plains and Great Lakes, numerous Natives are Catholic or Episcopalian. Furthermore, many Natives found missionaries sympathetic to their poor treatment by English, French, and American governments. Missionaries like Henry Whipple in the 1800s often advocated for the U.S. government to honor its treaties. They often objected to massacres of Natives. Bartolomé de Las Casas even wrote a book about how the Spanish government was being cruel to the Indians and how he objected to the cruelty on Christian religious grounds. As tribal people suffered increasing poverty, many Natives relied on the charity, support, and advocacy of missionaries to help them through hard times.

Today, as a consequence, Native Americans have differing and sometimes conflicting views about the missionaries and the religions they brought. Some embrace various denominations of Christianity openly. Some do so out of love for the teachings of those religions, some because those faith traditions are now family belief systems passed down through generations, and some because they actually fear their own tribe's culture and religion. The shaming practices of Christian missionaries created a legacy in many Native communities—tribal healers and spiritual leaders are sometimes gossiped about and called *bad medicine*. Other Natives don't want anything to do with Christianity or missionaries and deeply resent their intrusions into tribal communities and their assaults on tribal ways.

The differing views Native people have of missionaries are exacerbated by the role missionaries and churches played in running residential boarding schools for Natives. Those schools often used harsh physical punishment to discipline students for speaking their tribal languages. They cut the long hair off Indian children. And many of the staff members were documented to have sexually abused Native children in their care.

Were Indians ever slaves?

Yes. Spanish, French, English, and Dutch newcomers all tried to enslave the Native population. Columbus alone took many hundreds of Natives as slaves. But Native Americans were highly susceptible to diseases brought by Europeans. They also ran away every chance they had. And sometimes whole tribes fought to free their people or avoid enslavement. Within 100 years, Europeans began to rely more and more on enslaved people brought across the ocean from Africa, who were much more resilient to disease and less able to run away or resist by getting help from friends and relatives outside the community of enslaved people. Even so, by the time of the U.S. Civil War, it is estimated that around 15 percent of the enslaved people in America were still Indigenous.[30] Europeans never gave up on the idea of enslaving Native Americans. And in some parts of America, Indian slaves remained the norm for the entire colonial period. In California, for example, the Spanish created twenty-one missions, each with a Native slave population, and ran them from 1769 to 1833. Sometimes entire tribes were enslaved, as happened with the Chumash.

Was the swastika an Indigenous symbol before the Nazis used it?

Yes. Several tribes in the Southwest and Great Lakes used the swastika in traditional art and ceremony long before contact with Europeans. It was also widely used in the ancient cultures of India, Armenia, and northern Europe. In Native American traditions, it was seen as a representation of spirits in the four cardinal directions of the compass, moving in a clockwise circle—the circle of life. Ojibwe elder John Smith was photographed in the

early 1900s with beadwork that incorporated the swastika, and it was put on the uniforms for some of the basketball teams at Indian residential boarding schools in the early 1900s as well. It's not clear which ancient iteration of the swastika inspired Adolf Hitler to appropriate it for use as the Nazi symbol in the 1930s.

How was killing off the bison related to the Indian wars?

There were 60 million bison (also commonly referred to as "buffalo") in America at the time of first contact with Europeans, and the bison were a staple food for many tribes—Comanche, Tonkawa, Lakota, Arapaho, and more. Bison hides provided tipi coverings and clothing. Even their dung was used for fires. In the 1860s, a powerful confederacy of Cheyenne, Arapaho, and Lakota defeated the U.S. Army in the Red Cloud War and forced the Army to abandon three major forts and territory that encompassed most of five present-day states. The U.S. government wanted to subdue the tribes, but doing so by military conquest was proving to be especially difficult. It was then decided that the best way to subjugate the tribes was to eradicate their food supply and starve them into submission. General Philip Sheridan said of bison hunters, "These men have done more . . . to settle the vexed Indian question than the entire regular Army has done in the last 30 years. They are destroying the Indians' commissary."[31] Colonel Richard Dodge wrote in 1867, "Every buffalo dead is an Indian gone."[32] Undefeated in battle but

starving, Crazy Horse and other tribal leaders brought their people into the forts to surrender.

At first, the government had employed U.S. Army sharpshooters. After their initial efforts, they paid bounties on bison to private citizens. William "Buffalo Bill" Cody

A pile of bison skulls, 1870.

claimed he shot 4,282 bison in 18 months in 1867–68. In a shooting contest with William Comstock he killed 68 bison in 8 hours, all with his Springfield Model 1863. People hunted from trains, too, and one person reported shooting 120 bison in 40 minutes. Bison hides were tanned and sold for two dollars each. The bones were crushed and used to make bone china and fertilizer. Hides were made into machine belts for factories. White hunters killed 60 million bison, reducing the massive herds to just hundreds of animals by 1890. A conservation effort began with the Yellowstone herd in 1902; in Alberta, Canada, in 1907; and with the Theodore Roosevelt National Park in North Dakota in 1908. Today there are around 360,000 bison (mostly on private ranches). The European equivalent of the bison—the cow—now numbers 108 million in the United States and Canada.

Did Indians ever keep slaves?

Yes. Before European contact, Native Americans did not keep chattel slaves (humans owned by other humans as their property). But many tribes did take war captives and usually adopted the child captives as full-fledged members of the tribe. They sometimes took adult captives and assimilated them as well, through either marriage or ritual adoption. After European contact, some tribes in the Great Lakes and Southeast started to sell war captives to Europeans, who enslaved them as chattel slaves and had them work plantations or mines.

In the Southeast, the Cherokee and a couple of their neighboring tribes began to mirror European slaving customs. They evolved their agricultural practices to function much like Euro-American plantations, even keeping Black slaves as chattel property. The Cherokee in particular developed stratified economic systems, with some of their members being very wealthy and others quite impoverished. The actual percentage of Cherokee who owned Black slaves was small. But when the Cherokee were removed from the Southeast to Oklahoma on the Trail of Tears, many of their Black slaves were made to relocate with them and their descendants are still in Oklahoma. Over time, many of the Cherokee Freedmen, as they were eventually called, married into the tribe and even today are members of the

Cherokee Nation. Others did not marry tribal members and their offspring are not eligible for tribal enrollment today, which is based on proven descent from an original Cherokee tribal member.

RELIGION, CULTURE, & IDENTITY

Indian time means that we will do your ceremony until it's done. That's not an excuse to be late or lazy.

–Thomas Stillday, Red Lake (Minnesota)

Indigenous people are 4 percent of the world's population but they protect 80 percent of the world's biodiversity.

–attributed to Leila Salazar-López, The Plant Teacher

We understand that this government gives its subjects the freedom of worshipping as he chooses and we cannot understand why we are deprived of this privilege.

–Nodin Wind

They can't persecute a man for following his dream. Everybody knows that.

—Anna Gibbs

Life will break you. Nobody can protect you from that, and living alone won't either, for solitude will also break you with its yearning. You have to love. You have to feel. It is the reason you are here on earth. You are here to risk your heart. You are here to be swallowed up. And when it happens that you are broken, or betrayed, or left, or hurt, or death brushes near, let yourself sit by an apple tree and listen to the apples falling all around you in heaps, wasting their sweetness. Tell yourself you tasted as many as you could.

—Louise Erdrich

Why do Indians have long hair?

There are hundreds of distinct Indian tribes in North America, and their cultural beliefs and hairstyles are diverse. For many Native Americans, hair was and is viewed as a symbol of spiritual health and strength. Leonard Moose, an Ojibwe elder from Mille Lacs, said that hair was like medicine and if someone's hair was cut, their medicine would leak out. Moose claimed that when he was a child, if someone had a haircut, the parents would usually run the cut braid over a hot rock to seal the "wound" on the child's hair and prevent his or her medicine from draining away. Hair was spiritual strength or power but also a visible symbol of that power, and thus a source of pride and even vanity. All of these things combine to provide a distinct cultural perspective about hair.

For most Indians, hair was cut only under certain circumstances. Meskwaki and Mohawk warriors plucked hair on the sides of the head, a tradition that developed in wars where scalping was commonly practiced. Many Diné, or Navajo, cut children's hair on their first birthday and then do not cut it again. They believe that the purity of childhood preserves spiritual strength and that the haircut will enable greater development of that strength as the child grows. Among some tribes, hair was cut as part of tribal mourning customs, but this practice was not universal. You

Anton Treuer (left) often tells his sons Isaac (center) and Evan (right) that he may not have the best braids in the family any more, but he more than compensates with better beadwork.

can imagine how it must have felt for many Native children to have their hair cut against their will upon entrance into U.S. and Canadian government-run boarding schools. Today, there are still many Native Americans who wear their hair long and carry the cultural belief that the hair is a symbol of spiritual strength.

Hair is also a visible part of identity, especially for Native men. I am brown. But if I have a short haircut, I could pass for Latinx, Arab, Filipino, or Thai. My long hair makes me more visibly Native to others. It's an identity marker.

Do Indians live in tipis?

Not usually. Europeans do not usually live in straw huts or ride horses as their primary means of transportation—although there probably are exceptions. And Indians do not usually live in historic dwellings or travel by foot, dogsled, or horse. Questions like these often speak to the mythologized fascination with Plains Indians, as seen in *Dances with Wolves* and other movies. We cannot hold on to a stereotype of how any people are and use that to judge their authenticity.

Native Americans are diverse, and each group's practices have changed over time, but that does not diminish their authenticity. Today at sun dances, powwows, and other events, members of some Plains tribes set up tipis. The Haudenosaunee (Iroquois) use a longhouse for ceremonial functions. Many tribes in the Great Lakes use wigwams for ceremonies. In parts of the Southwest, hogans and pueblos are used for both ceremonial and everyday shelter.

I live in a modern house. I have a deck and a grill. I put up Christmas lights. I also build ceremonial wigwams at least twice every summer. We use saws and axes and metal knives, but all of the materials are what our ancestors would have used pre-contact. We make the string out of bark from basswood trees. We use maple and ironwood saplings. And we build the structures communally—there is a large group of us who do this together. We don't live in these structures. But we spend at least four weeks each summer using them every day for ceremonies. We are modern people, but we are ancient too.

What is fasting and why do Indians do it?

A *fast* is a search for a vision that will establish a relationship between the faster and the spiritual world. Many Indians believe the Great Spirit has a plan for everybody, and one never knows what it is, but fasting is a way whereby one can get a glimpse of it. By giving up food and water, the person who is fasting becomes disconnected from the physical world and more strongly connected to the spiritual world. This enhanced state makes it possible for a faster to be approached and "pitied" by spirits with the gift of a song, a medicine, the right to give Indian names, or the company of a guiding spirit.

For many tribes, a woman's power is her birthright, represented by her ability to bring life into the world through pregnancy and childbirth, and manifests when she comes of age. A man's spiritual power has to be earned through fasting.

The process customarily begins by giving tobacco to someone who knows about fasting. That person will provide instructions on how to prepare and when to go. Young people are often given a choice about fasting. For some tribes, that choice might occur when a parent or namesake offers a child charcoal in one hand and breakfast or candy in the other. Children who choose the food are not ready. When they choose the charcoal, they are ready.

There are many differences in the methods of preparation and fasting. Some people might use a sweat lodge. Some fast on a platform, some on the ground, some in a lodge or in a tree. Occasionally people will fast with others, but usually it's a solitary activity.

Males or females can fast any time of the year, but typically boys and young men are encouraged to fast, and spring, a time of new life, is considered especially strong. Medicines are sprouting, birds and animals are coming back from migration or out of hibernation. Physically and spiritually, the world is coming alive. It's possible to fast at any age, but fasts are most common in the spring of one's life, when it is easier to earn pity from the spirits. Adults have to sit out longer to make the same connections.

What are clans and do all Indians have them?

Clans, or totems, are birds, animals, fish, or spiritual beings or places that represent different families in many Native communities. Most tribes have clan systems. Most tribal stories about the origins of clans describe humans being adopted by the clan animal (raised by wolves, for example), or even people being animals that transformed into humans (a bear that became a man, for example).

At Cochiti Pueblo, there are two essential groupings—Turquoise and Pumpkin. Those groupings matter a great deal for the organization of some dances at the Pueblo but do not function like the clan systems of other tribes. Many, including the Plains tribes, have maintained sophisticated kin networks without clan systems. Others, like the Dakota, used to maintain clan systems and kinship networks but have since lost and discontinued their clan systems.

For most of the tribes in the Algonquian and Iroquoian language families, clans remain a critical part of tribal life.

In 1849, Ojibwe chiefs from Wisconsin presented a written petition in the Ojibwe language to the President of the United States, and enclosed this image, showing their authority to lead as vested in their clans (crane, marten, bear, merman, and bullhead). Their unity is shown in the lines connecting the heart and mind of the crane to all others. The crane was Chief Buffalo, head chief and spokesman for the bands who signed the petition.

In Iroquoian tribes, members follow their mothers' clan. The clan system is even incorporated into the rights of tribal members to participate in longhouse ceremonies. Ojibwe people follow the clans of their fathers. Forest County Potawatomi boys follow the clan of the father and girls follow the clan of the mother.[33]

For tribes that maintain beliefs in clan, it is customarily taboo to marry someone of the same clan. There are ingrained cultural concepts that vary from tribe to tribe for handling situations where one has a non-Native parent, from whom they would normally receive their clan. Some believe there is an automatic adoption into a certain clan or a necessary ceremony or ritual to obtain a clan for the person who needs one.

Where are the real Indians?

Once, when I was lecturing in France, a man in the back of the room raised his hand with great excitement. French guys never get excited at academic talks, so I took his question. And his question was, "Where are the real Indians?" I suppose he was looking for someone who just stepped off the set of a Hollywood movie with a feather headdress and a horse. I replied, "Where are the real Indians? Where are the real Frenchmen? There is a castle across the street, and there is nobody living in it. In fact, I don't see anybody riding up and down the street on horses with shining armor. I don't even see guys with berets and little pipes. Where are the real Frenchmen?"

All cultures change over time. What it meant to be French a thousand years ago, a hundred years ago, and today are all different. But a Frenchman can still be French even if he's traveling in China because he carries that identity inside of him. It's the same for Indians, who carry their identity with them. Many things inform identity, including heredity, connection to tribal communities, traditional lifeways, and tribal languages. Each of those parts of identity might be threatened for many Indian people, but what it means to be Indian is both complicated and very real, in spite of what movies and stereotypes say.

What does *traditional* mean?

That's a loaded question. Defining tradition is very subjective, depending on the culture. People from Pittsburgh who happen to be of German heritage might have a very different idea of what is traditional compared to the Pennsylvania Amish. Tradition is about much more than biology. Because cultures, languages, technologies, and values shift far faster than most people realize, it is hard to define.

For Indians, defining what is traditional gets further tied up in a sometimes-contested discussion of identity. For example, the community of Ponemah on the Red Lake Reservation in Minnesota has 100 percent traditional Ojibwe religious belief and funerary practice. No one has ever been baptized in that community. And the fluency rate in the tribal language there is the highest of all Ojibwe communities in the United States. Across the lake, in the community of Red Lake, on the same reservation, the tribal population is mainly Catholic. People in Ponemah define tradition by religion, traditional lifeways, and language. But people from Red Lake tend to emphasize heredity (blood), hunting and fishing, and reservation affiliation as more important parts of identity, Indianness, and tradition.

This example demonstrates how testy political discussions of tradition can be. Personally, I find the customs, practices, language, and beliefs of my ancestors to be defining features of tradition and central to my identity. But I also live in a modern world. I drive a car and wear manufactured clothing. Although my life differs from those of my ancestors of a few hundred years ago, I find much more in common with them in my own religious choices, cultural beliefs and practices, and language. I tried to make that distinction to the Frenchman who asked where the real Indians were (in the previous question), but it is important to recognize that the tension between old and new, modern and traditional, is ongoing and intense in Indian country.

Aren't all Indians traditional?

There is incredible diversity in Indian country. There are communities in Canada and remote parts of the Navajo Nation where fluency rates in Native languages approach 100 percent. In many other communities, there are no speakers left. It's the same with religion and culture. Each place has its own history. And it is usually through no fault of their own that many Indians do not speak their tribal language or grow up with their traditional religious or cultural practices. At the same time, while many forces and realities are beyond the control of any individual human being or community, there are some things Indians can exercise more control over. And, fair or not, it is necessarily up to Native people to take steps to stabilize traditional custom, practice, and language.

In the Upper Midwest, almost 30 percent of the non-Native population is of German heritage. But their families

Elias Treuer (above) knocking wild rice into a canoe. After the harvest, the rice is parched in kettles over a fire, and then danced on to separate the hulls from the kernels. Anton and Isaac Treuer (below) examine rice in a dance pit to see if the hulls are fully separated for winnowing.

have lived in the United States for as long as five generations. They don't speak the German language and have never lived in Germany. In fact, if you sent them to Germany, they might have a nice vacation, but they would be most comfortable when they came home to the United States. There is a difference between having German heritage and being a Deutschlander. And so too is there a big difference between having Native heritage and being, for instance, Apsáalooke (Crow). I believe strongly in the importance of tribal language, although I'm not so much of a fundamentalist as to say that non-speakers are not Indian. But the more divorced Indians become from tribal language, culture, religion, and custom, the more unrecognizable we become to our ancestors. How much can a people change before they are no longer the same people?

Why is it called a *traditional Indian fry bread taco*?

This question is as befuddling to me as "Where do the wood ticks go during the wintertime?" There is a traditional fry bread taco stand at every single powwow and many other secular and social events. Frankly, the words *traditional, Indian, fry bread,* and *taco* do not have any business even being in the same sentence. Taco? Really? Fry bread was created by resourceful Indians who were trying to subsist on U.S. government rations of lard and flour. It is certainly not traditional. Indians laugh at the irony, and I know I'm a sucker for one of those once in a while myself. But Indians need to wake up to the harsh realities of the world. Ironic

and humorous though it might seem, given that we have the highest rate of diabetes for any racial group in the world, mislabeling this concoction "traditional" is killing us. We have so many healthy foods in our traditional diets—wild game (roasted or boiled, not fried), fish, wild rice, berries, tubers, corn, beans, squash, pumpkins, sweet potatoes, and many other vegetables. Those foods are traditional and good for us, so I think the emphasis should go to them.

What is Indian time?

"Indian time" is another terrible misconception widely held in Indian country. Today the concept is sometimes used as an excuse to be late or lazy. But Native Americans in former times were neither. If you woke up late or took a lazy day, your children often went hungry. People worked hard and were physically fit in order to survive. In former times, Indians also worried a great deal about "bad medicine" and avoided offending people out of fear and respect. People did not show up late for social or ceremonial events out of fear they might offend someone who had the power to do spiritual harm to others.

Mille Lacs Ojibwe elder Melvin Eagle once told me that when he was a child, he and a friend were playing and laughing in a road and an old man walking by thought they were laughing at him. Melvin told his mother, who immediately made him take tobacco and gifts to the old man's residence to apologize and explain that he was not laughing at the old man. This care of relationships, like being on time, is a mark of respect. Today, among some people, I see a lack of work ethic and respect that would have horrified any Indian from a couple hundred years ago. According to Red Lake Ojibwe elder Thomas Stillday, *Indian time* simply means that we will do your ceremony until your ceremony is done, no matter how long it takes, with no shortcuts.[34] It is not an excuse to be late or lazy.

What are Indian cars?

Regardless of what may have happened in recent years, when we look back to BC (Before Casinos), we see that most Native Americans shared the experience of poverty. That experience still shapes Indian communities today, even in places where poverty is less a concern. The Indian car has been viewed by many as a symbol of this shared experience. The Indian car is the one that is falling apart—its bumper is held on with duct tape and bailing wire, and the tires are all "brothers from different marriages"—they don't match. I have a couple of cars in my yard that meet this description, but those vehicles do not define who I am. I make that distinction with purpose.

Today in Indian country, there is an incorrectly but widely held view that to suffer in poverty is to be authentically

Indian. Natives sometimes try to out-Indian one another. They play identity police. While poverty was a common experience, the negative parts of the culture of poverty are at odds with older, traditional Indigenous views of self. Pictures taken in the 1800s show people wearing decent pants and beautiful beadwork. They took pride in their personal appearance. They dressed up, especially for ceremony. Now, many Indians dress down, wearing jeans and T-shirts and leaving their beadwork in the closet when it's ceremony time, for fear they will be labeled stuck-up or seen as showing off. While the Native talent in artistry and beadwork is proudly on display at the modern powwow, it is absent from almost every other dimension of tribal life.

People dress casually. And not just for comfort. They sometimes celebrate their poverty because they mistakenly view an expression of poverty as an expression of Indianness. Our ancestors traditionally sought to improve their standard of living through hard work and personal pride in trade, diplomacy, and trapping. Today's embrace of the culture of poverty is at odds with the worldview of our ancestors.

I thought that Indians have a strong sense of ecological stewardship, so why do I also see a lot of trash in some yards?

If we were all true to the religious and cultural principles of our forebears, there would be many fewer problems in the world. The Bible has a lot of teachings about peace, but many Christians actively participate in war and have done so consistently for 2,000 years. It is true that many Native value systems and religious beliefs carry a deep respect for all animate and inanimate things—animals, birds, fish, and growing things. No matter how modest one's dwelling might be, traditional belief systems emphasize keeping it clean and treating it with respect. Although the sense of environmental stewardship attributed to Indians is sometimes romanticized, there is an authentic value of respect and reciprocity in Native interactions with the natural world.

At the same time, Indians, like all human beings, have sought to advance their position and make life easier for themselves, occasionally resulting in differences between belief and practice. Pressures on Indian land and livelihoods and European demands for furs all contributed to an Indigenous practice of harvesting beaver to extinction in some areas. Native Americans in the southern Great Lakes intentionally set forest fires to extend the range of the woodland bison eastward all the way to New Jersey. These actions created easier access to critical food supplies, and while they had a positive impact on the population of bison, they worked to the detriment of certain other flora and fauna. Controlled fires also created fire breaks to protect villages from wildfires (and forests from village cooking fires) and to enhance the productivity of certain crops such as blueberries. *Changes in the Land* by William Cronon and *1491* by Charles Mann do a great job of describing the ways that American Indians made their environments.

Trash bothers me, too, but the issue of trash in people's yards speaks to a larger concern. There has been a systematic attempt to assimilate Native Americans, and assimilation, historical trauma, and poverty have eroded traditional values of respect and pride in personal appearance and residence. Having fancy clothes, cars, houses, and other displays of wealth does not mean that one is more respected in Indian country. But in many Native communities, the traditional value and belief is that, no matter how humble or extravagant the dwelling, good spirits are attracted to clean places and bad spirits hide under clutter and garbage. When I see garbage in someone's yard, I am more likely to view it as someone being out of touch with their culture rather than a statement about the culture itself.

I see this issue as a reflection of the deeper one of poverty in Indian country. All poor populations have a similar issue. Those who do not own their homes take less pride in them. Many tribes manage their own garbage and recycling programs and coordinate youth activities to clean up their communities. Tribes are doing a lot to address this issue. Cultural values lend great support to that effort. But there's still plenty of work to do.

Are Natives at the front of environmental activism, or is that a stereotype?

Again, Natives do have a strong sense of environmental stewardship. Tribes and tribal people continue to lead in many environmental activism efforts. All Indigenous worldviews come from connection to an indigenous place—that means a special relationship to the earth. It's like that for the Sami in Scandinavia, Australian Aborigines, and all the tribes in the Americas.

I believe that we are all connected and what happens to the earth happens to all of us. That's a common tribal view. So for us, advocating for environmental issues is the same as advocating for human rights. A lot of Native people say, "Water is life." When we die, the water leaves our bodies. When we are born, water comes first. And we all need water to drink. We all depend on water and the larger environment to be healthy and we can only be as healthy as the environment in which we live. All the political fighting and economic striving people do is meaningless if we cannot breathe, drink, or eat because everything is contaminated.

The Menominee Nation of Wisconsin pioneered sustainable forestry practices in the 1800s and still teaches them to the world at the College of Menominee Nation. Tribal resistance to mining, pipelines, and thoughtless development has protected whole ecosystems. According to a study by Leila Salazar-López, "Indigenous people are 4 percent of the world's population but they protect 80 percent of the world's biodiversity."[35]

If Indians respect the environment, how come the Makah hunt endangered whales?

First of all, Native Americans have always hunted, fished, and gathered. And for many thousands of years, those efforts were done sustainably. Tribal people did not hunt animals to extinction. All the problems started when the first White guys arrived. There was a state hunting season on woodland caribou for all Minnesota citizens of all races well into the 1900s, when for decades it was known that the entire species was endangered.

The record and the view of most Natives support a practice of sustainable harvest and respect for the environment. It's not always perfect, especially when Natives have had to contend with non-Natives taking at a level and scope that far exceeded their own traditional use. In Minnesota, Wisconsin, and Michigan, this did tremendous damage to fish

A 2016 environmental march in solidarity with the Dakota Access Pipeline protestors at Standing Rock.

populations and made it hard for Native people to sustain their own use of their own waterways and resources, even on reservations.

For the Makah, who live on the Pacific Coast in the state of Washington, hunting whales with traditional tribal weapons and watercraft is not just an ancient practice to get food, it's an ancient ceremony that is important to the identity of the people. Their harvest (and other parts of their identity, such as the tribal language) has been restricted and assaulted for a long time, so revitalizing and maintaining a whale hunt is viewed by many tribal members as an act of sovereignty, a positive traditional identity development, and an important coming-of-age activity for tribal members. They harvest one whale per year. Japanese, Russian, British, and American whaling operations did tremendous damage to many whale populations over hundreds of years. The Makah practice did not damage whale populations—others did that. And harvesting one whale per year is not likely to negatively impact the entire population of whales. I think the Makah practice is acceptable and understandable and even worthy of support, especially since the Makah also spend significant time and resources advocating for and protecting the health and vitality of the ocean and other ecosystems in their area.

Do Indians have a stronger sense of community than non-Indians?

Definitely. For most Americans, living in this country has meant dislocating from motherland and mother tongue. An

American can move from the East Coast to the West and shift from being a New Yorker to being a Californian. Identity has become malleable. Native Americans have a stronger tether and bond to community. Even most Native Americans who leave their home reservations to work in cities will frequently travel home for family and community functions. And regardless of personal religious choice, it is exceptionally rare for Indians to have a funeral outside their home community, even if they've spent most of their life living off-reservation.

Some places have an especially strong sense of community. In Ponemah, on the Red Lake Reservation, no individuals own land. All land is held in federal trust for the benefit of all tribal members. Homesteads are established for families that live on the reservation, but those families cannot own the land on which they live. This situation makes it hard to get a loan for a house, but it has maintained a strong sense of community. The rights to homestead in a particular place are passed down through families. Almost all of the families on that reservation are living on plots of land that their parents and grandparents and great-grandparents, going back through generations, have lived on. Further, in Ponemah, the custom is to bury one's dead relatives in the front yard. Often many generations are buried in a front yard—which makes it a lot harder to sell the family farm and move to California. And although not every single member of every single family attends every funeral, at least *someone* from every family attends local funerals and brings food. They do this not just because they knew the person, which, given a community numbering 1,000, they usually do. They do it simply because they are members of the same community. The Pueblo also have a remarkably strong sense of community. When there is a dance or feast day, every family participates without question or resistance.

How are different gender identities and roles viewed in Native communities today?

Indian communities are very different today from the way they were when Europeans first arrived. Being a man or woman used to make a big difference in someone's eligibility to be a leader. Today it still has an impact, but not nearly as much. In Ojibwe communities, women are actually more likely to be elected to tribal office than men. In many other places, it doesn't make much difference. Among the Pueblo, it still does make a difference—usually only men become war chiefs and governors.

At Native ceremonies, being a man or woman often matters more than it does in politics. Ceremonial roles in Native communities have changed, but slowly and with great resistance. In politics, however, most tribes have entirely new structures to their governments. Democratic elections have replaced hereditary chieftainship in determining who runs the government on most reservations.

Although most humans are cisgender male or female (their gender matches their birth sex characteristics), some humans from all cultures have not neatly fit into these two gender categories. Many variations of transgender identity have been documented across the world and throughout history. Today, Natives show up just as varied as everyone else. To some degree, mainstream media and social views probably have a greater impact on the perspectives of young Native people today than the traditional values concerning gender roles or sexual identity. It is true that many Native Americans have a greater sensitivity to differential treatment based on race and gender and that Native Americans tend to vote for more Democrats than Republicans outside of Oklahoma, which may indicate a somewhat more liberal, modern political viewpoint on gender identity among many, but certainly not all, Native people.

What is life like for LGBTQ Natives today?

The experience of LGBTQ Natives is as varied as the experience of non-Native LGBTQ people. Some identify with and prefer the label *two-spirit*, but not all. While people from any marginalized group might be more sensitive to someone else's experience of marginalization or mistreatment, that is also not always the case. Homophobia and bigotry pervades all of North America, and Native spaces are not an exception. It can be tough for people who are part of more than one marginalized group.

We all need affinity space—places where we can go and be accepted for exactly who we are and where we don't have to explain everything in order to be understood. If someone is LGBTQ and Native, they may need some Native affinity space so their racial experience is shared by people around them. But they also need affinity space around their experience and identity as LGBTQ. Sometimes it can be a real challenge to find both in the same place. In an LGBTQ affinity space a Native person may feel racially isolated. And in a Native affinity space they may feel isolated or marginalized for being LGBTQ. My sister is a lesbian, and, when living in rural northern Minnesota so she could be close to family and her Native community, she felt like there were only two other lesbians around and she had already dated both of them. But the Internet and her personal and professional connections kept her connected with her lesbian affinity and dating world too, and she's married to the woman of her dreams now. But it wasn't always easy.

What's your perspective on Christian missionaries today?

There are many Christian missionaries, clergy, and laypeople doing work in Native communities today. Red Lake in northern Minnesota, to take one, has a Catholic church, school, and clergy there every day. Many other missionaries work with Indigenous people in Mexico and South America. For most Natives, it's hard to separate their history from present-day relationships. Missionaries have always done their work through schools and churches that have advocated the Doctrine of Discovery, and they often kept Native kids away from their parents during the boarding school era. Today, some Indians are Catholic, Episcopalian, Methodist, or Baptist and appreciate or even admire missionaries. But many more resent their continued presence in Native communities and view that presence as an effort to assimilate them to dominant religious traditions, language, and culture. They would rather have the missionaries simply leave them alone. Most Indians, whether they are Christian or not, would like to see the churches own their role in the history of oppressing Natives, and make a meaningful effort at educating about that history and addressing historic and contemporary injustice, something most churches and missionary groups seem reluctant to embrace.

Are a lot of Natives Christian today?

Yes. We don't have survey data to tell you how many or even roughly what percent of the Native population is Christian, but it's pretty high. In places like Oklahoma, Kansas, and Nebraska, the majority of the Native population is Christian. But there are quite a few people who follow traditional religious beliefs and more still who participate in the Native American Church, which combines Christianity with older Native beliefs and use of peyote. In Hawaii, where there has been a successful ongoing language revitalization effort, most of the population still uses Christian practices for weddings and funerals. At the same time, in the Great Lakes and Plains, there is a higher percentage of the Indian population that follows traditional Indigenous religious practices exclusively. In my many travels throughout Indian country, I have witnessed and sense a deep interest in revitalizing ancient and ongoing Indigenous beliefs and practices, and increasing disillusionment with colonial ways of thinking and doing things, including Christianity.

Is it true that the Pueblo and some other tribes combine Christian and traditional Native practices?

Yes. I have some great friends at Cochiti Pueblo in New Mexico, and I witnessed a really fascinating ceremony with them. When the Spanish colonized the Pueblo in the 1500s and 1600s, they built a church at the center of each Pueblo village and forced everyone to be baptized. The Pueblo had no choice but to comply or be killed, so they complied. But in secret, they brought each newly baptized child into the kiva (their main ceremonial structure) and washed off the baptism with a tribal ceremony. The Spanish were chased out of Pueblo country in 1680 in a major revolt against Spanish colonization. But even when the Spanish were gone, and even today with them long gone, the Pueblo people replicate that ceremony. Each child gets baptized and then gets the baptism washed off. It might seem easier not to do the baptism at all, but that's not the custom. The church and the kiva stand at the center of every Pueblo.

The Native American Church combines Christianity with traditional Native beliefs, the use of a water drum, and pre-Columbian use peyote. Quanah Parker, an early Comanche practitioner of the Native American Church, said, "The White Man goes into his church house and talks about Jesus, but the Indian goes into his tipi and talks to Jesus."[36]

Many Christian Natives also frequently participate in powwows and other dimensions of their tribal culture. Sometimes, the Christian churches in their communities use Indigenous symbolism, like medicine wheels and feathers, and tribal medicines, like sage, for smudging (burning to create medicinal smoke, like incense). Culture and religion are not the same thing, but they are connected.

What is Indian religion?

Because there is so much diversity in Indian country, there is no such thing as one "Indian religion." In the Great Lakes and other regions, some tribes have societies that require a religious initiation. Such initiations are conducted entirely according to ancient tribal customs but function much like baptism and confirmation do for Christians. Those ceremonies serve to place the initiates on a particular religious path and are often accompanied by instructions and expectations for a certain code of conduct. Other tribes have societies that are spiritual in nature but do not induct someone into a particular religious belief system.

For most tribes, though, religious belief is less focused upon specific ceremonies or induction into specific groups than on a set of values, beliefs, and rituals infused into everyday life. Because of this, Indian religion, spiritual perspective, and custom tend to be organic, somewhat fluid, and integrated into other parts of people's lives rather than a separate activity with a membership list.

In addition to the Native American Church, other Indian religious rituals have infused ideas, values, or even customs of Christianity with tribal practice.

The traditional tribal religions of all Native Americans revolve around belief in a higher power—a common creator for all people. But they often acknowledge spiritual power in all things and all beings—fish, animals, birds, and people. This is not polytheistic, but it is different from Judaism, Islam, and Christianity.

Why do Indians use tobacco for ceremonies?

Most tribal communities in North America use tobacco. Although customs vary from tribe to tribe, most Indians believe that any spiritual request made of the Creator or one's fellow human beings must be "paid" for. Tobacco is viewed as an item of not just economic but primarily spiritual value. It is a reciprocal offering. Some tribes, including all of the Pueblo, also use cornmeal with this same view in mind.

Some tribes, such as the Potawatomi and Ho-Chunk (Winnebago), cultivate their own tobacco. Other tribes make "tobacco" from other plants and medicines, especially the inner bark of red willow or dogwood. Often red willow tobacco is mixed with other medicines or cultivated tobacco to form kinnickinnick. Indian people who practice traditional religious beliefs and customs differentiate between the use of spiritual tobacco and the abuse of chemical-laden pleasure tobacco. When tobacco is used in ceremony, generally it is the least carcinogenic form and the smoking does not involve inhalation, somewhat mitigating potential health risks.

Isaac Treuer offering tobacco.

What are kachinas?

At Hopi, Zuni, Laguna, Acoma, Isleta, and other Puebloan communities in the Southwest, people use the word *kachina* to refer to spirits. If something is considered a kachina, it is believed to have spiritual power or presence. Examples include thunderbirds, the wind, special places, and even the souls of ancestors. It is believed that kachinas have relationships to one another just like people do. Some folks have identified over 400 different kachinas. The Hopi believe that many of the kachinas live around the San Francisco Peaks (near Flagstaff, Arizona). For the Zuni, many live in

the water near their pueblo. Regardless of where they live, kachinas travel to the people. They come to dance, eat, sing, bring gifts, and make it rain.

Many Puebloan people seek the help of kachinas through ceremony. They have dances and ask the kachinas for rain, good harvests, healing, fertility, and protection. Usually there are dancers who wear elaborate regalia to dress like and symbolically represent the kachinas. At these ceremonies, both the kachina spirits and the dancers are called *kachinas*.

The Hopi and some others in the Southwest have a custom of creating dolls that represent the kachinas. This custom started in the late 1800s. But now it is a highly specialized form of art. The dolls are not toys or idols for worship. They are supposed to look like the spirits so that they can be studied. It is believed that children will get to know the spirits better this way. The dolls are made of cottonwood, painted, and marked with unique symbols. In the mid-1900s, some of the Native artists who made dolls started to sell them to people outside the Native community for art appreciation rather than cultural use. Today a single doll can sell for as much as $10,000.

It seems like Indians have a deeper spiritual connection than people in many other religious traditions. Is that true?

Most Indian religious traditions are far less hierarchical, structured, or driven by rigid organization than Abrahamic (Christianity, Judaism, Islam) religious forms, making association and practice more natural and easier to access. For example, Christians rely upon the Bible to obtain moral teachings and religious belief. Someone who is not baptized is often denied or at least discouraged from participating in communion. For most Native ceremonies, anyone from the tribe with a good heart can attend and participate.

For many participants in Indian spirituality, there is no rulebook to govern their knowledge of the Creator. It is far more likely that someone would go fasting to obtain a vision, and rely upon that vision for their deeper understanding of the Creator and their relationship with the Almighty. There is much less power placed in the hands of a Native spiritual leader than in a pope, bishop, priest, rabbi, imam, or other religious official. But Indian religious leaders do have status and often receive a high degree of respect from people in their community.

Usually if somebody does not like what they hear or the substance of any particular religious form in Indian country, they are free to have nothing to do with it. And that won't significantly diminish their access to their religion or their status as a religious person among their peers. The same freedom does not exist for Catholics, for example, who would have a hard time practicing their faith without attending mass. There are a few exceptions to this higher degree of religious freedom within Native communities. Among the Pueblo, each community has one series of sacred dances, and there are not alternative dances or numerous spiritual leaders to choose among.

Access to genuine spiritual connection can be frustrating for many people, including Indians, especially those living in urban communities or places where traditional religious practice has become severely depleted or assimilated. Those frustrations are somewhat lessened by the fact that for most Indians, prayer is not a weekly event arranged by others, but a daily event that people do on their own. Further, access to even more complicated ceremonies and free expression at those ceremonies is less strict for many Native people, when they can get to them.

What is meant by Native "ways of knowing"?

Most Americans are familiar with a certain way of learning and problem solving. This way includes things like the "scientific method," where there is a theory, testing, data collecting, analysis, and so forth. We are used to reading and memorizing to learn things too. But some cultures have different ways of getting information. Those are often called *ways of knowing.*

One of my Ojibwe elders, Nancy Jones, provides a perfect example. She said that you can always tell when the bear cubs are born. It happens in the winter, between mid-January and the end of February. Even though this is a six-week window of time, Jones says that on the very day it happens, the weather always warms up. Even though there is snow on the ground and it's winter, the warm-up comes with a fog, which is the "breath of the bear," waking the unborn cubs. People who are used to the scientific

Nancy Jones (Ojibwe), Nigigoonsiminikaaning First Nation (Ontario).

method would question her assertion and ask for the data sets to prove it. They might even dismiss what she said as a "myth."

Several years ago, the Great Lakes Indian Fish and Wildlife Commission did a large study of bears using the scientific method. They recorded the weather, kept cameras in bear dens, and wrote down everything they observed. They saw that there *is* a six-week period from mid-January to the end of February when the bear cubs are born, and that every time they are born the weather warms up and there is a fog. A western scientific thinker would be tempted to assume that a warm-up in the weather must coincide with a change in barometric pressure, which triggers a physiological response in the bears, telling them that it's time to give birth. Let's assume that all of that is true. My question is, How did Nancy Jones know? The answer is that she had a valid body of knowledge and a different way to get that knowledge and interpret it. That's an Indigenous way of knowing. It's different from the western way. But it's still valid.

Often historic Indians have been dismissed as primitive—a few bands of roaming nomads in the wilderness without the technological mastery Europeans had. But Mayan and Aztec builders created structures that are still a marvel of engineering and remain standing today. The Anasazi, ancestors of the Pueblo people today, built numerous structures (without slave labor) across the Southwest that still stand thousands of years after they were built. Americans can't make a building last more than forty years in some places. At Chaco Canyon and many places in what's now the United

States, Mexico, and Guatemala, the buildings didn't just stand for thousands of years. They were constructed in ways that are hard to replicate even today. In some places, the sun could shine through a portal they constructed on the first day of the summer solstice and illuminate a basilisk a mile away—only on that day. And they built such wonders without many of the tools we would use to try to replicate their work, such as a transit or even a wheel. They knew things about science that were incredibly advanced and even ahead of their European counterparts.

What are some of the customs related to dating and marriage?

Native American dating and marriage customs varied a great deal historically. Some made arranged marriages, even polygamous ones (discussed earlier), but most had free choice. Americans couldn't imagine marrying for something other than love. When people were under a lot more pressure, the practical benefits of marriage—partnership and help, protection and provision—played a bigger role than they do today. Divorce happened in historic Native communities but less commonly than it does now. We could say the same things about European marriage and dating.

Usually Native families encouraged their young adults to make a good marriage choice without directly controlling it. One of my great mentors, the late Archie Mosay, was born in 1901. When his father was courting his mother, he used to walk for three days from East Lake, Minnesota, to

Balsam Lake, Wisconsin, to see her. They would go for walks and visit and fell in love, but her aunts always walked behind them to make sure they didn't do much kissing or anything else until after they were married. Today that sounds like a strange way to do things in both East Lake and Balsam Lake, even if it was cute. Most Native people today mirror mainstream society in their dating practices and customs. Teenagers and young adults have most of the say over their choices and timing in relationships.

What happens when a Native and a non-Native person date?

I know a lot about this question. My dad was White and my mom Indian. I am Native and look the part (brown skin, long hair). My wife is from what I jokingly call the Swedish-American tribe (blond hair and blue eyes). There are special challenges and blessings to being in an interracial relationship.

The blessings include bringing people together from very different backgrounds and experiences. It can be unifying and beautiful. And it can be empowering for a mixed-race couple that finds a way to do this effectively. There is always a diversity of lived experience and perspective in the relationship and the family. I learn a lot from my wife and vice versa. I think it helps us both see the world with more compassion and understanding. When my wife and I got married, we had an Ojibwe spiritual leader use a pipe with two stems and wrap us in a star quilt while he prayed for us. But my wife wore a white wedding dress that looked traditional in the European sense of the word. We had guests of every racial group you could imagine. It felt unifying on many levels.

There can be challenges to a racially mixed marriage too. People outside the relationship often have at least some low-level bias. They can come across as insensitive and sometimes even rude. That can make it harder for both

people in the relationship to be at ease when the larger families get together. Sometimes inside the relationship it just takes extra effort to understand someone whose racial experience has been different from yours. When we bring our whole family to ceremonies and my wife is the only White person around, I sometimes forget how uncomfortable she can be and need to remind myself to introduce her to everyone and pay more attention to her, so she feels more at ease. It's the same for me when roles reverse. But when two people of different backgrounds have a great love and good communication skills, dating and marriage across racial lines works just fine. The world is not colorblind, but love is.

What are some of the customs related to pregnancy and childbirth?

Customs vary so much from tribe to tribe that it is difficult to give an answer that shows the breadth of belief and practice. Many Indians believe that we do not have souls. Rather, we are souls. We have bodies, which are just temporary houses for our souls. The terms *soul* and *spirit* are interchangeable. The Ojibwe word for *body, niiyaw,* literally means "my vessel." The body is a container.

Many tribes believe that when a woman is pregnant, the spirit of her unborn child is hovering around her body, waiting to inhabit the fetus. (For example, a common belief in the Great Lakes region is that the spirit of the child actually chooses his or her parents. That spirit then comes to earth to hover around his or her mother while she's pregnant.) For this reason, and because in former times there was a much higher rate of infant mortality, there are many taboos around pregnancy.

Many Native Americans believe that abortion can interfere with the Great Spirit's "plan" for a new baby. While lots of Native people today are pro-choice, the decision to get an abortion or not is often influenced by this belief. Natives are frequently told that nobody knows better than the Great Spirit when someone's time should end. Many Indians choose not to have abortions because of this common belief.

To take another example, people in Indian country usually do not have a baby shower before the child is born; doing so would show the spirits that the family assumes the child will arrive and live. Earl Otchingwanigan (Ojibwe from Michigan) and other elders have often said that the cradleboard for a family's firstborn should not be made until the child is four weeks old. Once the cradleboard has been made, it becomes a family heirloom, and it can be passed from the first to the second to the third child without restriction.

Expectant mothers are told to be careful of what they say, as it can invite good or bad luck. In some tribes, mothers are told not to look at salamanders, snakes, or even cats. Many families instruct expectant mothers not to eat burnt food. In some tribes expectant mothers are told not to eat too many strawberries or blueberries to avoid giving the child blue or red marks on his or her body.

Expectant mothers in many tribes are also urged not to attend funerals. Birth and death don't mix. Everybody loves a brand-new baby—even departing souls. Out of fear that the departing soul might want to take a sweet baby with him or her, expectant mothers simply stay away. Even young children typically avoid funerals. If a child's presence at a funeral cannot be avoided, the custom for many tribes is to rub charcoal on his or her forehead. This is a "passover," so the departing soul will not see or disturb the child.

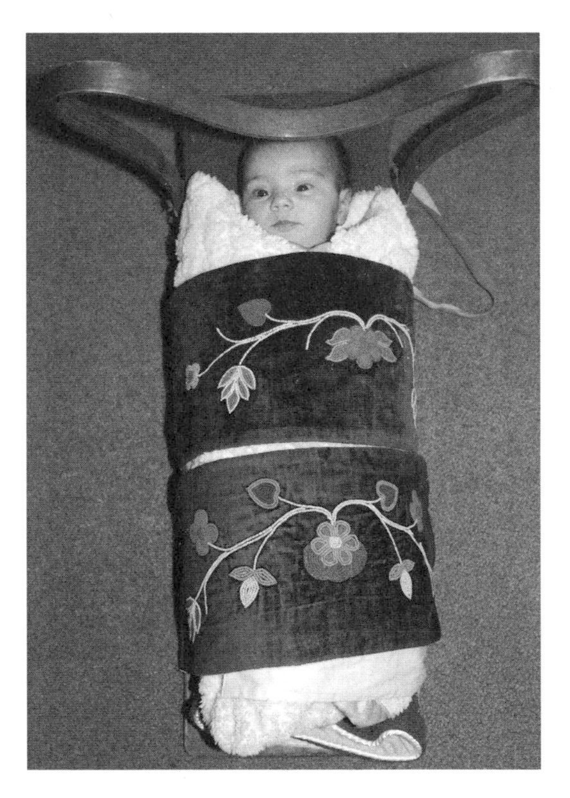

Luella Treuer in a cradleboard. The cradleboard entertains the child while keeping her safe.

There is also a great deal of variation in childbirth customs. According to Ojibwe spiritual leader Archie Mosay (Wisconsin), the parents made a tea out of catnip, called *namewashk* in Ojibwe, in order to give the new baby his or her first bath. Some families also lay the baby on a bed of moss so the child will bond with Mother Earth.

Many Native families save the placenta and bring it home. There are a few different customs concerning its proper treatment. According to Ojibwe elder Leonard Moose, the placenta should be put up in the east side of a white pine tree. The white pine is a symbol of wisdom and longevity, and east is the direction from which the sun rises and the source of all life. According to Earl Otchingwanigan, the placenta should be buried on the north side of a maple tree. The maple tree is the tree of life, and north is the direction at the end of the cycle. With all of these customs, tobacco is put out with the placenta.

A week or two after the umbilical cord has been cut, the dried end of the cord falls off and among Algonquian tribes is often placed in a pouch. If the child is being kept in a cradleboard, the pouch is hung on the crash bar for the cradleboard. If the child spends more time in an Indian swing, the pouch is tied on the swing. If the child uses neither a cradleboard nor a swing, the pouch can be hung on the wall near where they sleep. After one year, the spiritual connection between the baby and his or her umbilical cord fades. The cord end can be kept as a memento, but it no longer serves any physical or spiritual function. It is said that babies who did not have their cord ends saved for a year will spend the rest of their lives "looking for" them. They might want to open cupboards in strangers' houses or look through other people's medicine cabinets.

What are naming ceremonies?

Getting an Indian name is one of the most basic yet treasured customs in Native communities. Many tribal members believe that it is actually the spirits who name people, even though humans perform the ceremonies. Parents do not usually pick the name for their child; rather, the parents pick a spiritual leader to bestow a name.

For many tribes, including the Ho-Chunk, Meskwaki, Dakota, Lakota, and others, there is often an ancestral connection in the giving of a name. For tribes where the ancestral connection is important, the giving of a name creates a strong and lifelong relationship between the person receiving it and an ancestor who has gone on to the spirit world.

Other tribes, such as the Potawatomi, Ottawa, and Ojibwe, do not usually have an ancestor connection in the giving of a name. For those tribes, the names are usually obtained from fasting or dreams, and each name has a story behind it. Someone might see a vision or have a dream about a giant bear coming through the clouds and give the name "Bear." Some Ojibwe chiefs have used public names, in addition to their spirit names. Bagone-giizhig (Hole in the Day) and some other Minnesota Ojibwe chiefs even used their fathers' names so they could use their fathers' recognition and prestige.

Many Ojibwe tribal elders instruct people to have a feast four days after the birth of a child. The purpose of this first feast is to welcome the arrival of a new spirit in the world. In some places, the naming ceremony is performed at this feast. For others, it happens later. Both parents have equal say in choosing a name giver. The only requirement for name givers in most tribal traditions is that they have Indian names themselves.

No matter who is running a naming ceremony, some ideas about traditional Indian names are universal. Indian names are spiritual identification—how spirits know people. As described earlier, the Ojibwe word for body, *niiyaw,* literally means "my vessel." *Niiyawe'enh* means "my namesake." That word is used for both the name giver and the name receiver because it describes a spiritual gift that is housed in both of their bodies. The namesake relationship is for life. But a namesake is more than just the person who gives a name. A namesake acts as an adviser, guide, and role model, much like a godparent in other traditions. Namesakes are often important in other ceremonies throughout life.

Usually, if someone wants to ask for spiritual help, they approach a wise person and give tobacco. But when namesakes take tobacco, they are making a lifetime commitment. Later in life, someone can call his or her namesake and ask for spiritual help, even if the namesake has moved far away. Because namesakes accept tobacco on the day of the naming, they can smoke their pipes and pray for their namesakes.

Can a non-Native person get an Indian name?

In many tribes, Indian names can be bestowed upon anyone, regardless of race. The custom is open and widely shared. However, this practice is not universal among tribal communities. For some, names come from specific ancestors and cannot be given to someone who is not a lineal descendant. For others, names come from ancestors and can go to anyone, but family members are reluctant to give such a special personal honor to an outsider. Some tribes, like the Hopi and Pueblo, used to be more open to outsiders but got overrun by curiosity seekers; they have made many of their cultural customs more exclusive to protect their sanctity and to ease access for their own people.

If a non-Indian person wishes to obtain an Indian name, they should simply offer tobacco to a knowledgeable spiritual leader and ask what the custom is in that area. And should the answer be that Indian names are given only to Indian people in that community, they should respect the existing tradition.

What are coming-of-age ceremonies?

As in many cultures, coming of age is a special and empowering time in a Native person's life. Customs for this time differ from one tribe to another and are also usually very different for boys and girls.

In Indian country, menstruation is seen as a symbol of the spiritual power of women and their ability to bring life into the world. This view is different from common cultural beliefs in mainstream society, which often leave adolescent girls feeling dirty or embarrassed when their change of life occurs. For many tribes, a woman's spiritual power in relation to other spiritual powers is similar to the repelling effect of trying to push together two magnets: it's not bad, but it needs to be given its own space.

When a girl gets her first "moon" (monthly period), she is full of this positive spiritual power. It is a common belief that the power is so great it could interfere with other things. In former times throughout the Great Lakes area, when a girl got her first moon, she spent time alone in her own wigwam. It's difficult to do that today, so a girl might spend more time in her bedroom or another safe, private place. In times past, this separation was enforced in a very strict way—a young woman was secluded from men, from sacred items, and from many kinds of ceremonies. During this time, grandmothers and female namesakes instructed her on how to conduct herself as a woman.

Most Great Lakes tribes instruct girls to use their own dish and spoon throughout the year of their first menses. This practice teaches about how powerful they are and how to use restraint, how to be aware of their actions. Most girls store their special dishes in a bundle separate from other household items. Other commonly followed rules for the entire first year as a woman include these: don't go swimming, don't go in the water at all, don't step over anything, don't handle men's belongings, don't touch anything growing—new life, brand-new babies, puppies, and so on.

This is the start of the time when a girl can have a baby. She is instructed about the changes to her body and her rights and responsibilities as a woman. During her first year, an Ojibwe girl can't eat traditional foods until a feast is held where someone feeds her that season's food as it is harvested. This feast offers protection to the harvests: the woman's power is so great that if she eats the fresh wild rice, or blueberries, or fish without a feast, she could affect the crop in that area.

Once the final food is fed to an Ojibwe girl at the end of her first year as a woman, there is a more elaborate ceremony, during which all the women, including her extended family and her female namesakes, come to give teachings. These lessons might include:

> *You are a woman now. So, if you see a bunch of us sitting around, you come sit with us. You are one of us.*
>
> *You are a woman now, so you have a right and a responsibility to be respected by men. What that means is:*
>
> *No one can hit you;*
> *No one can call you names;*
> *No one can make you do something sexually that you don't want to do.*

Look around at your ceremonies. You'll see that there are jobs for women and for men. There is a place for women at ceremonies. Those places at those ceremonies show the balance of men and women.

Throughout your life, if you ever cannot avoid touching something you shouldn't, you can use gloves so your power won't interfere with the spirit power of anything else.

Cedar is a powerful medicine. It can be used as a smudge, as a tea, to sit on, in your shoes, even in your underwear. It acts as a barrier.

Refrain from most ceremonies during your monthly menstrual period. Stay back as far as possible. Exceptions are sometimes made for the most important and longest ceremonies, with added cautions.

Use your skirt. It is your spiritual identification as a woman. You should be proud of your womanhood. Watch your skirt to make sure it doesn't go over people or food.

Now that your first year is up, you don't have to eat on separate dishes anymore, but your spiritual power remains tremendous every time you have your moon.

Sometimes this training is misunderstood by those outside the cultural practice as a way to treat young girls unfairly or more poorly than everyone else. But the indoctrination of girls into the ranks of womanhood is accompanied by such strong and consistent reinforcements of positive power, right, and responsibility that the perception and practice in Indian country is one of empowerment.

Boys often receive instructions on their transition to manhood from a mentor before fasting sometime after their voices begin to change. However, the transition to manhood in many tribes can also be associated with taking on responsibilities as a provider for the people by hunting, fishing, trapping, and snaring.

In most tribes, both boys and girls can harvest wild game. A person's first successful hunt is usually a time of ceremony marking the transition to adulthood. The Ojibwe call the ceremony *oshki-nitaagewin*. Boys may be groomed a little more for it, but girls do *oshki-nitaagewin* too. The word means "to make a kill for the first time," and the ceremony is sometimes repeated for the first rabbit, fish, partridge, and deer.

When one first kills an animal, there is almost always an offering of tobacco. The hunter will actually speak to the animal killed. An effort is made to show the animal that he wasn't simply killed for sport. The animal has given up his life so that the people can eat, a self-sacrifice. It is usually taboo to waste one's kill. There are regional differences, but many animals have a body part that is considered special, that houses the animal's spirit. This part will be put out with tobacco. Some families cook the whole deer and invite the entire village when someone makes a first kill. It is now more common for a family to adapt to

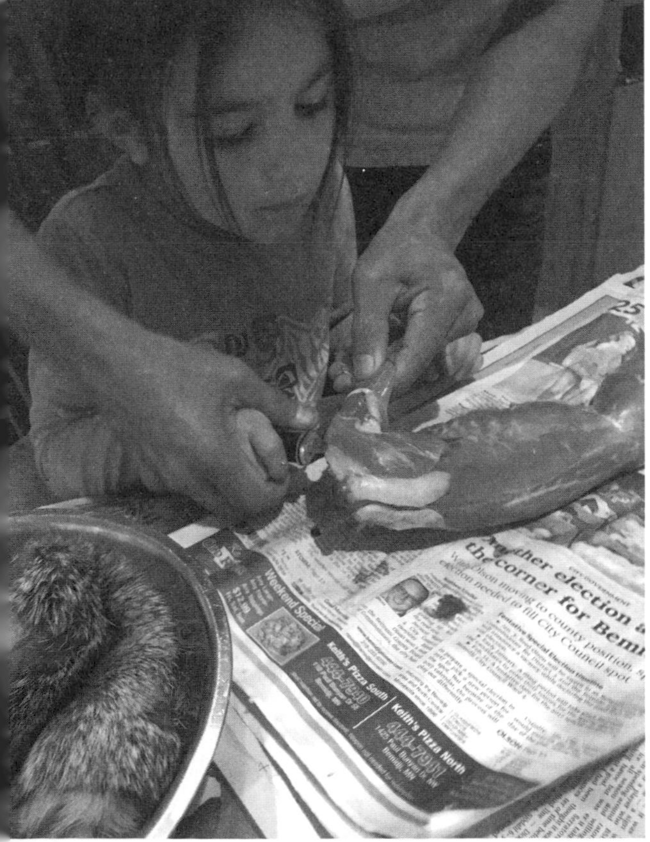

Becoming a successful hunter helps mark the transition to adulthood in many tribes. Pictured above are Isaac and Elias Treuer after a successful fall deer hunt. Below is Mia Treuer, processing a rabbit she snared in the winter.

modern life by cooking some of the deer and then packaging up the rest to give away.

At most first kill feasts, after a tobacco offering, someone approaches the hunter, takes a spoonful of meat, and offers the first bite to him, saying his Indian name. But the hunter has to refuse the first bite. Some people will offer the spoonful four times, and on the fourth time he can eat.

Ojibwe elder Mary Roberts (Manitoba) instructed young people to say something on the first refusal of the offered food: "No, I'm thinking of the children who have no one to provide for them." The food is returned to the pot, a new piece of meat is taken and offered, and the hunter refuses again, saying, "No, I'm thinking of elders who can't get out into the woods to hunt for themselves." So the food is put back; a third spoonful is offered, and again he refuses: "No, I'm thinking of the people who came here today to support me." When offered a fourth bite of the food, he can eat it. Then the hunter is told, "You just changed your life. You are now a provider for the people. And every time you kill an animal, these are the things you think about: children who have no one providing for them, elders who can't feed themselves, your family, community, and supporters. And to reinforce this, you now have to give away your entire remaining kill. You are not hunting for glory. You are hunting for food and to provide for your family and community. It's important that you have respect for your family and the animals." The young hunter is then thanked with hugs and handshakes and formally acknowledged as having changed from dependent to provider.

How come everyone's laughing at a traditional Indian funeral?

Not everyone is laughing. Grief is real and difficult for people of all cultures. But for many tribes, belief in the afterlife is deeply held. In my Ojibwe culture, we do not believe in heaven or hell. Everyone goes to the same place when we die. Unlike in funeral customs for many Judeo-Christian traditions, a grieving family does not invite a priest to preach. The entire funeral is for the person who died. Food, songs, prayers, and instructions on how to reach the spirit world are given to the deceased. The process is often long and complicated, but it heightens the sense of a departing soul's arrival in the spirit world, respect for tradition, and celebration of a life lived and an even better destination for the departing soul. People grieve at traditional funerals, too, but the grief is lessened by the spiritual process and ritual. There is also usually a lot of community and family support. In many Native communities, all families, even those not related to the deceased, cook and bring food to wakes and funerals.

The Ojibwe bury their dead in shallow graves, put a hole in the casket, and even make a hole to the spirit house that is placed over the burial site, all to enable the soul to visit its body. Since the spirit of the departed is believed to be emotionally attached to its body, this gives time for the attachment to lessen. But after four years the spirit house is allowed to disintegrate and return to earth.

Do Indians charge for participation in their ceremonies?

For the most part, only fake medicine men do that. Mille Lacs elder James Clark once told me, "If you give someone a dollar for a ceremony, the spirits will look at it and think that it's a pretty small blanket." Most ceremonies involve a ritual gift of tobacco. For more important ceremonies, there is usually a food offering and a cloth item such as a blanket. Even more elaborate ceremonies may involve other types of gifts, clothing, and sacred items.

Money is a new concept, so its use in ceremony is usually uncommon. There are some occasions, such as ceremonial drums, where members may give money instead of a homemade or store-purchased gift, but that is different from charging others for helping them. Sometimes spiritual leaders travel great distances at personal expense to assist others, and those seeking their help may give them gas money, but that is also different from their charging a fee. Most tribal members view charging for ceremony as "bad form," and some even consider it taboo.

What is a sweat lodge?

A sweat lodge is small, dome-shaped frame made out of tree saplings that is covered with bark, mats, blankets, or canvas.

Rocks are heated in a fire outside the lodge and brought inside. Water is poured on the rocks similar to a sauna. While sweating in the sweat lodge, people smoke pipes, sprinkle medicine on the hot rocks, sing songs on hand drums, and pray. In addition to prayer, sweat lodges are used to purify people in preparation for fasting, participating in a Sun Dance, or other ceremonies. It's one of the best-known and most widely practiced Indian ceremonies today. As a result, there is a great deal of variation in practice.

Sometimes the ceremony has been copied or even abused by outsiders. In October 2009, a White man named James Arthur Ray charged money to non-Native people to participate in an "authentic Indian sweat lodge ceremony" in Sedona, Arizona. He had dozens of people packed into a small lodge and kept it too hot for too long. Three people died: Kirby Brown, James Shore, and Liz Neuman. Ray was convicted of three counts of negligent homicide.[37] In this case it seems quite clear that the person running the ceremony was an irresponsible fake medicine man who took advantage of non-Native people fascinated with Indian spirituality. I see his actions as criminal and spiritually wrong. Sweat lodges are commonly used by true Native spiritual leaders from many communities, but the physical experience never endangers human life when done responsibly and the event is carried out with a true desire to help others rather than make money from their needs.

A scene from the first Longest Walk protest in 1978, led by the American Indian Movement, which helped spur the American Indian Religious Freedom Act.

Do Indians still get persecuted for their religious beliefs?

Yes. In 1883, the U.S. commissioner of Indian Affairs created a "Code of Indian Offenses" that was used to make Native religious practices illegal.[38] Then the U.S. government sent Indian agents a memo called Circular 1665, which told the agents to ban and break up tribal dances, religious ceremonies, and giveaways, even after Indians became U.S. citizens in 1924. Circular 1665 remained in use until 1933. The first amendment to the U.S. Constitution established freedom of religion, but it was insufficient to provide for the religious freedom of Indians the way it did for Americans of other races.

In 1978, the American Indian Religious Freedom Act sought to remedy that. This law required all government agencies to eliminate interference with Natives' free exercise of their religion. Even after the repeal of Circular 1665, state and federal agencies had routinely denied unemployment benefits to Natives who used peyote, and federal and state agencies denied Natives access to sacred sites when those sites were located in parks and forests managed by government agencies. The 1978 act made it illegal to do these things.

However, even today, many Natives struggle to freely practice their religions. In 2008, Damien Bad Boy, an enrolled member and resident of the White Earth Reservation (Minnesota), was continually harassed by the city of Mahnomen, which claimed that his sweat lodge (on his

Peyote.

private property) violated city building codes, fire codes, and noise ordinances. He went to court and eventually settled a civil suit. The city has never changed its laws or tried to negotiate with the tribe to allow for traditional sweat lodge use.

Bad Boy's case was not unique. An Indian in Tennessee had his sweat lodge destroyed by the local fire department several times in the 1980s. And many tribes and tribal members cannot access their own sacred sites or sacred items. There are a great number of sacred items in museums and private collections owned by non-Native people. And many sacred sites are on private land owned by non-Native people or on nonreservation, government-owned land that still restricts access in spite of the American Indian Religious Freedom Act. The Native American Church uses peyote (a drug made from cactus) and so do some tribes, but use of peyote has often been illegal. Native Americans in federal or state prisons are often allowed access to only Judeo-Christian religious leaders. Tobacco and traditional medicines are not allowed in prisons or most schools. Although conditions have improved over the past century, there are many ways in which free practice of ancient custom remains difficult for Indians.

What sports are most popular for Natives today?

It depends on where you look. In the Great Lakes, Northern Plains, and especially in Canada, hockey is still big. There are several Native hockey players in the NHL right now. In the eastern Great Lakes, from New York to Michigan, lacrosse is huge. A lot of Native lacrosse players continue into college and other lacrosse leagues. Baseball was a really big deal in the 1950s and 1960s in most Native communities, but it's less popular now. A lot of Native kids

Evan Treuer, playing lacrosse with a Native league in Bemidji, Minnesota.

ABOVE: Bronson Koenig (Ho-Chunk), one of many Native basketball players in the collegiate and professional ranks.

LEFT: A shot from the 2019 Native American Basketball Invitational, courtesy of the NABI Foundation.

play football. But far and away the most popular reservation sport today is basketball. Every Indian community I go to there are kids shooting hoops. In Montana, Arizona, New Mexico, Minnesota, and other places, reservation high school teams often make it to the state basketball tournaments. Those kids can play. And sometimes whole communities travel to the games to watch their young people play. It's a lot of fun and pretty inspiring too.

What music is most popular for Natives today?

I have raised nine Native kids and I feel like they have embraced every kind of music under the sun. Most of them love hip-hop. Some like really weird and eccentric modern music. One of my kids is in show choir (glee club) and loves to sing everything catchy on the radio from every decade. I see a lot of other Native kids with this diversity of musical taste too. I love 1980s music. My mom liked Elvis and the Beatles. At the same time, my whole crew loves to powwow. So we listen to Pipestone, Northern Cree, and everything else in that genre. There is some really cool fusion music too, like A Tribe Called Red, which combines powwow music with modern beats. And there are a lot of Indigenous spoken-word artists, like Thomas X, that my kids like too.

Why do Indians have so many kids?

I have nine kids myself, so it might look like I'm not fighting stereotypes on this question. For me, having a large family wasn't a goal or even a plan. I just woke up one day and they were all there on edge of my bed asking for food. But I don't know many people from any racial or ethnic group who have families this big anymore.

Throughout history, many ethnic or racial enclaves have been famous for their large families. For Indians, it is true that many tribes have a culturally ingrained love of family. But the same can still be said for many cultures across the globe nowadays. The larger family size in many parts of Indian country is less because of culture and more because of other variables. Poor people tend to have children at a younger age and to have more of them.

Access to and knowledge of birth control, as well as prenatal and postnatal care, have improved dramatically in Indian country over the past several decades. The birth rate is going down. The trends that have slowed the birth rate throughout the industrialized world are slowly reducing the birth rate in Indian country too. Having six children or more in a family was very common for the grandparent generation and even many in the parental generation, but is quite rare for Indians raising families today.

POWWOW

So you want me to choose between going to powwows and being with you. Well, I made up my mind. Come here pretty girl, give me a kiss goodbye.

—Ojibwe round dance song by Pipestone Singers

What is a powwow?

The word *powwow* comes from a term for spiritual leader in the Narragansett and Massachusett languages, which Europeans later mistakenly used to talk about many types of Native events. Although Ojibwe drum ceremonies, traditional Dakota wacipi dances, and some other tribal ceremonies are sometimes referred to as *powwows,* today's events are usually social, not ceremonial, and are widely practiced all over North America. They usually last anywhere from one to three days, and they are open to people of all tribes, genders, ages, and races. Powwows are mainly dance events, where people wear elaborate beadwork, feathers, and other regalia and dance to a wide array of songs performed by numerous drum groups, each with anywhere from five to twenty singers. The powwow is a somewhat new cultural form, although one of the most vibrant in all of Indian country, and especially popular with young people.[39]

Many tribes had different types of drum ceremonies and war dances at the time of first contact with Europeans. Powwow grew from these ceremonies into a more secular dance with people from many tribes. It used to be that each eagle feather worn by an Indian represented a deed done in battle—a kill, wound, or scalp—so wearing a feather bonnet, bustle, or dog soldier hat marked one as a fearsome warrior. Often, warriors and chiefs proudly displayed their feathers at treaty signings and diplomatic events, showing their military might, parading into the compounds of U.S. Army forts, for example. This custom evolved into the current grand entry, where Indians of all ages and genders parade into the dance arbor, although it is still veterans who lead. Styles of dance from the Omaha (grass dance), Dakota (war dance), Ojibwe (jingle dress), and other tribes were freely shared across tribal lines.

In the 1960s and 1970s, tribal governments in many places began to spend more money to support powwows, encouraging participation by providing meals and even money to dancers and singers. The custom grew into sometimes extravagant displays and even competitions with prize purses for best singing and dancing in multiple categories. Some of the wealthiest tribes, such as the Mashantucket Pequot, sponsored powwows with total prize purses of more than $1 million. Even less well-off tribes like Leech Lake have devoted hundreds of thousands of dollars to support powwow customs. The practice is vibrant because an overwhelming majority of the tribal population participates in powwows, and the custom transcends lines of religious choice, tribe, and race. Access is easy, and the creativity of Native artists and musicians finds fertile ground in the music and regalia. Today tribes and tribal people distinguish between two main types of powwows—traditional powwows, where there is no competition dancing or singing, and contest powwows, which offer prize money for best dance and song performances. The Canadian Aboriginal Festival (historically held in either Toronto or Hamilton, Ontario) is a powwow that routinely attracts over 40,000 people. The Gathering of Nations (held in Albuquerque, New Mexico) has over 70,000 participants. Powwows are a big deal and they are here to stay.

Powwows also offer safe, sober environments that bring communities together and usually involve people of all ages, making them a healthy social option. Some tribal members, though, feel that the financial support given to powwows would be better spent on other, even more important initiatives, such as tribal language and culture revitalization.

What do the different styles of dance mean?

There are many styles of Indian dance. The “men’s traditional” style typically includes a feather bustle worn on the back, elaborate beadwork, and a dog soldier hat, feather headdress, or roach (made of porcupine and deer hair with feathers on top). This kind of dance regalia comes from the older war customs, in which warriors earned feathers in battle and displayed them at war and scalp dances (but not always in battle). Today, it is not expected that those who wear such regalia have “earned” their feathers by military deeds, although the feathers are still highly respected. Because in former times each feather represented a human being who was killed or wounded, a feather that is accidentally dropped in the powwow arena is usually picked up only by military veterans, who use a special song to dance around it and retrieve the fallen “comrade.” Traditional dancers mimic the actions of warriors and hunters scouting for enemies or game.

Another common men's dance is the "grass dance." Originally a distinct style used only in the Omaha Grass Dance Society, it spread to other tribes, became very popular in the 1970s, and remains so today. Dancers do not usually have feather bustles, although they do often have head roaches made of porcupine and deer hair, sometimes with a feather or two. The body of the outfit includes an apron with long fringe that mimics the action of grass blowing in the wind. The dancers themselves spin, turn, and shuffle their feet as if they were moving in tall grass, all to the beat of the drum.

Men's "fancy dance" comes from the older traditional style. It includes many elements of traditional regalia, but usually with bright colors and double bustles that are not always made of eagle feathers. The dancers display rapid footwork and even gymnastic moves—spinning, cartwheeling, and jumping. Among the most popular styles to watch, fancy dance is much more widely practiced at competition powwows than at traditional ones.

There are other styles of men's dance as well, most of which involve mimicking the actions or motions of birds or animals. There are also many styles of beadwork. The eastern Great Lakes tribes often use more floral designs, while the western Great Lakes and Plains tribes often favor more geometric patterns, but dancers are free to create whatever they wish. Although some people purchase their dance regalia, most make their own or have family members help them, and use personal colors given to them at their naming ceremonies, from dreams, or while fasting.

In older dance forms that came before powwows, women did not always dance in all tribes, but that's not the case at powwows (and even many ceremonies) now. Powwow dancing is as popular and widely practiced among women as it is among men.

The "women's traditional" dance has many variations in regalia. Southern Plains style often incorporates elk teeth to show off the hunting skill of a woman's partner. Western tribes sometimes make use of the cowry shell, although that item has religious significance for many Great Lakes tribes and is less common in that area. Typically, the outfits have elaborate beadwork and very long fringe, and gentle dance motions rock the fringe back and forth. Often, women's traditional dancers ring the outside edge of the dance arbor in a circle around the men.

The women's "jingle dress" style involves a long, tight dress covered in numerous jingles, often constructed from snuff can lids or other metal. The jingles make a swooshing sound. The jingle dress style evolved from an Ojibwe man's dream of the dress around the time of World War I. The jingle part of the regalia is believed to have healing power. Sometimes jingle dress healing songs are performed at traditional powwows, but usually the secular version of the dance is on display. A more ceremonial use of jingle dress dancing, for healing, is usually done to ceremony songs at various drum ceremonies. There it is accompanied by food offerings, prayers, and the giving of gifts.

Women's "fancy shawl" is the other popular form of female dance. The attire involves a colorful dress and shawl.

There are many categories of powwow regalia for men including traditional (left), grass (center), and fancy (right).

2

Women's powwow regalia is just as varied as men and includes traditional (left), jingle (center), and fancy shawl (right).

The dancer spins and moves her arms to mimic the actions of a butterfly coming out of its cocoon and flitting about the arena.

Why are "49" songs sung in English?

The "49" is one of the few partner dances exhibited at powwows. The music is different from other powwow songs—slower and syncopated (with an accented rhythm). Partners hold hands and move in a long line, twisting and winding around the arena, following the moves of the lead couple. The music uses English in part because this dance is inspired by French and English partner dance customs but also because is it an especially popular form of music among young singers. Over time, tribal song composers have tried to entertain with wit and even popular culture lines, such as "you got the right one, baby," and "good ol' fashioned Indian lovin.'" It's part of the modern culture of the music.

How come there are prize purses at powwows?

Not all Indians are happy about the recent emergence of the contest powwow, although it is a huge part of the life of many Native people today. Competition for prize money in various styles of dance and singing comes from the rodeo part of powwow's origins. In the 1900s, the dances became more rigidly stylized and social and less ceremonial. Today, tribes with significant financial resources often offer these large prize purses to draw numerous singers, dancers, and spectators. It is seen as a way to show local hospitality, raise the profile of the host community in Indian country, and demonstrate authentic culture to outsiders.

Most tribes also sponsor "princess" and "brave" competitions for young people at powwows. In addition to dancing, young competitors give speeches (often in the tribal language) and do community service. Winners are named "princess" or "brave" for their communities and lead all the other dancers into the arena at the start of each powwow grand entry. Someone who wins princess or brave is usually expected to attend as many powwows as possible for a year to represent their community, and at the end of the year, the outgoing princess or brave will sponsor a giveaway at their home community's powwow.

Some Indians oppose the expansion of contest powwows over traditional powwows and other cultural activities. They say that placing a financial value on participants' abilities to sing and dance takes over older cultural ideals of community cohesion, inclusiveness, and respectful generosity. Tribes and tribal people are agents of their own cultural change. The modern powwow is a welcome, healthy gathering of people from many communities. It is a joyous social event and source of community pride. But it is not a substitution for traditional religion or ways of life.

Can non-Native people dance at powwows?

Yes. Although there may be rules against outsiders' participation in ceremonial events and customs for some tribes, powwow has no such official barriers. Furthermore, as the number of Indians with light complexions has grown over the past few decades, many non-Native people may even be assumed to be Native at powwows. The powwow emcee will announce to the audience if there is a special honor song or exhibition song for a style of dance that is limited in any way (such as to grass dancers only or to family members of someone who passed away). Otherwise, powwow music is considered and often called *intertribal*—open to people of all tribes and races.

Do women sing at powwows?

Yes. Women from all tribes sing in a variety of social and ceremonial functions, but there are rules that differ from tribe to tribe. Some types of ceremonial music are exclusively male and other types exclusively female. In many places, men sit around the powwow drums and do the drumming and most of the singing, although women can and often do stand or sit behind the men, singing with them, usually an octave above to the same melody. In the Northwest, women will often sit at the drums and sing with the men.

The first ceremonial drum that the Dakota gave to the Ojibwe came through the vision of a Dakota woman who "saw" men singing at the drum and women sitting behind the men, singing with them. That practice carried over to social forms of singing on large drums for the Ojibwe, Menominee, Potawatomi, and others. For those tribes, it is not seen as an exclusion of women but rather as the greatest way to respect the vision of the woman who "gave birth to the drum." Tribal people respect the traditions of the host communities for both ceremony and powwows, including their different gender rules about singing.

What is the protocol for gifts at powwows?

Visitors are not required to give gifts at powwows, where it is the host community's responsibility to show generosity to others. Toward the end of the powwow, the host community usually sponsors a giveaway, during which they make large piles of blankets and other goods and distribute them to dancers, helpers, and spectators. Sometimes, a family will sponsor a giveaway. Once in a while, a family that is having a hard time might ask for a blanket dance to receive donations for travel or health care. Contributing money during a blanket dance is a free will donation.

TRIBAL LANGUAGES

This is our language. It is the sound of the waves crashing on the shore, the sound of the wind in the pines, the rustle of the leaves in autumn. It is the sound of the birds singing in the forest and the wolves howling in the distance. This is our language, from which we obtain life, our means of knowing who we are, this sacred gift, bestowed upon us by our creator.

—Gordon Jourdain, Lac La Croix (Ontario)[40]

How many tribal languages are spoken in the Americas?

There were around 2,300 tribal languages spoken in North and South America before sustained contact with Europeans (500 in what's now the United States and Canada and 300 in Mexico, with the remaining 1,500 spoken in South America). There are now around 650 total in all of the Americas (with just 150 of those spoken in the United States and Canada), and the number is shrinking quickly. All world languages are members of families, such as the Germanic or Romance language families. And languages in the same families (like English and German) have some similarities, although they are not always understandable to one another. There are 56 Indigenous language families in North America and over three times that number in South America. Sometimes Native American languages spoken by groups that are next to each other (like Ojibwe and Dakota) are as different as Chinese and English.

Which tribal languages have a chance to be here a hundred years from now?

Of the 150 tribal languages spoken in the United States and Canada, only 20 are spoken by children. They include Ojibwe, Cree, Ottawa, Diné (Navajo), Hawaiian, Tiwa and Tewa (Pueblo), Hopi, Apsáalooke (Crow), Mohawk, Havasupai, Cherokee, Inuit, Yupik, Aleut, and Lakota. But even

Anna Gibbs was one of many Natives from the Baby Boomer generation whose first language was an indigenous language. She eventually became a published author, language resource, and the first woman known to have officiated at traditional Ojibwe funerals and medicine dance. Red Lake's first Ojibwe immersion program was named in her honor.

most of these tribes do not have any monolingual speakers of the languages. Usually, English is used for some aspects of daily life (school, job, or social). Even in remote parts of the Navajo Reservation (Arizona), Ni'ihau (Hawaii), or Lac La Croix First Nation (Ontario), where there are groups that have 100 percent fluency in the tribal language, mainstream media is coming in via the internet and English is starting to become the peer language for some of the youngest age-groups. People are worried about the future of tribal languages everywhere in the United States and Canada. In Mexico, some of the thirty Mayan languages have large numbers of speakers (6 million total), including significant groups of monolingual speakers, and their future seems certain in some places.

Why are fluency rates higher in Canada?

They aren't that much higher. Like Indigenous communities throughout the Americas, most Canadian First Nations, Inuit, and Métis communities are in language crisis. The missionary activity started early in the colonial experience there, although the residential boarding school system began (and ended) later in Canada than in the United States. That timeline, coupled with the geographic isolation of some communities in Canada (accessed primarily by floatplane or boat), has helped to keep rates higher in a few areas.

Some communities also have unique circumstances. Manitoulin Island (in the Georgian Bay of Lake Huron) has a large tract of unceded Indian land that provided a higher degree of isolation and eased some of the social and government language pressure seen in other parts of Ontario. Another example is a large group of Dakota who escaped military attack and persecution in southern Minnesota in 1862 by settling in Canada. Because of that experience, their descendants have been especially tenacious about language revitalization in recent years, creating a living resource for today's Minnesota Dakota communities in their own language revitalization work.

It seems like tribal languages won't give Native people a leg up in the modern world. Why are they important to Indians?

In fact, tribal languages do give Indians a leg up in the modern world. I have written a lot about this in my book *The Language Warrior's Manifesto: How to Keep Our Languages Alive No Matter the Odds*. The Waadookodaading Ojibwe Language Institute in Reserve, Wisconsin, has operated for twenty years, and the kids there routinely do better than other Native kids on state-mandated tests administered in English, even while the teachers do not speak to the kids in English until the higher grades. Tribal language education is a powerful tool for the development of everything from brain function to basic self-esteem.

Indian people value their languages for many other reasons as well. They are cornerstones of identity, and their use keeps us recognizable to our ancestors. They are defining features of nationhood. The retention of tribal languages tells the world that we have not been assimilated, in spite of 500 years of colonial effort to achieve that. They are the only customary languages for many ceremonies, a gateway to spiritual understanding. And tribal languages carry unique tribal worldviews. They define us as distinct peoples.

Why should tribal languages be important to everyone else?

I always tell the deans and president at Bemidji State University, where I work, that when people call for the "Department of Foreign Languages," to be sure to direct them to the English Department. Tribal languages are modern, domestic languages. They are the first languages of this land and the first languages of the first Americans. These facts alone should make their retention especially important.

But additionally, there are the proven links between academic achievement and cultural and linguistic competency for Native youth. These show that everyone should want the most successful strategies employed to bridge the educational and economic achievement gaps for Indians, so that Natives can be the best possible neighbors and need fewer entitlements to deal with poverty, reducing the tax burden for all. But even more important, the survival of tribal languages and cultures is a test for the morality of our nation and its ability to provide for the needs of all of its citizens. If the government can enable and support the retention of cultural and linguistic diversity, its strength and moral position is obvious, rather than tainted.

What are the challenges to successfully revitalizing tribal languages?

Some tribal languages have no speakers left and very few written resources. The Hebrew language was revived almost

2,000 years after people first quit speaking it, but in a form highly altered from its original use and with the help of lots of written material and a large population of people committed to seeing Hebrew live. The deck is stacked against many Indian tribes accomplishing something similar. The places that have a good chance of success have a critical mass of fluent speakers and growing resources (books, audio programs, computer software, and operating systems that support the target language). The challenges are finding these language resources, certified teachers fluent in the target language, and financial support. Often tribal government support is limited because many tribes don't have enough money, or because tribal leaders do not see the value of preserving their own languages. Lighting the fire for a major revitalization is challenging in many places, even where the potential is great.

When were tribal languages first written down?

Some tribes did write before European contact. The Mayans had a unique system of writing. The Ojibwe used symbols written on birch bark to preserve critical information. But the formal writing systems developed for most tribal languages were introduced after European contact. Missionaries wanted the Bible and other religious texts to enter the minds and hearts of Indians as quickly as possible, and some did a lot of work with tribal languages to achieve that goal. Most systems used roman letters. Some, like syllabics (employed for Cree and Ojibwe), used unique symbols.

Sequoyah, a Cherokee silversmith, developed a syllabary for Cherokee. His syllabary—the first to be independently created by a member of a nonliterate people—was formally adopted by the Cherokee Nation in 1825 and is still used today, recently being incorporated as a language on the Apple computer and iPhone operating systems.

Many tribal languages were never written. Why are they written now?

At one point in time, White people never used cars, so why do they use them now? Because it makes life easier and more efficient. Indians also at one point did not have cars, or electricity, or writing systems for most of their languages. But those things can improve quality of life or ease of communication. Still, there is not universal agreement about the writing of tribal languages. The Pueblo are among the strictest in their insistence that the language remain oral only. Most tribes accept the writing of tribal languages but may not agree on specific writing systems. In most places, there is an increasing awareness that writing can be a useful part of developing needed resources, preserving critical information, and stabilizing languages.

Why is it funnier in Indian?

All languages have their words made from smaller parts of words called *morphemes*. In English, those morphemes come from the language's Germanic roots, and from Latin, Greek, and many other languages, so everyday speakers of English do not usually know the roots of words. But the opposite is often true for tribal languages, whose speakers know the deeper meanings behind their words and can then communicate on two levels—using words and what's behind them. That makes it easier to have plays on words, puns, descriptions, and names converge in ways that give greater meaning and humor to many situations.

In Ojibwe, for example, the word *giboodiyegwaazonag* means "pants" or, literally, "leggings that sew up the hind end." Ojibwe people must have thought pants were hilariously impractical in a cold-weather climate where one had to take the entire works down to go to the bathroom, when someone with a skirt or breechclout and leggings had quick and easy access. Even today, when Ojibwe people regularly wear pants instead of breechclouts, the word still makes people chuckle.

How do tribal languages encapsulate different worldviews?

Just as morphemes carry possibilities for humor, they carry deeper and more resonant meanings that shape attitudes. In Ojibwe, for example, the word for an old woman, *mindimooye,* literally means "one who holds things together," describing the role of the family matriarch. In English, *old woman, elderly woman,* and *aged woman* all speak to age rather than to a more respected position for elder women in society. Many women dye their hair, get Botox injections or face-lifts, and rarely admit to their true age in order to combat the appearance of growing older, because the worldview of many English language speakers doesn't value the role and appearance of older women. But in the Ojibwe language, there is a revered place for elder women, one reflected in core values, actions, and the language itself. You don't have to tell Ojibwe speakers to respect their elders. The respect is built right in with every word one would use to

Mille Lacs elders making Ojibwe books.

refer to them. Even the gender-neutral term for elder in Ojibwe, *gichi-aya'aa,* literally means "great being."

Why don't tribes do more to support language and culture?

This is a very important question, and because it touches my work, I have some strong opinions on the topic. Language and culture receive little support in many places, even where tribal language and culture are strong enough to have a good chance of revitalizing tribal societies.

Priorities compete for tribal support. Poverty is a real problem in most Indian communities in the United States and Canada, and many tribes have well-designed and much-needed programs to combat it. But tribal governments also spend a lot of money on powwows and charitable donations to non-Native organizations like churches—a painful irony. For most tribes, powwows are a new cultural form, one that did not come from their people. And churches and missionary organizations were at the forefront of efforts to assimilate and change Native Americans. Their role in advocating for removal to reservations and their participation in the residential boarding school experiment did tremendous damage to many Indian people and communities. But it's relatively easy to support a local powwow that people understand and enjoy, and to give money to a church that many tribal leaders and members belong to.

Learning a tribal language is hard. Many tribes have very few or no speakers left, making prioritizing tribal language or ancient cultural ways much more difficult. Indian cultures and identities are changing very rapidly. Many tribal members find it easier to redefine what it means to be Indian, with greater emphasis on things like holding a tribal enrollment card, rather than trying to preserve and revitalize cultural forms and a concept of identity that is more recognizable to their ancestors.

Supporting tribal language and culture also involves taking a good hard look at one's self and community. This dynamic is especially challenging because it is language and culture revitalization that offer our greatest opportunities for strengthening political, economic, educational, and community health.

POLITICS

You can plant the seeds of a stronger nation; you can plant the seeds of a better future for your children and your children's children.

–Oren Lyons

What we now call an Indian nation was a modern invention born at the moment of treaty.

–Scott Lyons, *X-Marks: Native Signatures of Assent*

What is sovereignty?

Sovereignty means "self-rule." Indian nations are sovereign because they rule themselves—they have their own governments, police, fire departments, and business operations. Tribal sovereignty is the basis for most of the different legal and political conditions on Indian reservations. Treaty rights, casinos, and different tax laws are possible in Indian country only because tribes are sovereign. That sovereignty often helps tribes to protect tribal languages, cultures, and land in ways that would be impossible if it did not exist.

Sovereignty is what makes a tribe different from a cultural group like the Amish. The Amish have preserved unique cultural traditions and languages, but they are still subject to federal and state laws. The Meskwaki Nation (Iowa) and other tribes have preserved unique cultural traditions and language but are not subject to all state and federal laws. Thus, the Meskwaki exercise independent control over their reservation and make their own laws about things like casinos and taxes. They are sovereign.

Tribal sovereignty is a powerful political authority, but it is not absolute. There are some limits to it. Over many decades, the U.S. and Canadian governments have tried to diminish the political power of tribes and their sovereignty with some, but not complete, success. Native nations do not maintain their own armies, for example. The U.S. and Canadian federal governments have significant power over some aspects of tribal life and law. Specific dimensions of tribal sovereignty—including treaty rights, gaming, criminal law, and taxation—are detailed throughout the rest of this book.

Why do Natives have reservations or First Nations?

Natives used to own all of North and South America. Reservations (in the United States) and First Nations (in Canada) are not gifts to Natives from the U.S. or Canadian governments: they are parts of each tribe's original homeland that the tribe held on to—the parts that were not sold or taken. When tribes made treaties, they sold much of their land, but those treaties also formally accepted tribes as independent governments and owners of their retained, reserved lands—another major difference between Natives and other racial or ethnic groups in the United States and Canada.

Starting in the 1830s, three Supreme Court cases in the United States, often called the Marshall Trilogy (after Chief Justice John Marshall, who wrote the opinions for the Court), again affirmed the special status of tribal governments and their reservation lands. Those cases made it clear that state governments did not have jurisdiction on reservations or over Indian people. Reservations are nations, not just cultural groups, landholdings, or communities. In Canada, the status of reservations was affirmed by legislation, constitutional reform, and 22 distinct tribal self-government agreements. Both the U.S. and Canadian governments tried to limit tribal nationhood at times, but the basic reason for the existence of reservations and First

Nations remains the same—they are our original homelands and the tribes and U.S. and Canadian governments signed numerous treaties and other agreements that said we get to keep them forever.

Why isn't being American or Canadian enough? Why do Indians need reservations today?

Reservations are home to around half of the Natives who are official members of tribes. Like most Americans and Canadians, Natives love their homes. The connection that Indigenous people have to their reservations and First Nations is really strong. In numerous places, many generations of family members are buried in the same ground. Nobody wants to give that up. And there are special places and ceremony sites on reservations that are sacred to many tribal people.

But the preservation of Native-controlled land is about more than special places and ancient histories. The continuation of tribal government is a continuation of tribal self-rule. Many Natives feel that their ancestors paid very dearly—and they themselves are still paying dearly—for the right to have their reserved lands and tribal governments. Reservations and First Nations are nations, and the people carry powerful patriotism for their nations. It is true that there are plenty of problems on reservations, ranging from poverty to substance abuse in some places. Quite a few reservations and First Nations have unemployment rates over 50 percent, and most have unemployment rates over 20 percent. Tribal governments are trying to fix their problems through education and employment opportunities. The federal government has been unwilling to do much about Indian poverty. Tribal members see the greatest hope for addressing these and other problems in Indian country in the programs of their tribal governments.

Native Americans often laugh at the misconception that reservations are nothing more than concentration camps. Some people even think there may be barbed wire or other physical obstacles to the free travel of Native Americans. That view is just plain untrue.

In addition to all the reasons that Natives love their homelands and need their tribal governments, many draw attention to the fact that the federal governments of the United States and Canada promised to reserve those lands and tribal governments forever as partial payment for the land they got through treaties. If nations like the United States and Canada go back on that promise, their own integrity is compromised and the cultural and economic well-being of the tribal population would suffer.

If Natives in the United States and Canada have their own nations, how did they become United States or Canadian citizens?

In the United States and Canada, enrolled tribal members are also citizens of the countries where their tribes are located—dual citizens. The process by which Natives became U.S. citizens in America was a little complicated. For some tribes, this happened for all of their members by treaty. This was the case for the Cherokee in 1817, more than 100 years before most Indians became citizens. Some tribes had special citizenship provisions when they went through allotment (a process I will say more about later). For others, in 1918, the U.S. government realized that many thousands of Natives had fought in the U.S. Army in World War I, but could not vote or enjoy the benefits of American citizenship. They remedied that by an act of Congress that year—but just for male Native veterans who filled out an application.

This era was still the height of assimilation policies, and a lot of missionaries and government officials wanted Indians to be American. Another law—the Indian Citizenship Act—was passed in 1924. That legislation made all Natives born in the United States American citizens. Many states still forbade Natives to vote since voting rights are governed by states, not the federal government. Some of the state laws forbidding Natives to vote were repealed in 1957, and the rest were countermanded by the Voting Rights Act of 1965, which dismantled Jim Crow laws in the South.

Many Natives welcomed American citizenship, but not all. Mohawk, Onondaga, and Seneca Natives objected to their American citizenship. They said they had fought with the Americans as allies in World War I but that they wanted only their Native citizenship. Today, all Natives born in America are U.S. citizens and, if eligible, tribal citizens as well.

In Canada, the Canadian Citizenship Act of 1946 declared Canadian citizenship separate from that of Great Britain but excluded many Canadian First Nations people and most of the Inuit population. The act was amended in

1956 to include all First Nations, Inuit, and Métis people as Canadian citizens.

What is a non-federally-recognized tribe?

There are many Native people in the United States who lost their land dealing with the British, French, Spanish, Dutch, and even Russian governments. But some did not have a treaty with the United States, and as a consequence the U.S. government has not usually recognized them as a Native American tribe. Federally recognized tribes have always had a formal process for dealing with the U.S. government—through Indian agents in the 1800s and through the Bureau of Indian Affairs in recent years. That process, while frustrating and paternalistic, has funneled resources to the tribes and helped maintain their political identity.

Non-federally-recognized tribes do not have this. In spite of that political reality, many such tribes have maintained their culture, identity, and even language. Sometimes, a non-recognized tribe will petition for and receive federal recognition if they can prove their cultural and political continuity. Sometimes they are unsuccessful. The Lumbee in North Carolina, for example, are a large tribe that has yet to be recognized by the federal government. Some tribes, even though they cannot get recognition from the U.S. federal government, are recognized by state governments. That helps affirm their political identity, but does not open the way for federal financial resources to support tribal operations. The U.S. government also terminated over

100 tribes in the 1950s, removing their federal recognition. Some of the terminated tribes, like the Menominee, were reinstated, but most were not. They aren't Indians in the eyes of the U.S. government anymore.

In 1898, the Curtis Act opened the Cherokee, Choctaw, Chickasaw, Seminole, and Creek (Muscogee) reservations. (This was an amendment of the Dawes Act, which is covered later.) Some land was allotted to tribal members and 90 million acres were given to White settlers. This legislation also changed the status of these five tribes, abolishing long-standing tribal courts and government operations. All of these provisions enabled Oklahoma statehood at the expense of the tribes. The tribes adapted and maintained recognition through the state of Oklahoma rather than the federal government, but at a great cost. On July 9, 2020, the U.S. Supreme Court ruled that the Creek lands lost via the Curtis Act were in fact still within the reservation. This significant case could alter the formal status of these five tribes and have major implications for the tax status of their land and businesses as well as law enforcement jurisdictions. It strengthens the sovereign status of these five tribes.

What's it like for Natives who aren't part of a recognized tribe?

It can be very frustrating and sometimes painful for Natives who aren't part of a federally recognized tribe. If their tribe is not recognized, or if they are not eligible for enrollment in a federally recognized tribe even though they have Indian blood in their veins, other people often think that they aren't "real" Indians. It hurts when non-Native people don't see you for who you are, and it sometimes hurts worse when your own people don't accept you. They aren't eligible for many of the scholarships and other supports that go to enrolled members of federally recognized tribes. People who are not enrolled are usually not eligible for tribal housing. Children of an enrolled parent in some places can no longer keep property in the family when the parent dies. Socially and politically, they often feel invisible as Native people.

What is the status of Alaska Natives?

Alaska became a state in 1959. The United States was long done making treaties with Indians by then and that fact left the status of Alaska's many Indigenous people a big legal question mark. The Native people in Alaska obviously had a deep sense of community, and many lived by hunting and fishing and spoke tribal languages. They were Native but were not recognized the same way that tribes who had treaties with the U.S. government were. In 1971, the U.S. government tried to sort that out by passing the Alaska Native Claims Settlement Act. It created twelve regions in the state and organized all of the many tribal groups in each region into a "corporation." These corporations held and still hold rights to natural resources. Each of these twelve corporations, and a thirteenth established for descendants of Alaskan Natives no longer living in Alaska, were compensated for the land they lost and some of the resources on that land. This act was an effort at restorative justice, although the amount of the money received in no way made up for the suffering of Alaskan Natives or their continued poverty. It did not provide Alaskan Natives a status as powerful as the treaty status of federally recognized tribes elsewhere in the United States, but it did help preserve for them a measure of political and economic power.

Why do Indians have treaty rights? What other rights do they have that differ from those of most people in the United States?

There are two main reasons why Indians have certain rights that other Americans do not. The first has to do with treaties. When the U.S. federal government wanted land from Indians, negotiators had to pay Indians or promise them different things in order to get the land. Tribal leaders had a different concept of land ownership than Europeans. The main thing these leaders insisted on was the right to hunt, fish, gather, and travel on all of their lands, including lands soon to be ceded to the federal government. Often, the U.S. government got title to Indian land but agreed to allow Indian people to retain their right to use the land. These rights, often called *usufructuary rights,* are the basis of the treaty rights that many Native Americans enjoy today. They explain why hunting seasons and methods are sometimes different for Indians on Indian land than they are for other people and why tribal rights sometimes extend outside reservation boundaries. These provisions are part of the payment the U.S. government made for the land.

The other major reason Indians have different rights is that state governments have no authority over reservations or tribal governments except for individual criminal cases in places where Public Law 280 is in effect. (More on Public Law 280 later.) And in the U.S. Constitution, all rights not specifically granted to the federal government are reserved to the states. As a result, most of the basic regulations and civil laws that Americans deal with on a day-to-day basis come from state government rather than the federal government. Enrolled members living on reservations in the United States thus

Keller Paap (Red Cliff Ojibwe) exercising his treaty rights to spear fish.

fall under tribal jurisdiction for most aspects of their lives. In Canada, tribal sovereignty works differently than in the United States, but the right to hunt and fish is a matter of the jurisdiction of First Nations for the most part and is usually far less restricted than for other Canadians.

What is allotment?

Allotment took place in the United States from the middle of the 1800s until 1933. The government took reservation land, which was held in trust for the shared use of all tribal members, and split it into pieces to be owned by each tribal member, with the remaining "surplus" sold to settlers and private companies. The profits from "surplus" land sales were then to be used by the Department of the Interior to pay for assimilation programs for American Indian people. Some tribes had their reservations allotted by treaty. Most reservations were allotted by an act of Congress called the Dawes Act, which enabled this policy on tribal land in the United States in 1887. Of the 155 million acres of land held in trust for Indians on reservations at that time, 50 million were allotted to tribal members, usually in 160-acre parcels. The remaining 105 million acres of land were deemed "surplus" and sold cheaply or given away for free to White settlers. The Oklahoma Land Rush in 1889 was one of the most famous cases where reservation land was given away for free to White settlers after allotment. Over 50,000 White settlers staked claims to 2 million acres of free homesteads in Oklahoma inside Indian reservations that year.

It would have been better for Indians to avoid allotment or make sure that all of the land allotted went to Indians instead of White settlers. One of the reasons the government created the policy was to open reservations to timber, mineral, and land speculators and settlers through that "surplus." But the land allotted to Indians quickly flew out of their hands as well. There were legal protections of Native allotments—Indians were not supposed to be able to sell their allotments for twenty-five years. But numerous White land speculators broke the law and Natives lost their

The Oklahoma Land Rush of 1889.

land anyway. While the Dawes Act was in effect, from 1887 to 1933, the federal government passed many amendments to the legislation to limit trust protections and make the sale of Indian land easier. As a result of this policy, Indians kept less than 10 percent of their own reservations in many places.

A few reservations, including Red Lake (Minnesota) and Menominee (Wisconsin), were able to avoid allotment. Usually, the success of communities in avoiding allotment had less to do with a kind American government than it did with the tribe's geographic isolation, or other political considerations. In Red Lake, for example, the government asked for allotment, a major land cession, and relocation all at the same time. The tribe ceded some land but avoided allotment on the main reservation they retained, and the people never had to relocate. Even today, all land at Red Lake is held in trust for all tribal members. Red Lake and the few other tribes that avoided the policy are the exception rather than the rule, however: allotment was the means by which two-thirds of the overall reservation tribal land base was lost.

What is clouded title?

Most reservations in the United States have both tribal land and land that is owned by private citizens. On many of those reservations, non-Native people own most of the private land. A fair number of those people have titles to that land that are "clouded." *Clouded title* means that proof of rightful ownership is not clear, usually because the land was taken from Natives illegally. Multiple parties claim a right to the titles of clouded parcels—like the Indians who should have inherited their family allotment and the children of a White farmer who bought the land from a timber company that took it illegally from the Indians.

As discussed earlier, between 1784 and 1871, the U.S. government signed 370 treaties with American Indian people to obtain 720 cessions of land. The lands remaining in tribal hands were subject to a lot of land fraud, lease fraud, and mineral lease fraud, especially during the allotment era (1887–1933). Simply put, there were resources on reservations that outsiders wanted. And those who wanted the resources did not always have great respect for the rightful Indian owners of the land.

As an example, Joseph Auginaush, an elder from the White Earth Reservation, once showed me a twenty-four-dollar grocery receipt. He explained that a grocery clerk from nearby Roy Lake went to the allotment officer at White Earth and demanded the Auginaush family allotment to pay for the family's grocery bill. The grocer took their family's entire 160-acre allotment. The grocer sold the allotment, but the people he sold it to then had land with clouded title. The Auginaush family was never paid for the theft, and had no court hearing or formal notice of the land transaction. Theirs was a typical case.

After generations of ownership by non-Native people and many sales of those parcels of land, non-Native families who did not commit fraud and have lived on reservations for generations now cannot get clear title to their own land; as a result, they have lower property values and must deal with a stressful process to sell their land or give it to their children. Many Indians were ripped off, and their descendants have been unable to access the land they should have received as a birthright.

A law that declared all current owners as the rightful owners of land on reservations would simply legalize the theft of many of those parcels from Indians. This solution would be neither morally nor legally right in this country, which has valued property rights above most others. But a law that granted land parcels to the descendants of the original owners would disregard the rights of inheritance and ownership of many non-Native families. Fixing this mess is not easy and many parcels of land on reservations continue to have clouded title.

Is something being done about clouded title?

There have been attempts to clarify clouded title on Indian reservations. By 1946, when the U.S. government established the Indian Claims Commission (ICC), tribes had already filed 219 land claims cases in the U.S. Court of Claims. The commission of three judges eventually settled 285 cases but was authorized to offer only money for land lost because of fraud. However, many tribes wanted their land back, not money, and the commission did not solve all land conflicts. In 1978, the federal government passed legislation ending the ICC and sent the remaining 170 undecided cases to the U.S. Court of Claims. The Oneida and Lakota cases are among the most famous. The Lakota refused their large court-ordered financial settlement, insisting upon the return of ancestral lands. The Oneida had many complications because of their relocation from New York to Wisconsin and state interference in the federal-tribal relationship. They have had several court cases about land and jurisdiction issues, and some have yet to be resolved.[41]

In 1996, another court case tried to address all of the Indian land fraud. *Cobell v. Salazar* was finally settled in 2009. In the end, it provided money for tribal scholarships and direct payments to tribes and to some individual Natives. But not all people and tribes were happy with it. The settlement focused on trust funds and trust lands, most of which originated under the allotment policy. Only Native Americans who were enrolled members and could prove fraud on parcels of land, or funds that the U.S. government administered on their behalf, had permission to work through an incredibly long and cumbersome process to receive partial compensation. Most Indians didn't have paperwork, proof, or lawyers. Some of the payments were huge, and some good came of the case, but it did not administer justice to all, and it is impossible to go back and find a different solution now.

If tribes had hereditary chiefs, how come there is a democratic process for selecting tribal leaders in most places today?

From 1779 to 1934, the U.S. government systematically dismantled tribes and tribal leadership structures. They did this with treaties signed between 1784 and 1871, but also with acts of Congress and a steady wave of White settlement and displacement of Natives from the beginning of the American nation. They moved Indian people onto reservations—often concentrating many chiefs and their people in one place—and then put non-Native Indian agents in charge of tribal affairs. In 1934, the Indian Reorganization Act changed the U.S. bureaucracy that dealt with Indians (the Office of Indian Affairs, soon to be renamed the Bureau of Indian Affairs) from a supervisory agency to an advisory agency.

This was a major policy change, but it still took decades for tribal people to organize modern governments. When they did, there was a lot of variation, from more traditional leadership structures to (more commonly) democratic forms. The U.S. government gave draft constitutions to tribes, but those constitutions were flawed, based on a corporate governance model rather than a political one with checks and balances. In corporations, the chief executive officer (CEO) has a lot of power, and there are not many checks and balances on that power. In the United States, the President, Congress, and Supreme Court balance one another and are supposed to stop one another from abusing their power. Tribes are still (with varying degrees of success) trying to fix those draft constitutions and remake tribal government in their own ways. The Indian Self-Determination and Education Assistance Act of 1975 enabled the U.S. secretaries of the interior, health, education, and welfare to contract with and make grants directly to tribes, which served to further strengthen tribal powers. In Canada, the Constitution Act of 1982 codified First Nations agreement to use democratic elections and even regional and national representation of their First Nations in larger organizations, most notably the Assembly of First Nations, which advocates on their behalf of all 634 First Nations across Canada.

What's the Indian Reorganization Act?

The Indian Reorganization Act (IRA), passed in 1934, changed the role of the Office of Indian Affairs (soon to be renamed the Bureau of Indian Affairs) from a supervisory agency that managed every major facet of Indian government (without tribal input or representation) to an advisory one. In a short time, tribes developed modern tribal governments much as they are today, and the era of Indian self-determination began. Tribes could once again have greater say in designing their own futures. The IRA also stopped further allotment, which helped stabilize what was left of the tribal land base.

The IRA was welcomed by many tribes, but it did not fix everything wrong in U.S. Indian policy. The U.S. Department of the Interior still kept lots of power over tribal affairs, tribal citizens had few rights or protections, and the new government structures after the act did not usually reflect traditional tribal values. In some cases, the IRA also merged separate tribes into confederated tribal governments. For example, Sandy Lake (Minnesota) was established as an independent reservation in 1855 and had always had its own chiefs and independent political structure, but after the IRA it was folded into the Mille Lacs Reservation, where it had a district representative but no longer functioned independently. Many people from that community still feel betrayed, isolated, and disempowered by the change.

Do Indians ever work together politically and economically?

Yes, Indians work together, and sometimes with great positive effect. There are national and international Indigenous organizations like the National Indian Education Association and the National Congress of American Indians tackling issues from environmental protection to political and economic reform. At the tribal and grassroots levels, there have been many efforts to address

Current president of the National Congress of American Indians, Fawn Sharp.

health, education, economics, and language and culture revitalization. Some have been incredibly inspiring.

Each tribe in the United States is its own sovereign entity—a Native nation. They independently make their own decisions, subject only to the Major Crimes Act, Public Law 280, and other federal limitations on tribal sovereignty. However, in some places, those Native nations have pooled their political and economic resources to work cooperatively.

As an example, the Great Lakes Inter-Tribal Council (GLITC) has twelve member reservations in Wisconsin, some of which have very different tribal heritage, languages, and cultural practices. The conceptual framework for the council is to empower all its members politically and financially.

Another example is the Minnesota Chippewa Tribe (MCT), which operates differently from the GLITC because technically the MCT is a tribe that has six member reservations. Usually each reservation is its own tribe in a legal sense. The MCT reservations have much in common: language, culture, history, and treaties, some of which were signed by leaders from most of the member reservations. In fact, the Nelson Act of 1889, which implemented allotment for most Ojibwe in Minnesota and addressed other land issues for them, created some of the impetus for starting the MCT. Several independent Ojibwe nations shared interest in tracts of land and money from the sale of that land, which was officially held "in common" for all of them. When modern tribal governments were created after the 1934 Indian Reorganization Act, establishing the MCT two years later seemed like the easiest way to deal with the land and money issues for the member tribes in the future. The MCT administered trust lands for member tribes for a long time, but over the past twenty years, Leech Lake and other tribes have been slowly asserting greater individual control over trust land and tribal leases.

The MCT was designed to enable cooperative work and greater political clout. But it has had other effects as well. One of the reservations, White Earth, makes up one-third of the MCT's tribal population (and one-third of many revenue streams). White Earth has often been frustrated in its efforts to pass major, meaningful constitutional reforms because the other member reservations do not agree with their changes to tribal citizenship, and do not want to release White Earth from the MCT because they would lose control over more of the money that comes to the larger tribe.

Although the MCT, GLITC, and others like them are formal governing arrangements between tribes, many nonbinding cooperative efforts exist as well. The leaders of all the Pueblo meet together at times. Blackfeet, Apache, and other tribes have cooperative councils, usually focused on shared culture and language efforts for all reservations from the same tribal group rather than political governance.

Why do so many Indians live in urban areas today? What is relocation?

Some reservations have unemployment rates over 50 percent. Anyone who lives in a place with limited opportunities for financial betterment or even basic survival seeks a way out.

That's how America filled up with immigrants, and it is part of the explanation for how so many Indians left reservations. It's also true that Indians have a high rate of marriage to people of different races, which helps bring a lot of Indians off-reservation. One study found that 61 percent of Native women and 54 percent of Native men married someone from a different race. This was higher than the rate for Asian women (37 percent), Asian men (16 percent), Black women (12 percent), Black men (25 percent), and White men and women (both at 7 percent)—the highest rate for any racial group in the United States.[42]

Also, some reservations, like Leech Lake (Minnesota), own less than 4 percent of their land due to policies like allotment. Even enrolled members have a hard time finding housing on the reservation and are forced to look elsewhere. Enrollment criteria for reservations are a major source of contention as well: there are now more than twice as many Indians self-identifying for the census as there are enrolled members (tribal citizens). The non-enrolled Indians are not eligible for tribal housing and other programs.

In addition to all of these variables, the U.S. government made it official policy to move Indians from reservations to urban areas in the 1950s. The government gave tribal members one-way transportation and rental assistance for their first month in a major city. Thousands of Indians took advantage of the program, believing they would find greater financial opportunities in cities. Milwaukee, Minneapolis, Chicago, Denver, and Oakland developed large Indian populations as a result of this policy. But relocation failed to deliver the financial betterment it promised. There was still a racial barrier to getting a job for people of color in the 1950s and 1960s, and Indians who moved under the policy were soon even more impoverished than their reservation counterparts. Still, the establishment of substantial urban Indian populations was a permanent change.

What is life like for urban Indians today?

About half of the enrolled tribal members in the United States and Canada live off reservations, mainly in urban areas. The number of self-identified Natives living off reservations is even higher. I lived in Milwaukee for four years and in Minneapolis off and on when I was going to graduate school. When I lived in a big city far from home, I spent a lot of my time getting back to the reservation for drum ceremonies, powwows, and to spend time with my family. Every person is different, but many urban Natives keep connections to their home communities. Travel can be expensive, though, and we become who we hang out with. Some Native families have been living in cities for generations. We adapt to those environments. Sometimes urban living makes it harder to do things like hunt, fish, gather, and farm. For some of us those activities feel kind of foreign. And that can create internal conflict as we, like all humans, try to figure out who we really are. At the same time, for many Natives, there are better job and educational opportunities in urban areas, and we want to do well and feed our families as much as everyone else. However, the possibility of betterment on reservations is changing as many tribes are truly accelerating in job creation on reservations and many have even built tribal colleges and other opportunities for every kind of ambitious Native.

What is termination?

The U.S. government did a lot of experimenting with Indian policy. Although the Indian Reorganization Act (IRA) of 1934 opened the self-determination era, only two decades later the government was looking for ways to diminish tribal sovereignty and terminate it altogether, which is exactly what this policy was about. The government compiled a list of tribes from the most "acculturated" to the least, with plans to end their political existence. The government saw termination not as a punishment but rather as the final step in successful assimilation. The more assimilated the tribe, the more likely they would make a successful transition to being only American and nothing else.

As the government proceeded to terminate the sovereign status of tribes one at a time, it quickly became clear that the policy was a disaster. One prominent example was the Menominee, who had pioneered the world's first sustainable forest harvesting program and banked $10 million with no help from the U.S. government. Without legal standing as a sovereign nation, Menominee land and business operations became taxable. They lost their management team and soon the very land on which they harvested trees. The new Menominee "corporation," which owned the former reservation lands, had to sell the land in order to pay the taxes on the remaining land. The revenue stream diminished and then disappeared; they had to shut down the operation. Tribal members had no jobs. Tribal member Ada Deer said, "It was like burning your house down to stay warm in the winter."[43] The federal government had to spend more in welfare payments to tribal members than it had cost to support the Menominee tribal government, and Menominee County became the poorest in the state of Wisconsin.

After years of sustained protest, the terminated Menominee were reinstated, as were some other tribes, such as the Klamath, Coquille, and Catawba, in the 1970s and 1980s. Most of the other 109 terminated tribes were never reinstated.[44] Many continue to struggle to gain a return of status. Any trust that tribes and tribal members had for the federal government was shattered once again.

Why do Indians have their own police and courts in some places?

Tribes are sovereign, and that status gives them the right to govern themselves. Police and courts are part of self-governance. Unless a treaty or act of Congress limits tribal sovereignty, it is unhindered. For this reason, tribes have different laws about gaming and gambling, hunting and fishing, and many other things. Most tribes have now developed their own law enforcement and justice centers and staff.

Despite the fact that the right of tribes to build their own police and courts has been there since the Indian

Reorganization Act of 1934, some tribes have not done this. The U.S. government controlled reservations for decades and systematically dismantled tribal leadership structures in most places. Only since 1934 have tribes been able to assume greater control over their own governments. Building courts and successfully managing police forces takes a lot of logistical support and money. Although federal grants can support a tribe's efforts to build police and court systems, government support is never enough, and most tribal court and police administrations have to compete with one another to get the funding, get legislative support to secure funding in the congressional budget, or pay for these systems themselves. Every one of those things is difficult. It takes time to develop qualified police officers, lawyers, and judges. Tribes are sometimes reluctant to spend the resources needed to create a court if they can staff it with only outsiders. Therefore, tribes with small populations or limited financial resources have been somewhat less likely than larger tribes to develop police and court systems, although there are exceptions. The federal government has also passed legislation like Public Law 280, which further eroded the jurisdiction of tribal governments in some states, but those laws are complex and not in place on all reservations.

Why does the FBI investigate murders on some reservations?

Most lawyers do not understand Indian law and jurisdiction very well, and most everyone else understands even less.

Before the treaty period, tribal leaders used to have the only say about matters of justice in their communities. Over many decades through the 18th, 19th, and early 20th centuries, the U.S. government systematically attacked and eroded the authority of tribal leaders.

One of the first major legal changes in tribal sovereignty came in response to the U.S. Supreme Court decision in the case of *Ex Parte Crow Dog*. A Lakota man named Crow Dog killed another Lakota named Spotted Tail in 1881. Tribal leaders convened a traditional tribal council and decided that Crow Dog would have to pay money to Spotted Tail's widow and provide for her well-being for the rest of his life, and furthermore, exiled him and his entire family for four generations. (Leonard Crow Dog, a well-known spiritual leader for the American Indian Movement, is the last of the four generations to live in exile from the main community at Rosebud.) Spotted Tail, who had been acknowledged as a chief by General George Cook in 1876, was someone who had cooperated with the U.S. government rather than resisting. Many non-Native officials felt that Crow Dog was getting away with "the red man's revenge." They arrested him, tried him for murder, and sentenced him to hang.

Crow Dog got a lawyer and fought his case, eventually winning a major decision. The court ruled that the Lakota could not be subject to the jurisdiction of a federal, state, or territorial court, and that the ability of tribes to address such offenses was an attribute of tribal sovereignty that had not been specifically ended by an act of Congress. They said neither the states nor the federal government had the power

Crow Dog.

to hang Crow Dog. There was a public outcry in the United States about Indians getting away with murder. Afterward, many lawmakers used that sentiment to develop a new policy approach that would strengthen the U.S. government's power over Indians on tribal land.

The Major Crimes Act (1885) gave the federal government jurisdiction over major crimes between Indians on Indian land. (Crimes that involved non-Native people on reservations were already matters of state jurisdiction.) From 1885 on, federal authorities investigated Indian-on-Indian cases of murder, rape, arson, manslaughter, burglary, larceny, and assault with deadly intent. Initially, this was done through the White Indian agent on each reservation. Courts of Indian Offenses, administered by the U.S. government, were the venues through which justice was administered to Indians. Eventually, as the Office of Indian Affairs became advisory rather than supervisory, the FBI assumed the role of primary investigator for Indian-on-Indian crimes on Indian land. The Major Crimes Act was amended many times, and the list of offenses expanded significantly.

All of this was intricate enough, but the federal government later passed legislation that sought to give some state governments authority over criminal affairs in Indian country too. The new law, Public Law 280, further complicated the arena of jurisdiction in Indian country. Essentially, the federal government has authority over major crimes everywhere in Indian country, *unless* Public Law 280 has specifically granted that jurisdiction to state governments.

Most of the criminal law in America is state law, not federal law. Murder is not a federal crime in America, but each state has declared murder illegal. Some states have the death penalty while others do not. Reservations are the only significant exceptions to state jurisdiction when there is a murder. It makes a difference. There is bias against Natives in both state and federal courts. But truth-in-sentencing guidelines are harsher at the federal level. And the complex jurisdictions produce very different outcomes for Native offenders. Study after study has found that Indians do more time for the same crimes than other Americans do.[45]

Why do state law enforcement agencies investigate murders on some reservations? What is Public Law 280?

In 1953, the U.S. federal government wanted to get out of the Indian business, and Public Law 280 was passed as part of a new series of legislative attacks on tribal sovereignty. It has had a major impact on many tribes.[46] This congressional act originally applied to tribes in only five states—Oregon, Nebraska, California, Wisconsin, and Minnesota. Eleven other states were later added to the list. Many states declined the jurisdiction when it was offered to them, because it would require them to provide services to tribal members that the federal government had previously funded.

Until Public Law 280, tribes had authority over their own reservations except for major crimes. (The federal government controlled reservation courts and government before the Indian Reorganization Act in 1934. Major crimes had remained under federal jurisdiction since passage of the Major Crimes Act in 1885.) With Public Law 280, states specifically named in the law would assume all criminal and limited civil jurisdiction over Indians, including over major crimes in some places. The complex web of state criminal law now formally applied to Indians in several states for the first time in history.

In the 1950s, tribal governments were new, weak, and unaware of Public Law 280's implications, so the law passed without the consent or consultation of most tribal leaders in affected communities. It soon became clear how deeply their sovereignty would be affected by state jurisdiction.

A few exceptions to Public Law 280 exist in states where it was applied. At Red Lake, in northwestern Minnesota, Peter Graves successfully had their reservation exempted from Public Law 280. Red Lake developed and maintains its own criminal code, court system, and police force (through the Bureau of Indian Affairs). The federal government intervenes and assumes jurisdiction over major crimes, but the state of Minnesota has no authority at Red Lake. That is why when a school shooting occurred there in 2005, federal law enforcement agencies investigated.

As another example, the Bois Forte Reservation (Minnesota) was initially subject to Public Law 280, but it succeeded in getting an exemption in 1975. It also maintains its own courts, police, and legal code. Tribes facing impending termination, like the Menominee, were also exempted.

Bois Forte and Red Lake are now exploring ways to use their courts to exert jurisdiction over major crimes as well.

In 2009, for instance, a Bois Forte tribal member burned down the tribal headquarters and was charged with arson under the Major Crimes Act, but Bois Forte also charged him with arson in tribal court. The dual charge was not double jeopardy because the United States and Bois Forte are separate sovereigns under the law. The tribe eventually "stayed" their charge so the man did not have to do two sentences in this case. But in the long run, tribes hope to supplant other agencies in criminal affairs on their reservations with this tactic. It has the potential to expand tribal jurisdiction and reduce the role of the Major Crimes Act in undermining tribal sovereignty.

As tribes have become better educated about sovereignty and the law, and better funded, most have developed their own court systems and police forces. A few have negotiated agreements with state, county, and municipal law enforcement agencies to clarify jurisdiction and support funding for tribal law enforcement operations. Pressure is also growing for a repeal of Public Law 280 or a case-by-case exemption for many reservations. Many tribes have had success in legal challenges to the civil authority of states over Indians in Public Law 280.[47]

Don't tribes ever investigate murders on Indian land themselves?

Yes. States have formal jurisdiction in murder cases where Public Law 280 is in effect, and the FBI has formal jurisdiction in murder cases in all other parts of Indian country. However, tribal police do a great deal of investigative and police work related to murder and drug charges on reservations. Tribal police often exercise arrest and search warrants, cooperate with the FBI and other law enforcement agencies, and participate in joint task forces to make their communities safe.

Should Leonard Peltier be freed?

In 1975, two FBI agents were murdered in South Dakota. This event occurred shortly after a major police and military action at Wounded Knee on the Pine Ridge Indian Reservation. The video documentary *Incident at Oglala* and a special report on *60 Minutes* have now made it clear that the two most damaging pieces of evidence used to convict Leonard Peltier of the murders should not have been admissible in court. One was a ballistics report that was clearly made up by the FBI. The other was an affidavit from a woman named Myrtle Poor Bear, who later stated that the FBI coerced her by threatening to permanently remove her children from her home if she didn't sign the document.

Many people feel that Leonard Peltier was made into a scapegoat and punished for a crime he did not commit. Those who argue for his release also often state that we owe it to the families of the murdered FBI agents to find their true killers. If Leonard Peltier had received a fair trial or a retrial without the clearly tainted evidence, he probably would not have been convicted. But did he kill those FBI agents? Maybe not, but I don't know.

Was the American Indian Movement good or bad?

I do not agree with everything that the American Indian Movement (AIM) or its leaders have done or said, but I do believe that AIM did more good than bad. Ojibwe and other Indians in Minneapolis founded the American Indian Movement in 1968.[48] The movement was soon catapulted to national fame for its powerful protests—they fought injustice across America, usually by taking on the U.S. government and sometimes by taking on tribes.

Some AIM members participated in the takeover of the federal prison at Alcatraz in 1969, although they did not

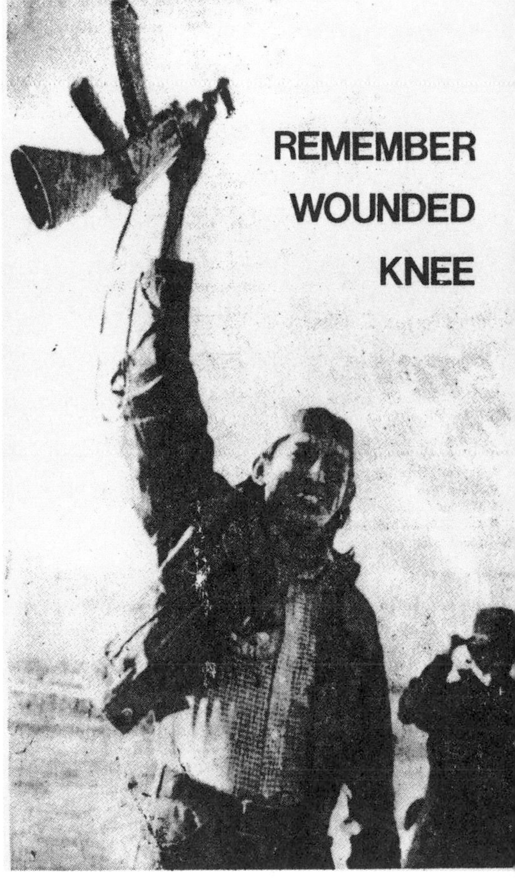

Bottom left: Marchers during the Wounded Knee Occupation by the American Indian Movement, 1973. Top left: A scene from the Trail of Broken Treaties, 1972, which culminated in the takeover of the Bureau of Indian Affairs by the AIM. Top right: A poster showing AIM member Bobby Onco (Kiowa) after the ceasefire agreement between AIM forces and federal marshals at Wounded Knee.

organize that event. The movement did organize a takeover of the Bureau of Indian Affairs in 1972. Members also burned the Custer courthouse to the ground and occupied the Wounded Knee Trading Post in South Dakota in 1973. This sort of activism raised the group's public profile and the issues that motivated it, and, as a result, many Americans heard, felt, and came to understand Indian discontent with government policies for the first time. But the protests did little to bring new government action or to address the underlying issues that caused so much unrest in the Indian community.

AIM's greatest achievements are the ones for which it is less well known nationally, but far more appreciated by Indians.[49] AIM was initially created to deal with Indian urbanization and poverty in Minneapolis. In 1968, it founded the AIM Legal Rights Center, which provided free legal assistance to Indians. As of 2020, it has served more than 30,000 people. In 1968, the movement also founded the AIM Patrol, which sought to police the police, document cases of police brutality and racial profiling, assist Indians with legal grievances, and advocate for victims of crimes. The AIM Patrol evolved over time: in 1986, when a serial killer was targeting Indian women in Minneapolis, the patrol provided free protective escorts for Native women who needed to walk or ride to work, school, and shopping centers. In 1979, AIM also developed the American Indian Opportunities Industrialization Center, a successful job training and placement program for Indians.

The American Indian Movement also offered innovative leadership in education by pioneering the first Indian-culture-based K–12 school in Minnesota. The Heart of the

Earth Survival School was created in 1971, and it graduated more Indians than all of the other Minneapolis-area schools combined for two decades. Heart of the Earth underwent some serious struggles and eventually closed, but its historic achievements in serving urban Indian youth and inspiring other tribal school initiatives are remarkable.

What is the Indian Child Welfare Act?

The Indian Child Welfare Act (ICWA), introduced in 1978, sought to address a horrific problem in adoption and foster care of Native children. Expert testimony (including surveys conducted by the Association on American Indian Affairs and other organizations) indicated that as many as 35 percent of Native children were separated from their homes by adoption or foster care.[50] In Minnesota, as much as 25 percent of the infant Indian population was being adopted. Minnesota's out-of-home placement rate for Indians was five times that of non-Native children. More than 90 percent of the adoption and foster placements were with non-Indian families. The trend disempowered parents in the raising of their own children and disconnected Native youth from their families, reservations, and culture.

Social service agencies had major oversight and procedural problems. Most of the Native kids removed from their homes never had a social worker visit those homes. Racial bias was prevalent. Many tribal members were terrified of losing their children—not because they were bad parents, but because they were Indian.

The Indian Child Welfare Act was the first serious legislative attempt to counteract these tendencies. It provided mandates to state courts and county social service agencies for placement of children who were removed from their homes, prioritizing placement with (1) preference of the child and parent, (2) extended family, (3) other tribal members, and (4) other Indians. It also required that agencies notify tribes of cases affecting their members, and it granted tribal courts and agencies the right to intervene on behalf of their children's welfare.

The Indian Child Welfare Act was a big step in the right direction, but there were many problems with it. First, the law had no teeth: there were no fines or punishments for individuals or agencies that did not comply. It was also difficult for caseworkers to know if a child was Indian—some Indians look brown, others Black or White. You can't always tell who someone is just by looking. And social workers often did not check records or even ask if a child's identity wasn't obvious to them. Most of the lawyers and judges never see the children in the cases they argue and decide. It was especially hard for any of *them* to know what tribe the child was enrolled in (or even if the child was enrolled).

Finding qualified Native homes for placement was also difficult. Canadian Indians living in the United States and Indians whose tribal affiliation was not known were not covered by the act because they were not "federally recognized." The act also provided no means or guidance for education or training social service workers about Native culture, history, language, or even the act itself.

All social service agencies were so grossly underfunded that, even after passage of the act, the trends in foster care and adoption for Indian children were barely affected. Furthermore, while foster care placements usually involved a house visit by a social worker, even years after the act only a small percentage of the Indian foster care removals did. Legal processes also take time. Often tribes received no notice, or late notice, of a proceeding, and by the time they tried to intervene and advocate, the affected children had already been removed from their homes for years.

Today, state social service agencies must develop permanency plans, such as a CHIPS (Children in Need of Protection or Services) petition, within one year of initiating litigation, and communication between tribal and county agencies has greatly improved. Judges routinely ask social service workers about site visits in many states as well. Some state and tribal governments signed agreements that require states to pay for foster care placements ordered by tribal courts. Some states passed additional legislation, like the Minnesota Indian Family Preservation Act, which sought to strengthen and expand some provisions of ICWA. Minnesota saw a 92 percent decline in Indian adoptions and a 66 percent decline in the Indian foster care rate over the first two decades after ICWA.

In spite of that dramatic improvement, the effects of these laws have been insufficient. Indians still have the highest foster care and adoption rates of all racial groups in the United States, and, in most states, Indians' percentage of the foster care and adoption caseload is ten times their percentage of the overall population. Much more needs to be done to ensure tribal involvement in child welfare processes, provide racial sensitivity training and cultural education for county social service workers, reduce unnecessary removals of Indian children from their families, and connect removed children to their communities and culture.

What is blood quantum, what is tribal enrollment, and how are they related?

Blood quantum is the percentage of a person's racial lineage that can be documented as Indian. Tribal governments keep lists of enrolled members, otherwise known as tribal citizens. Eligibility for enrollment in most tribes in the United States is dependent on blood quantum, rather than biological descent, residency, or place of birth. This is the political definition of Indianness in America. In Canada, being an official tribal member is referred to as "status." Blood quantum was less critical for enrollment in Canada than in the United States, but over the past 20 years, First Nations governments have actually moved in the direction of stricter criteria for enrollment. The politics of exclusion work a little differently in Canada, but the dynamic is similar to what we see for tribes in the United States.

Blood quantum was first used in Virginia in the 1700s to restrict the rights of people with half or more Native ancestry. By the 1930s, the federal government and many tribes were using blood quantum to determine who was eligible for tribal citizenship. The fractions are expressed up to sixty-fourths—one might have a quantum of 37/64.

Criteria for tribal citizenship vary from tribe to tribe. Some, like the Pueblo, are very exclusive. Others, like the St. Croix Ojibwe (Wisconsin), require prospective members to prove 50 percent Indian blood. Most tribes still require prospective members to prove that they have at least 25 percent Indian blood, although some will now accept lineal descent. Most tribes also do not acknowledge Indian blood from other tribes. Fathers who are not named on birth certificates or who don't sign voluntary recognition of paternity papers do not typically have their blood counted.

There are many more self-identified Indians than enrolled members of Indian tribes.[51] Some of those self-identified Indians have thin ties to Native communities; they know only that someone way back in their family tree might have been Indian. Many other self-identified Indians grew up and now live in Native communities, have dark skin, and even speak tribal languages, but are still not eligible for enrollment.

Tribes have a clear right to decide who belongs to them and who does not. The primary alternative to blood quantum as the most important criterion for membership is lineal descent: to open membership to those who can demonstrate they have a direct Indian ancestor. But opening enrollment to more members might result in a flood of returnees, potentially allowing people who have never lived on the reservation to take over tribal politics and reduce the political power and economic resources of those who have lived there the longest. The tribes that have casinos and give payments to their members have further reason not to expand tribal membership, for fear of diluting benefits to current tribal members. In California, over 2,500 tribal members have been disenrolled by their tribes in recent years, and every one of those tribes operates a substantial casino.[52] The economic and political climate on reservations is divisive just when it needs to be inclusive.

Unfortunately, the enrollment records used to determine blood quantum are highly flawed. The original blood quantum calculations at White Earth (Minnesota), for example, were compiled during a lawsuit over land fraud in the 1910s by eugenics-trained scientists Albert Jenks and Aleš Hrdlička, who measured head shape, analyzed hair thickness, and scratched enrollees' skin, noting pink marks as evidence of non-Native blood.[53] By reducing the number of official full-bloods at White Earth from over 5,000 to 127, they vastly diminished the compensation that the U.S. government had to pay for land fraud. Amazingly, their lists—built on exactly those tests—still constitute the database for determining blood quantum and tribal enrollment at White Earth today.[54]

There are people whose tribal enrollment records show 100 percent blood quantum, meaning that, on paper, they are biologically 100 percent Indian. But many of those people have one relative way back in the family tree who is not Indian. There are many people whose tribal enrollment record says they are 25 percent Indian when they and their communities know for a fact that their blood quantum is much more. As a result of this crazy system, many Indians who by most measures would count as full-blooded cannot get enrolled.

While the Indian population in America is growing very rapidly, the enrolled population is advancing much more slowly and is even declining on some reservations. A demographic report on the Salish and Kootenai tribes of the Flathead Reservation (Montana) showed that the death rate has now eclipsed the enrollment rate and a current slow decline in the enrolled population will accelerate significantly after 2020.[55] The tribes appear to be breeding themselves into extinction, completing what forced assimilation could not accomplish. The criterion of blood quantum for tribal membership is a tremendous source of frustration for many Indians who want to belong to, vote for, and serve their tribes and people as bona fide members, but cannot. The net result is that more than half of America's self-identified Indian people suffer the drawbacks of discrimination and history and current community problems, but enjoy none of the benefits of tribal membership. And the debate about identity fuels the bad feelings and paralysis that have plagued tribes for decades. Hurt people hurt people—and lots of hurt Natives take their pain out on one another in the arena of tribal politics and enrollment fights.

Blood is part of identity, but the stuff on the inside matters more than exterior color, hair type, and height of cheekbone. Participation in culture and knowledge of the tribal language do not directly match someone's percentage of Indian blood, but these things often affect identity and tell us who we are more deeply than color. By extending the privileges of tribal citizenship only to those who have a certain racial pedigree and ignoring all other variables of identity, tribes are actually participating in racism. They are not just excluding non-Indians but also alienating and excluding identifiable Indians who have Indian blood, language, and culture. That is not okay.

Many Indians believe that if tribes are ever going to be effective in attacking the root of the problems that plague their communities, they must open the doors to tribal membership for all their people.[56] Concerns about being overrun by newcomers could be somewhat eased by making prospective members apply in person on the reservation. In New Zealand, Australia, South America, and Central America, blood quantum has never been the primary measure of legitimacy or citizenship for tribal peoples, and its absence has not harmed Indigenous people. In the United States and Canada, the most important questions for an Indian tribe or First Nation are not about us as a race. They are about us as nations.

How has tribal enrollment affected you personally?

I am not an enrolled member of any tribe, although I have enrolled relatives from Leech Lake, White Earth, Mille Lacs, and Red Lake reservations in Minnesota. But errors in enrollment records can be corrected, and I have hopes of being enrolled eventually, either at Leech Lake (where my ancestral village of Bena is located and most of my family is from) or White Earth (where my mother was enrolled).

For you to understand the depths of this question in the lives of Indians who are not enrolled, though, it's easiest for

Anton and Blair Treuer with their nine children, Jordan, Robert, Madeline, Caleb, Isaac, Elias, Evan, Mia, and Luella, and their first grandson, Kendrick.

me to simply tell you about my children. We have a large blended family, with nine children who don't all have the same biological parents. They are all identifiably Native in appearance, and they have grown up around Ojibwe ceremonies, language, and lifeways—snaring rabbits, harvesting wild rice, and processing maple syrup. For all of them, being Indian is something they are, believe, and do. It has nothing to do with a piece of paper or blood quantum. But five of my children are enrolled members at Leech Lake, one is enrolled in a Canadian First Nation, and three are not eligible for enrollment.

They learned about enrollment very young. One year I took the kids to Leech Lake's community Christmas party.

When they lined up with other reservation children to receive a gift "from Santa," tribal employees handed one present to each of my children on the tribal enrollment list and told their unenrolled siblings that they could not receive a gift. Being rejected by anyone is painful, but being rejected by the people with whom you identify most strongly, and the community or government that represents them, is excruciating. For the rest of their lives, six of my children will get to vote in tribal elections, receive modest college scholarship assistance from their tribes, and participate in tribal fish harvests. Three will not. Six will be eligible to run for tribal office. Three will not. My beautiful, smart kids are some of the most culturally knowledgeable people of their generation, so the tribes lose too, because only six of these incredible kids get to represent their tribes as bona fide members.

Enrolled or not, all of my children know who they are, but I cannot protect them all from the very real pain of exclusion by their own tribes. Exclusion from a petty Christmas ritual, yes, but also from the deep sense of belonging that accompanies tribal citizenship.

What's it like for Natives who don't look Native?

For all people, racial identity is affected by many things. Color matters, of course. If I introduced myself as a White man, everyone would be really confused because my skin is very brown, even though biologically I am just as White as I am Native. But color is only part of the equation. Culture matters too. A Pueblo Indian, a Makah, and a Potawatomi might be racially profiled the same way, and look similar to one another, but their heritage, languages, cultures, ceremonies, and communities are very different. And race is also partially about consciousness—how we see ourselves. Many Natives are interracial—we might look brown, Black, or White. Those who look Black or look White are commonly mistaken for Black or White, because color shows up first and first impressions have an effect. While that's understandable, it can still be very painful for those who have strong Indigenous culture and consciousness to be misidentified.

Misidentification often happens when we meet people outside Native spaces. But it happens inside Native communities too. And that can be especially hard. Sometimes interracial Indians feel like they aren't Native enough to be accepted by their own people, and they aren't enough of anything else to be accepted in those communities either. As the number of interracial Natives has grown, more and more Indians are understanding and accepting that we don't all look the same. That's the trend, but it's not a guarantee of acceptance and respectful treatment either inside or outside Native communities.

How come some tribes ban the use and sale of alcohol?

The U.S. federal government used to regulate—and for a long time prohibit—the sale of alcohol on Indian land. Some of the current tribal laws against alcohol stem from these old U.S. Indian liquor laws. However, in this day and age, it is up to each tribal government to decide if they will ban the sale of alcohol on their land. Many tribes have removed the restriction. Some have removed it recently because many non-Native casino visitors like to drink. In other places, tribes have insisted that their reservations remain "dry." In addition to the problems that many Native communities have with substance abuse, many tribal members see drinking alcohol as a practice contrary to traditional cultural values.

Do all Indians have drinking problems?

No, but a lot of people have a problem seeing it that way. If someone walks into a crowded bar and sees 200 drunk White college students, they do not say, "See, all White people are drunks." But if someone walks into the same bar and sees 200 drunk White college students and one drunk Indian, it is likely that they would at least think if not say the same about Native Americans.

Over the Thanksgiving holiday in 2010, Station 280 (a St. Paul, Minnesota, bar) produced a poster featuring a scantily clad Native American woman posing provocatively. She was standing in front of a drawing of a happy cowboy with his arm around an Indian man who was passed out drunk. The poster read, "Drink Like an Indian, Party Like a Pilgrim." The poster was built on negative stereotypes about Indians and alcohol—that Indians have drinking problems, that Indian men can't handle their liquor but White men can—with the additional gratuitous sexual objectification of Indian women.

The stereotypes of alcoholism and Indians are complicated by the reality. Substance abuse is a problem in Indian country. We cannot rewrite history, nor can we rewrite well-documented statistics. Many reasons explain the widespread substance abuse in the tribal population. The evidence for genetic predisposition to alcoholism is conflicting and not always conclusive. However, environmental elements, historic factors, and issues of poverty all play heavily into this problem.

At the same time that there is a problem with substance abuse in Indian country, it surprises some people to know that a large percentage of the U.S. and Canadian tribal population abstains entirely from the use of alcohol. These people are motivated by the fact that for many tribes, alcohol is considered taboo in traditional ceremonial circles, and because there are many recovering alcoholics in Indian country. It also demonstrates that when Indian people are true to their beliefs and customs, they can find value systems and places that support and reinforce the culture of mental and physical health, free from substance abuse.

The widespread negative stereotype of the drunken Indian strengthens an Indigenous sense of otherness and dislocation from mainstream society. And because traditional ceremonial lifestyles and belief systems are threatened in many places, many Native youth have internalized negative stereotypes of themselves. It is not enough to tell Native kids be proud of who they are, if we do not at the same time tell them who they are. The struggle of connecting young people to their traditions is made worse by school systems that consistently provide opportunities to learn about others, but very few for Native kids to learn about themselves. We have a lot of work to do.

Is there a solution to substance abuse in Indian country?

There is no easy answer. If there were, we wouldn't have a problem. Issues of poverty, joblessness, historical trauma, violence, and substance abuse are all deeply intertwined. It is impossible to target one of those issues effectively without addressing all of the others. Indians and non-Indians alike have been scratching their heads for decades without making major progress on curbing substance abuse.

The most promising solutions we have lie in the realm of cultural revitalization. Decades upon decades of consistent effort to assimilate Indians have damaged Native communities in horrifying ways. The more disconnected Native people have become from their motherlands, languages, and cultural ways, the more dysfunctional they have become. And as outsiders have attempted to change Indians over the years, Indians have felt more and more isolated and misunderstood. This helps explain why culturally based treatment programs are much more successful for Indian addicts than mainstream programs.[57] In a few places, major efforts have revitalized traditional tribal language and culture. In those places, we often see a parallel strengthening of community cohesion, declining rates of substance abuse, and improvement in academic achievement.

For Native communities, these examples are the most promising effort to bring meaningful solutions to the people. For others, it is important to realize that America's greatest strength and greatest potential in helping Indians lies not in attempting to assimilate and integrate them further, but rather in respecting and supporting the cultural and linguistic diversity that makes this country truly great.

Why did COVID-19 kill so many people at Navajo Nation and other reservations?

The novel coronavirus (COVID-19) killed many people all over the world in 2020, but it had a disproportionate impact at Navajo Nation and some other reservations. The reasons for this are not well understood yet, but some of them seem obvious. On the Navajo reservation and in many other tribal communities, people have big families and lots of regular contact with one another. Houses and hogans (traditional Navajo lodges) are small. A lot of tribal members don't have running water, which makes it harder to wash your hands. All these things make it harder to stop the spread of any contagious disease.

Additionally, a lot of Native people have heart and respiratory conditions that make a disease like COVID-19 a lot more lethal. Many tribal communities are farther away from hospitals and clinics, so it is harder to get help when people need it. There are still 160,000 speakers of the tribal language at Navajo as well, and quite a few people who speak only that language. When they go to a hospital, a lot of things get lost in translation. The federal government also delayed and failed to deliver on a lot of the financial resources promised to tribes to combat the spread of the virus. That made obtaining protective equipment like masks and treatment equipment like respirators a lot more challenging in Native communities. Native health professionals and tribal leaders have been working hard to address all of these issues. Another coronavirus or other disease is likely to spread around the world at some point, and lives are saved when we are prepared.

Why are Indian politics often such a vipers' pit?

Why are American politics such a vipers' pit? Politicians and political processes everywhere are pretty contentious, but there are additional complications in Indian country. Indian communities are small, and tribal leaders, while responsible to all tribal members, sometimes play favorites and appoint their own family members to important positions. That is sometimes unavoidable in a small community, but in some places its effect is that every time there is a tribal election, some people lose their jobs because the new person has supporters or family members they want to appoint to those positions. When that happens, the electoral process is loaded with the angst and hope of not just voters who care about the political and economic future of their people, but of tribal citizens who are worried about their personal job security.

The biggest problem in tribal politics has very little to do with people and much more to do with the structure of tribal government today. The U.S. Constitution provides checks and balances. If the president does something outrageous or illegal, he can be impeached. The courts can check legislation and make sure that laws are not too oppressive. The executive and legislative branches have to come to agreement on spending money. But the constitutions of most tribes, given by the U.S. government, were drafted on a corporate governance model, without effective checks and balances. In many of those places, if the tribal chair is accused of a crime and the tribal court rules against the tribal chair, the tribal chair can appoint an appellate judge with no need for approval from others, and see to it that the appellate judge overrules the lower court's decision.

Many tribes have now revised the constitutions that the U.S. government handed to them. But constitutional reform is difficult for any government. And many tribal governments have yet to effectively improve their structure. Without an effective system of checks and balances in the structure of the tribal governments, things function well when tribal leaders have good integrity, but fall apart when they do not. Tribal leaders in the United States and Canada are no more prone to corruption than any politicians anywhere else—but they are also no less prone. The primary difference is in the structure of the governments.

The other problem with politics in Indian country is that Indigenous values and leadership structures are not at the center of tribal politics. In many places, hereditary chiefs from numerous communities were smashed together in one small place. With so many families and communities represented, nobody could be hereditary chief of them all. And the fault lines, factions, and cliques that plague many Indian communities today had their beginnings at the start of this reservation period, with the very identities of the people. Combine that with the fact that being a tribal leader in the modern world involves networking with governments and bureaucracies that have a colonial way of doing things—the U.S. government, the Bureau of Indian Affairs, and many other political and financial institutions.

Tribal politics are complicated. The work involves an understanding of financial and legal contracts. Yet the constituents to which tribal leaders are responsible are often unfamiliar with and especially untrusting of those institutions and processes. This distrust makes it far easier for tribal leaders to be misunderstood or demonized. And it also makes it easier for tribal leaders, some of them unfamiliar with modern financial and political processes themselves, to make mistakes.

In spite of all those pressures and complications, there are still many wonderful tribal leaders who have worked through the problems with great integrity and helped make their communities safer, healthier, and more prosperous. That's pretty amazing.

I heard that a lot of Indians serve in the U.S. military. How do they reconcile their service with the fact that the U.S. Army killed so many of their people?

Indian people have fought in every American war from the Revolution to Afghanistan. And Indians have served in the U.S. armed forces in larger numbers on a per capita basis than any other racial group in every conflict since World War I, before they were even U.S. citizens. Many Native

General Douglas MacArthur, Commander-in-Chief of the Allied Forces in the Southwest Pacific Area, on an inspection trip of American battle fronts, met representatives of five different American Indian tribes in one United States Army unit. Left to right: S/Sgt. Virgil Brown (Pima) Phoenix, Arizona; First Sergeant Virgil F. Howell (Pawnee) of Pawnee, Oklahoma; S/Sgt. Alvin J. Vilcan (Chitmatcha) of Charenton, La.: General MacArthur; Sgt. Byron L. Tsignine (Navajo) of Fort Defiance Arizona; Sgt. Larry L. Dokin, (Navajo) of Copper Mine, Arizona. (US SIGNAL CORPS PHOTO)

AFTER USE, PLEASE RETURN TO—
Information - 1001 Mdse Mart
Office of Indian Affairs,
Department of the Interior,
Chicago

OFFICE OF INDIAN AFFAIRS
RECEIVED
JAN - 3 1944
Washington, D. C.

RELEASED FOR PUBLICATION
DEC 31 1943
(2)
WAR DEPARTMENT

Americans enlisted for financial reasons. The service remains a way to earn money, provide for one's family, and escape from poverty on the reservations. Many who serve also seek a place in their families' military histories and the bonds with fellow soldiers that can be forged only in combat. Many tribes have famous military traditions, and serving in the armed forces is also a way to gain respect within their tribes and use the position of warrior to speak at ceremonies, carry eagle staffs and flags at powwows, and remind others of their people's proud warrior heritage. Native women serve in the military at a rate just as disproportionate as Native men. That translates to a special acceptance and honor in the Native world just as it does for the men who serve.

Native soldiers are typically well aware that the flag they serve under also flew over armies that massacred Indians and many others throughout its history. But they serve the U.S. military proudly. According to Gulf War veteran and Mille Lacs tribal member Sean Fahrlander, "I said that if I have to protect White people in order to protect my people, I'll do it. Don't ever forget—this *land* is still my country."[58]

What's it like for Natives who serve in the U.S. military today?

I am the first generation in my family not to serve in the military. Many of my uncles served in Vietnam and Korea. My father and grandfather served in World War II. My namesake was a World War I veteran. We can trace our military

Sean Fahrlander (Mille Lacs Ojibwe), Gulf War veteran (U.S. Navy).

history all the way back to some of the most famous battles between the Ojibwe and Dakota in 1700s and 1800s. I grew up hearing their stories and those of my good friends who served in the Gulf War and later operations in Iraq and Afghanistan.

The Army tries to get everyone to function as a soldier rather than a warrior—to follow orders and wear uniforms rather than show their individuality. My relatives experienced this aspect in a positive sense, as an equalizer. People could go only so far with racism because they had to respect the uniforms and the ranks everyone carried. But in Vietnam, Native servicemen were placed on point (in front of other troops) and long-range reconnaissance patrols at a higher rate than their White counterparts. That meant they were in greater danger. And it was harder for anyone with less money or education to opt out of service when there was a draft. That wasn't fair, and the unfairness was racially predictable, something which extended to their service time as well. My grandfather actually wrote "White" on his enlistment papers when he signed up to fight the Nazis in World War II, to make sure he wouldn't be mistreated. It's hard to say what the reasons are, but Native Americans, while serving in the military in greater numbers per capita than other racial groups, have not been promoted to high-level officer positions in equal measure. Indians in the service know this. They see the unfairness. But they see the honor of their service and the respect they earn from people from all racial groups for their service too.

How do Indians feel about the use of Geronimo as the code name for Osama bin Laden?

On May 2, 2011, U.S. Navy SEALs killed Osama bin Laden, architect of the 9/11 terror strikes against America. The U.S. military used Geronimo as the code name for Bin Laden in that action. Audio snippets from the raid included the lines "We have a visual on Geronimo" and "Geronimo is KIA."

The real Geronimo was a legendary leader among the Apache and remains an iconic symbol of resistance, pride, and power to many Native people. Many Indians viewed the code name as a slap in the face and an effort to recast a tribal hero in the role of villain, terrorist, and enemy of the United States. The use of Geronimo as Bin Laden's code name may have been a thoughtless blunder on the military's part, but that oversight hurt the morale of many Native soldiers, who, again, still serve in the U.S. military in higher numbers on a per capita basis than any other racial group in the country.

When I heard the use of this code name in the media coverage right after Bin Laden's death, I immediately thought of my grandfather Eugene Seelye, who enlisted in the U.S. Army, putting his life on the line and earning a Purple Heart in the European theater of operations during World War II. He gave so much to his country, and I wondered when his country would drop its callous disregard for Indians and reciprocate with a little respect.

What do you think about some tribes trying to legalize marijuana?

Several tribes have discussed legalizing marijuana even in states where marijuana remains illegal for recreational use. It seems likely to me that eventually recreational marijuana use will be legalized across the United States. Eleven states have already legalized it. Others are moving in that direction. Tribes are not governed by state authority, and there is a legal route for tribes to pass their own laws about marijuana and other things, as they have already done with gaming and gambling in many places. Leaders of some tribes see an opportunity to open some of the first recreational marijuana businesses in their areas, generating jobs for their people and new sources of much-needed revenue for their tribes. Those in favor of legalization also cite the high number of nonviolent recreational marijuana users who get incarcerated, removing them from their jobs and families and making them burdens to society instead of load-bearing citizens.

This is one of those topics that has divided opinion in Indian country. I certainly agree that people should not be incarcerated for offenses that do not pose harm to society or their fellow citizens, and recreational marijuana use falls into that category. To me, that is a problem with punishments defined in our criminal codes. Whether or not tribes should legalize pot is a different question. I do not support legalization myself, even though I am not likely to win that argument over the long term.

First of all, I believe that legalization sends the wrong message to our own people. People assume that legal means acceptable. And marijuana, while nowhere near as damaging as the opioids and methamphetamine that kill people every day from overdoses, is still proven to affect brain development and function even when not under the influence, especially in users under age twenty-five. It can be a gateway into other kinds of drug use. And our people need space from substance abuse and help healing from it, not more exposure to substances. I also think that tribes being early adopters of legalization sends the wrong message to the rest of the world. We become what we do. If the Ojibwe harvest wild rice and engage in commercial fishing of walleye, then we are seen as the wild rice people and the walleye people. If the Salish harvest salmon, they are the salmon people. If the Lakota ranch bison, they are the buffalo people. I am down with all of that. But if we become major producers and sellers of recreational marijuana, we become the pot people. That does something to our perceived identity and I think it hurts us more than it helps.

Do Indians vote Democrat or Republican?

Both. Just like other folks. There are rich Natives and poor ones, urban and rural, Democrat and Republican. There are some who refuse to vote in any American election and many more who vote in all elections. In many places, if you removed the tribal vote alone, several major elections would have had different results. In Oklahoma and some parts of the Southwest, many Natives vote Republican. In other parts of the country, Natives tend to vote Democrat. But nothing is set in stone. John McCain, a Republican, had a lot of support in Indian country because of his consistent record advocating for tribes and tribal sovereignty. That support was probably generated more in spite of him being Republican than because of it. But the idea that Natives all vote one way or that they are not swing voters is not accurate.

Are things getting better for tribes?

Yes, things are getting better. The political and economic power of Native nations has grown tremendously, especially following the development of casino gaming. Tribal leaders are more used to and effective at operating in the American and Canadian political systems, and the public has become slightly more aware of and knowledgeable about what is happening in Indian country, which helps generate outside support.

In spite of all that, there remains an incredible amount of work to be done. While poverty and substance abuse still plague most Indian communities, they may not be the greatest threats to survival. The Seminole (Florida), for example, have eliminated poverty for their people. They were even able to write a check to the state of Florida to help fill a major shortfall in the education budget for the entire state, which of course bought them a great deal of love from their non-Native neighbors. But if you ask the Seminole what keeps them up at night, they usually respond, "Language and culture loss."

Tribal leaders across the land work very hard, many of them with great integrity, to climb the mountain to political empowerment and financial prosperity. While these are worthy goals, my fear is that they will manage to climb that mountain to the very top, look around, and say, "Oh my God, we just climbed the wrong mountain. We should have been climbing the mountain of language and culture revitalization while we had the chance, while we had the speakers and the cultural carriers and the opportunity." After all, why would we need sovereignty and tribal government if we were completely assimilated with the rest of society? And if Indians have a hard time answering that question for other Indians, they're going to have a really hard time answering it for everyone else.

ECONOMICS

Money is like health. Having it is no guarantee of happiness. But the absence of it can make one miserable.

–attributed to Suze Orman

Do Indians get a break on taxes, and if so, why?

Some Indians do get a break on some taxes in the U.S. All Indians, whether they are enrolled members or not, must pay federal income tax. All Indians must also pay property taxes in the county or municipality in which they own a house—unless they live on tribal trust land (reservation land owned by the federal government and kept under control of a tribe), which is the case for a small percentage of Indian people. All Indians must also pay state income tax unless they are enrolled members who get all of their income from their tribe and live on their reservation, leaving only a small number of Indians exempt from state income tax. In Minnesota, for example, only 23 percent of enrolled Indians live on a reservation.[59] Only some of those get all their income from that reservation. All Indians must also pay sales tax on everything other Americans do, with the exception of vehicles.

The reasons for these complex tax rules lie in history. A state government has no jurisdiction over Indians on Indian land unless the federal government specifically gives that authority to states (e.g., by Public Act 280). That is why Indians living on Indian land, who get all of their income from their tribe, pay federal but not state income tax. Sales tax works similarly—tribal governments do not have to pay or charge state sales tax. But Natives who buy anything off their reservation do, and that's most of what Native people buy. Many tribes have negotiated compacts with the states they are in, by which those tribes agree to pay certain state taxes they are not normally required to pay, such as sales tax, in return for a monetary payment from the state government to support tribal programs.

Many Americans feel that it is simply unfair that Indians should not be taxed on all things, in all the ways that most Americans are taxed. And unfairness seems very un-American to them. Most Indians counter that there is nothing in their entire history that was fair to them. When weighed against traumas from the loss of their land to assimilation policies to the way the government continues to ignore poverty in Indian country, the small tax benefits that go to a small percentage of tribal members hardly seem worth fussing about. Tribal leaders also frequently point out that they supply many in-kind services to non-Native people by plowing roads, providing police protection and fire service on reservation lands (where many non-Native people live), and bearing the expense for those services to tribal members, which county and state governments would be obligated to provide if the tribes did not.

Both many opponents and supporters are unaware that any significant change to the tax status of Indians would require revisiting the U.S. Constitution and many of the treaties the United States signed with Indian nations. Opening those legal processes would probably cost the U.S. government and its taxpaying citizens far more than they would save by living with the status quo. The special tax status of tribal members is part of the structure and payment that

the United States had to agree to in order to obtain the rest of America from Indians. There is no way to redo one without redoing the other. In Canada, First Nations members pay the same taxes that all Canadians do except for a limited exemption for personal property tax defined by Section 87 of the Indian Act for First Nations members living on First Nations. That usually exempts provincial sales tax on vehicles, but does not apply to the Métis and Inuit. First Nation tribal property is not subject to property tax, but parcels owned by individual members off-reserve is taxed.

Do Indians get a break on license plates?

In the United States, Indian nations are exempt from the authority of state governments with the exception of jurisdiction shifts in places where Public Law 280 is in effect. For this reason, many tribes license motor vehicles to their members independently from state agencies. State governments, wanting to get their hands on some of the revenue stream from licensing, and to keep records of all tribal vehicles in the state system for law enforcement purposes, have negotiated compacts with many tribal governments that allow state governments to access tribal vehicle licensing information (with some limitations). In return, enrolled tribal citizens can exempt themselves from state vehicle sales tax if the automobile dealer agrees to deliver the vehicle to the member on the reservation. They can also get and renew license plates directly from their tribe at a subsidized rate.

Why should Indians be eligible for welfare if they are not taxed the same way as everyone else?

Indians are U.S. citizens and shouldn't be denied the benefits that go to other U.S. citizens simply because they happen to be enrolled in a tribe or because they are members of a certain racial minority group. Further, the U.S. federal government has legal obligations to provide for the health, education, and welfare of American Indians. Reneging on that responsibility would be not only morally but legally problematic. And finally, welfare funds and benefits are distributed through county social service agencies, but are not paid for by county or state government. Welfare benefits are paid for by the federal government and sent to states in block grants to distribute to their citizens. Because Indians are not exempt from federal taxation, it is bogus to assert that they are not paying into the pool that finances welfare.

In addition, a great nation can be only as happy as its least happy citizens. When the unemployment rate in the United States reached over 15 percent in the 1930s, they called it the Great Depression. Massive public policy initiatives sought to remedy the nation's economic woes. Well, the unemployment rate in Indian country has never been below 15 percent. For Indians, the "Great Depression" began in the 1800s, and it has never ended. The unemployment rate in some tribal communities is 50 percent, although most see rates around 20 percent. While a couple of tribes, like the Florida Seminole, have successfully eliminated poverty for their citizens, they are the exception, not the rule. And the fact that the first Americans continue to suffer so much makes a sad statement about the health of American democracy. We should be doing more for Indians, not less.

Are Indians all living in extreme poverty?

No. Some tribes, such as the Pequot (Connecticut), the Seminole (Florida), and the Mdwakantonwan Dakota (Minnesota), have successfully eliminated poverty for all of their enrolled tribal citizens. Many other tribes have reduced the unemployment rate from 50 to 20 percent. In over a dozen counties in Minnesota and sixteen counties in in Wisconsin, tribes are not just big employers but the largest employers of all. You'd better be nice to Indians there; you'll probably end up working for one someday. This dramatic improvement has largely been brought about by casino gaming. But anyplace where 20 percent of the population is unemployed has a problem. In Nevada and South Dakota, tribal gaming enterprises are not monopolies, and unemployment is 50 percent or higher in many of their tribal communities. So, there is a diversity of experience with poverty for Indian people in the United States today. A few groups are well off. Many groups are improving but are still very poor. And some groups still have most of their citizens living in abject poverty.

Are Indians all rich from casinos?

As stated earlier, a few groups are well off, many groups are improving but still poor, and some see most of their people living in severe poverty. Casino gaming has affected some Native Americans far more than others. For tribes that have a monopoly on gaming in a region and very small numbers of tribal members, casinos have had a dramatic impact on their members' financial status. But for most Indians who live in rural areas or come from tribes with large numbers of members, the impact has been much smaller.

Each tribe is an independent nation, with no legal obligations to other tribes. Casino profits are not shared by all tribes in America. Wealthy tribes often engage in philanthropy with less fortunate tribes, and in Wisconsin, all tribes agreed to share a small percentage of gaming revenues with one another. But those developments have not come close to leveling the dramatic wealth disparities among tribes, even in Wisconsin. In Canada, the sovereignty of First Nations has not superceded that of provinces, and tribes cannot build

The Seminole Hard Rock Hotel & Casino, Hollywood, FL.

casinos if provincial law doesn't allow for it, making the impact of tribal gaming negligible for First Nations.

How has casino gambling affected Indian communities?

Gaming and gambling are not governed by federal statutes, which is why some states, like Nevada and South Dakota, have legalized many forms of gambling but others, like Minnesota, have not. Indian gaming got its start in the late 1970s, when the Seminole Indians of Florida ignored the state's gaming laws (which allowed church bingo but nothing more) and developed a high-stakes bingo operation. The local sheriff tried to shut it down, but the tribe filed for an injunction, which was appealed all the way to the Fifth Circuit Court of Appeals. The decision, *Seminole Tribe of Florida v. Butterworth* (1981), upheld the right of the Seminole to develop gaming operations without regard to state laws. It was another sovereignty victory for tribal governments and a huge eye-opener for tribes in states that had not legalized casino gambling.[60]

Legal challenges to tribal gaming continued after *Seminole v. Butterworth*. However, the U.S. Supreme Court ruled in *California v. Cabazon Band of Mission Indians* (1987) that California could not regulate gaming on Indian land when it allowed other gaming, such as the state lottery, elsewhere in the state. *Cabazon* removed the final obstacles, and tribal gaming began to proliferate across the country. Within two years, hundreds of Indian nations developed some type of high-stakes bingo or casino-style gaming operation. Federal legislation followed in 1988 in the form of the Indian Gaming Regulatory Act, establishing clearly that all tribes were within their rights to build casinos.

Many Indians worry about negative impacts of gaming on tribal members because they disproportionately frequent the casinos. Increased rates of gambling addiction, exposure to secondhand cigarette smoke, and what many view as an unhealthy and untraditional environment in the casinos are among the greatest worries. There is also significant concern about the misinformed assumption that "all Indians are rich from casinos," which has led many granting agencies and regular citizens to believe that tribes do not need outside help in fighting poverty or developing programs. The influx of money to tribes through gaming has also increased internal political strife and accusations of mismanagement and embezzlement. Some of those accusations are well founded; others are not.

The Mille Lacs Ojibwe (Minnesota) used casino income to build a new health clinic and new schools, establish an all-band-member retirement plan, purchase health insurance for all tribal members, purchase a bank and many businesses—and still save half of their casino revenues. The financial and political power they wield speaks well for the potential development of gaming operations in Indian country, even though it makes sense for tribes to have diversified business plans and not rely on gaming alone to pay for their needs. It is up to tribal members and their governments to make the decisions they believe are best for them.

How have per capita payments affected Indian communities?

Per capita payments are payments to each tribal member from a portion of casino profits or other businesses. Most tribes will probably never be able to offer them, since they have so many tribal members relative to their income. However, some communities with small populations and large casino operations have recently begun to pay a portion of their casino proceeds directly to tribal members.

The payments create huge dilemmas for tribal governments and members. Members want the payments, and they pressure or vote in leaders who promise to start or increase them. The policy often puts stress on the bottom line for tribes that stretch margins to make per capita payments and diverts revenue from deserving programs (health, education, housing). The issue of per capita payments becomes a catch-22 for tribal officials, who find it politically impossible to reduce the payments but difficult to expand other businesses and programs when significant funds are diverted to the per capita payments.

For recipients, the payments are well-intended and welcome assistance, but some feel that per capita payments are a double-edged sword that do more harm than good. Tribes often put aside per capita payments for minors and give them large lump-sum payments at age eighteen. This timing accelerates negative behavior for some youth, who want to party with the largest check they have ever received, and often discourages further education or career development. In addition, tribal members who used to supplement their income and feed their families by farming, gardening, hunting, and harvesting cactus, pine nuts, wild rice, berries, and fish, but who now receive per capita payments, are far less likely to participate in those traditional lifeways, providing another barrier to healthy living and further eroding traditional culture. Finally, tribes that can't really afford to make per capita payments have actually been exploring ways to cut spending on social services and education in order to make these payments, in response to tribal member demand.

What is the future of Indian gaming?

I believe Indian gaming will not last forever. It will end not because politicians hate Indians but because they see opportunity. The economic and political climate in the United States has made it very difficult for both Democrats and Republicans to accomplish their campaign objectives without committing political suicide. Democrats can raise taxes only so high before they get voted out of office; Republicans can cut education and entitlements only so much before they get voted out of office. It is far easier for both parties to do something like an end run around Indian gaming at the state level. I believe state governments will increasingly develop and expand non-tribal gaming enterprises to bridge revenue shortfalls, which will cause Indian gaming to be less profitable due to increased competition. The political backlash in Indian country is far easier for most politicians to deal with than the potential backlash from the general public for doing other things.

Are tribes affected by many states legalizing gaming in non-Native spaces?

Yes. States like Nevada and South Dakota legalized gaming long before tribes started operations, so the tribes there never had a monopoly on gaming. The fact that these first adopters of gaming were usually closer to population centers than the reservations were also gave them a leg up. Tribal gaming therefore never became big in these states. As a result, tribes and tribal people there have had to seek other ways to address poverty and create economic opportunity. State governments in Illinois, New Jersey, and other places have allowed some limited but significant gaming. Those entities directly compete with tribes and divert business from tribal operations to these state-run or private casinos. These have not driven tribes out of business, but they do reduce their income.

What should tribes be doing to improve the economic condition of their citizens?

Tribal governments are working hard to improve the economic well-being of their communities. Gaming has obviously given them a major boost over the past thirty years. My primary frustration with the business development plans of many tribal governments, though, is that they often do not think beyond the casino doors. There are exceptions, of course, such as the Sault Ste. Marie Ojibwe, who operate over thirty different businesses. State governments are trying to directly compete with tribes in sports betting, lotteries, and casino gaming. Tribes will have more competitors in that area in the future. They should expand in other areas for more diverse and stable business opportunities.

For example, tribes could better employ their very special tax status in the United States. Pharmaceutical corporations often go to Puerto Rico, which also has a preferable tax status. I would like to see tribal governments trying to bring that kind of business to reservations. It would generate numerous jobs, most of which would pay well. Making this effort would also enable tribes to diversify their business investments.

There's much more to improving the economic well-being of an entire people than a sound business plan, though. America remains the richest nation on earth, but its citizens have not all been rewarded equally. Wealthy tribal nations have not always succeeded in raising the standard of living for all of their citizens either. In addition to having a sound business plan with diversified enterprises, tribal governments should provide strategic assistance with education, health care, and housing to supplement state and federal programs. They need not provide direct handouts but should give support that incentivizes healthy living and self-sufficiency.

There is an entitlement mentality in Indian country that I see as a problem. At Leech Lake (Minnesota), for example, the tribe pays for all band member funerals, provides fuel assistance, and gives other emergency financial relief. People are poor, and this assistance really helps them make ends meet and get through hard times. While the assistance is welcome, worthwhile, and expected by all tribal members, those benefits use up so much tribal revenue that it makes it hard for the tribe to provide other services. It would be political suicide for anyone in the tribal government to stop such programs. But support for health, education, language, and culture programs is often hard to generate. Many entitlements are extended for all tribal members, not just those in financial need. What seems fair actually deprives some tribes of resources to help those who need it most. Many other tribes make similar decisions with their money. And while the federal government treated Indians unfairly in many different ways, we cannot afford to sit around and complain about it. We need to do something about it.

EDUCATION

There are but two lasting bequests we can hope to give our children. One of these is roots, the other, wings.

–Hodding Carter

What were Native residential boarding schools?

One of the most harmful parts of the war on Indigenous culture was the residential boarding school system.[61] Beginning in the late 1800s, missionary, military, and government officials advocated for the removal of Indian children from their homes to better teach them in the English language and American culture. Captain Richard Henry Pratt, superintendent of the Carlisle Indian Industrial School, the first of many Indian boarding schools, said, "Our goal is to kill the Indian in order to save the man."[62] The idea of the schools had less to do with giving children an education than with taking away their culture. Children were sent to schools as far from home as possible in order to discourage runaways and inhibit parental contact. Their clothes were burned and their hair cut. They were strictly forbidden to speak tribal languages. At Carlisle and many other schools, children spent half the day working in fields or digging ditches and half the day in class. Attendance at Bureau of Indian Affairs (BIA) boarding schools or church

Pratt with Carlisle students, 1881.

mission schools was compulsory for Indian children—home schooling and public schools were not options for most Indian youth in the late nineteenth century.

The BIA schools came under criticism after many children began to die from malnutrition and diseases like tuberculosis; their bodies were not sent home for burial. The commissioner of Indian Affairs defended the situation in 1899, saying, "This education policy is based on the well-known inferiority of the great mass of Indians in religion, intelligence, morals, and home life."[63] There were 25 such schools in operation that year, with 20,000 new students every year. Parents did have the option of sending their children to mission schools instead, but those schools were usually just as

Tom Torlino (Navajo), a Carlisle student from 1882-1886, before and after entering the school.

harsh in suppressing tribal languages and culture and even more likely to expose students to sexual molestation, which was commonly reported.[64] Problems were not immediately known to parents, who often thought that their children would receive work opportunities upon graduation and at least three meals a day at the schools, which was more than many families could provide. Canada followed the American example and soon swept up a huge percentage of the First Nations, Inuit, and Métis population into the schools too.

The experience was devastating for most families. On returning home, many children could no longer recognize their own parents and could not speak the same language. The jobs people hoped would be

Carlisle students, 1900.

available for graduates never came to be in the country's racially polarized climate. Children often felt they could not fit in either on or off the reservations, and those feelings, together with the terrible poverty in most places, simply added to the growing problems on the reservations.

The schools came under increasing scrutiny as more than half the children at Carlisle had trachoma by 1900 and an influenza outbreak at Haskell in 1918 killed more than 300 students.[65] Official modifications did not change the dynamic, and Carlisle closed in 1918, but other schools actually continued to increase their enrollments. In 1928, the U.S. government commissioned the Merriam Report, which blasted the schools for poor nutrition and health care for

Native student burials at the United States Indian Industrial Training School in Lawrence, Kansas, now part of Haskell Indian Nations University.

students, insufficient clothing, exceedingly harsh physical punishment, and the breakup of tribal families. The next commissioner of Indian Affairs, John Collier, began to reform the BIA school system. It took many years, but after World War II, day schools started to dominate the educational experience of Indian children in the United States. Four BIA-operated boarding schools are still in existence today, but their policies have been reformed. In Canada, though, the residential schools for Native youth dominated Indigenous education well into the 1970s.

The long-term effects of the residential boarding school system are profound. People learn how to parent by how they are parented, and with as many as three generations of Natives in the United States and Canada forced to go through boarding schools, a critical piece of the social fabric was severely damaged. Many Native families have rebounded from the effects of boarding schools, but their blessings come in spite of the system rather than because of it. Of the remaining 150 tribal languages spoken in the United States and Canada, 130 are likely to go extinct in the next 30 years because only elders speak them.[66] Residential boarding schools are among the main reasons for this.

One of the goals of the residential boarding school system—educational achievement for Native youth—was directly hurt by the education policy itself. Many Natives developed or deepened distrust of politicians and educators as a result of their experiences in residential boarding schools. Today there is an astounding achievement gap for Native youth. One of the reasons is the distrust many family members have of schools. Many Native parents do not feel comfortable at school conferences and choose not to attend, limiting their ability to provide positive intervention or support for teachers in bettering their children's education. If the residential boarding school experience had not psychologically crushed so many Natives and alienated them from their own culture, this part of modern education for Indigenous people would be very different.

How come 50 percent of Indians are flunking their state-mandated tests in English and math?

There is an achievement gap for many groups of the population in America and Canada, but, on closer examination, that "achievement gap" is really an "opportunity gap." Poverty is one of the factors that strongly contributes to that gap. Children growing up in poverty are far more likely to have a whole set of circumstances that hinder their advancement in education. Most of these causes and effects are well documented. Education was unfairly denied to Black American youth for a long time. Native youth carry the history of residential boarding schools and historical trauma: education was a tool used to assimilate them. As a result, many Indians rightly question whether modern education is still designed to assimilate. When I went to school, I often heard from my Native peers that my education, especially toward my advanced degrees, meant that I was assimilated. I was called an "apple"—red on the outside but White inside—because I was well educated.

The modern educational system in the U.S. has a long way to go to be more inclusive of Black and Latinx communities and curricula, but the system is starting to respond to those communities. There are strands in the social studies curricula for all states that require education about topics like the civil rights movement. Yet all that one can be sure of learning about Indians is a sugarcoated version of Christopher Columbus and Thanksgiving. Eighty-seven percent of school districts teach nothing about Native anything after 1900.[67] As a result, young Native learners often feel like the curriculum in most American schools is still designed to make them more White.

Those who develop state curriculum guidelines do not intend to alienate anyone or limit their opportunities, but that is exactly what they do to Native students. An Indian student in the modern educational system will navigate many curricular strands before high school, but the teachings about the people who made the country great (not them), the heroes, presidents, and cultural icons (not theirs), the success stories (not them), and the culture and history of great civilizations (not theirs) hurt their self-esteem. The omission of Indians from the curriculum means that Native children can go to school and learn all about the rest of the world but not about themselves.

The opportunity to learn about oneself is not the only gap that negatively affects Native kids' academic performance. The skill sets emphasized in modern education (math and reading) are great for some things and from some perspectives—but not all. Native people often have different

The First Thanksgiving, 1621, an early 20th-century painting by Jean Leon Gerome Ferris.

values, different skill sets of emphasis, different learning styles, and different cultures. None of those differences are well supported in the modern educational system. All of these factors contribute to the opportunity gap for Native youth.

Such uncomplicated depictions of Thanksgiving continue to this day, including in schools.

Is there anything that works in the effort to bridge the achievement gap for Native students?

Some schools run by tribes and the Bureau of Indian Education meet No Child Left Behind or other education policy requirements every year. But throughout the United States, Indian youth underperform and underachieve in many places. Often, only half the Indian youth in a given school district are passing their state-mandated tests in English and in math. Everyone is scratching their heads trying to figure out how to remedy the situation.

To me, the answer is quite simple. We need to transform the schools that educate Indian youth from places designed to assimilate into places that enable people to learn about themselves and the rest of the world. This approach is a big part of the success for tribal schools that are making the grade on state-mandated tests. In Wisconsin, the Ojibwe language immersion school Waadookodaading has had very high pass rates on state-mandated tests administered in English. But the teachers there never instruct Native youth in anything other than the tribal language until the highest grades. That says a lot. And we should all pay attention. Assimilation does not create educational achievement, but access to tribal language and culture for Indian youth does.

A lot of tribes are developing their own schools, libraries, and tribal colleges. Putting Natives in charge does not solve all the problems. But it does increase the chances that educators will be responsive to the needs of the students in front of them and their communities.

How does education policy affect Indian country?

All schools in the United States rely heavily on funding from state governments. This is true for all public schools, most private schools, and all tribal and charter schools. Without state-supplied per pupil funding, most schools would not be able to operate.

The federal government wields influence in the equation by pressuring states with education policies such as No Child Left Behind (passed in 2002) and Every Student Succeeds (passed in 2015). And state governments in turn pressure school districts to generate educational achievement among their students. Money follows success.

There are many problems with a policy like No Child Left Behind. It holds schools accountable for the achievement of their students at a certain level. It does not matter if the teacher brings a kid from the first-grade reading level to the eleventh-grade reading level. If that kid is in twelfth grade, the teacher still failed. Every Student Succeeds granted more room for variance in accountability measures, but schools are still pressured to teach to a test rather than to a more holistic array of student needs. The challenges are pronounced in Indian country, where the educational achievement (opportunity) gap is severe. This has brought tremendous pressure on many school districts that serve a lot of Native youth. Some are in very rural areas: Should these schools close, most of their children would face a bus ride of an hour and a half in each direction to get to and from school. While accountability is necessary and understandable, the accounting measures should consider more than achievement. They should also consider progress from one benchmark to another, demographics, and other variables in constructing a fair measure of teacher and school performance.

No Child Left Behind, Every Student Succeeds, and other similar policies have long been pressuring those who educate Indians away from teaching tribal language and culture and toward teaching math and English reading. While those pressures may be slowly shifting, the heightened sense of alienation and distrust in Indian country will take far longer to lessen.

Do Indians all have a free ride to college?

Indians do not all have a free ride to college. Most tribes have scholarship programs, usually requiring a high grade point average. Some of those programs are very well funded, but many others are not. Also, most scholarships are extended only to enrolled members of federally recognized tribes. Considering the many issues with tribal enrollment in the United States, there is a great deal of unfairness and discrepancy in scholarship benefits for Indians. Tens of thousands of scholarships are offered across this country for all sorts of reasons, and Native scholarships make up their own small part of that number.

Many Americans feel that Indians are somehow financially privileged in the realm of education. Although only a small percentage of Indians get significant financial help with college, I believe it would be perfectly fair if all Indians did get a free ride. Through not only historic experience but also direct government policy, many Indian people have been made to suffer. They suffered not just in the 1800s during the height of violence; they suffer today. The Native population is disproportionately unemployed and impoverished. Financial opportunities have been slow in coming to Indian country. Considering all that America does to address poverty throughout the world, including funding the United Nations and the World Bank, it is high time for this country to do more for its Indian citizens. And rather than handouts, I think educational benefits would be perfectly appropriate.

What are some myths and stereotypes about Natives?

I've been taking on stereotypes throughout this book, but here is a frame for doing it yourself that may be helpful. In her TED Talk "The Danger of a Single Story," Chimamanda Ngozi Adichie said, "The problem with stereotypes is not so much that they are incorrect as they are incomplete." If we focus on part of someone's personality and ignore the rest, we don't get an accurate picture of them. It's the same for someone else's culture or historical or racial experience. Sometimes stereotypes are wildly contradictory. One says that Indians are all rich from casinos. Another says that they are all living in squalor on reservations. Neither is a complete explanation, even though many tribes are running multimillion-dollar businesses and half of the tribal population lives in poverty. Half the tribal population lives off reservations too. Other stereotypes abound. One says that Natives are all drunks. Many Natives (including me) don't drink. Another says that Natives are warlike. Yet another says that they are super-spiritual. Look for the whole story and you'll get a lot closer to the truth.

Is anyone getting it right in Indian education?

Yes. I have been really impressed with what the Native Hawaiians are doing. They have 22 Hawaiian-medium schools where Hawaiian is the language used to teach all day every day. They went from fewer than 1,000 speakers

Traditional Hawaiian music and greetings like this are more than cultural enrichment at Hawaiian-medium schools like Nawahi (pictured here)—they are central to the curriculum and their mission of positive Indigenous identity development for all learners.

there to 23,000. And the truancy rates have dropped, the test scores have gone up, and many graduates are going to college. The same can be said for the aforementioned Waadookodaading Ojibwe Language Institute for Ojibwe in northern Wisconsin, the Akwesasne Freedom School for Mohawk in New York, and many others. There is no simple solution, but I think that schools which support and really provide for positive identity development for Native learners—the opportunity to learn about themselves as well as the rest of the world—are having the greatest success.

SOCIAL ACTIVISM

Can there really be justice on stolen land?

—Gyasi Ross

Just as the oppressor, in order to oppress, needs a theory of oppressive action, so the oppressed, in order to become free, also need a theory of action.

—Paulo Freire

The earth is mother of all people, and all people should have equal rights upon it.

—Chief Joseph

Though it may cost me my liberty, it is my duty, and I will continue to speak and act also, till the wrongs of my people shall be righted.

—Hole in the Day

Why was the Dakota Access Pipeline protest such a big deal?

From April 2016 to February 2017, there was a massive tribal protest at the site of the Dakota Access Pipeline where it was to cross the Cannonball River on the Standing Rock Reservation in North Dakota. Eventually, thousands of protesters cycled through the site, some staying for the entire

A scene from the Dakota Access Pipeline protest, 2016.

duration of the protest, and others coming for short periods of time. The protest failed to stop the pipeline from being built, but it succeeded in raising consciousness across America and around the world about the environmental and racial impacts of the oil pipeline protest. The protest also brought an evolution in protest movements when Black Lives Matter and other social change groups worked cooperatively with the Native community. This kind of bridge-building work between different social justice movements did not begin in the Dakota Access Pipeline protest, but it seemed to mature and accelerate here.

As long as people buy gasoline and oil, someone is going to figure out how to get it out of the ground and to market.

The camp at Standing Rock.

There are no harmless ways to do that. Whether the oil comes in a truck, a train, or a pipeline, there will be environmental damage and risk involved in moving it from one place to another. The main source of conflict is in how pipeline companies routinely go about their business. If they drew a route for each pipeline that gave full consideration to minimizing environmental risk, and engaged with tribes, states, and municipal governments in good faith, there would likely never have been a protest at Standing Rock or so much tension about ongoing pipeline projects now. But that's not what they do.

Pipeline companies draw routes for pipelines that make environmental concerns a smaller priority than generating

the most money for the company. If that means they cross a river ten times instead of one time because it's a shorter and faster route, they do that. If a tribe or municipal government has a problem with the pipeline, they often build it up to the edge of the "problem" area, then build it from the other side of the "problem" area, and afterward pressure that area and its government to give in because the rest of the pipeline is already built. That's exactly what happened at Standing Rock.

Pipeline companies also often listen better to White constituents when they have concerns than they do to tribes and tribal people. When Energy Transfer Partners (ETP) wanted to build the Dakota Access Pipeline, White citizens in Bismarck, North Dakota, objected. Energy Transfer Partners changed the route of the pipeline to accommodate them. One hour's drive away, at Standing Rock, the tribal government objected to the route as well. They were ignored, and ETP built the pipeline up to the edge of the reservation, and from the other side of it, farther east along the pipeline route. The tribe objected to the pipeline because it was to go right across the Cannonball River, their only source of drinking water on the reservation. If the pipeline leaked (and all pipelines eventually leak), it could make it unsafe to drink the water in their community or swim or fish there.

Eventually hundreds of protesters set up camp along both sides of the Cannonball River to block the construction site for the pipeline. There was still an opportunity for ETP to try diplomacy and talk to the tribe, to calm things down and find a solution that everyone could agree to. But they refused. The protest grew. Then ETP hired a private security firm to deal with the protesters. They used attack dogs and tear gas. Several protesters were hurt. Press coverage grew. The Obama administration refused to take action to either approve or deny the pipeline for a long time. Had they taken a stand, that also could have resolved the growing crisis.

Energy Transfer Partners pressured politicians to send in military support. Tensions were high. The North Dakota state government strongly supported ETP. For example, North Dakota educational administrators said that any Native families at the protest were keeping their kids out of school illegally. There were some families there with children. But those children were signed up for home schooling, and many were from South Dakota rather than North Dakota. College students from the University of Mary in Bismarck volunteered at a home-school resource center at the protest camp, which kept a library for the kids. But North Dakota officials declared the children were truant and said they would initiate legal action to have the kids removed from their families and placed in foster care. In other words, officials weaponized the education and social services programs of the state to interfere with the free speech rights of parents whose ideas they did not like.

Another example: some of the land off the reservation where protesters were camped was owned by White ranchers. In North Dakota it is illegal for corporations to own farms and ranches, in order to protect family farms. But ETP worked out a purchase agreement with the ranchers so they could buy the land the protesters were on and charge them with trespassing. The sale was supported by North Dakota state officials, even though it broke their own law about corporations not owning farms and ranches.

Support for the protesters grew nonetheless. The Menominee sent truckloads of firewood. Many tribes brought food and blankets. More and more police, marshals, and military personnel arrived.

Donald Trump was elected president in November 2016, and it became clear that any potential support from Barack Obama for the position of the Standing Rock tribe would immediately be overturned by Trump once he was sworn into office. After Trump's inauguration, he signed a presidential memorandum, and the protest site was cleared by law enforcement personnel. The end of the protest was somewhat anticlimactic because many of the protesters left ahead of the police actions, because of cold weather and the harsh treatment many received from law enforcement. That treatment included many protesters being strip searched in the cold—some being forced to bend and squat while naked. Members of the press like Amy Goodman were accused of rioting and numerous other charges. Over 500 people were eventually arrested. Many are still doing time.

I went out to Standing Rock twice during the protests. What I saw there was very different from what the press often reported. I saw a large sign that read:

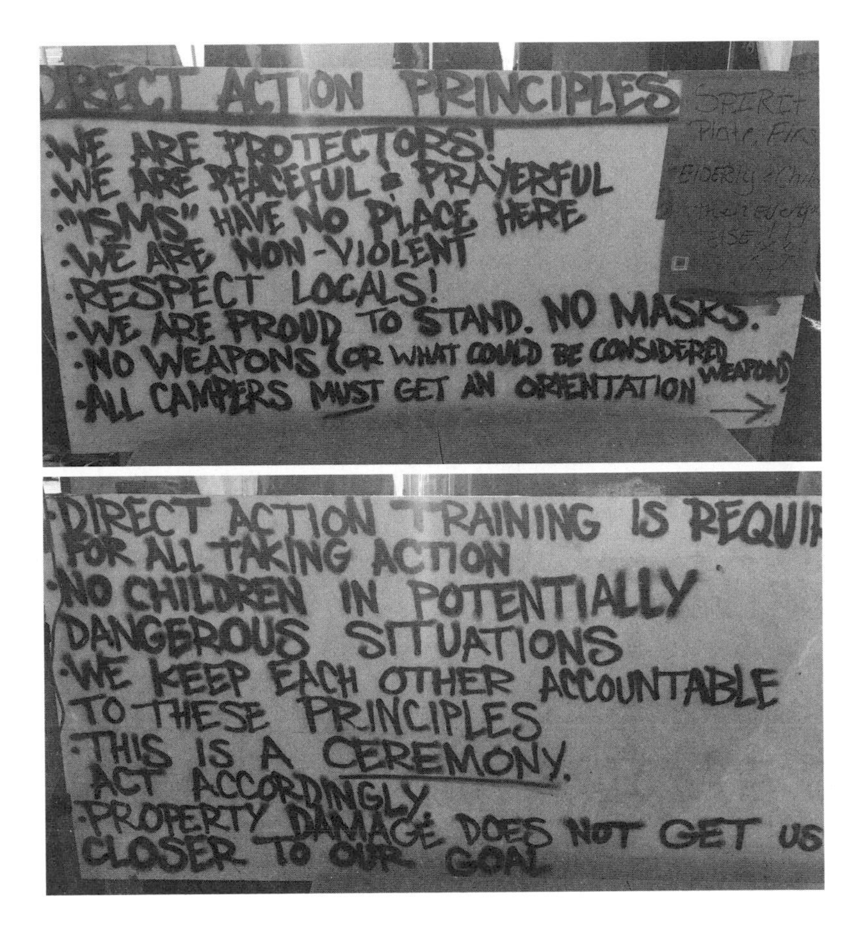

We are protectors. We are peaceful and prayerful. "Isms" have no place here. We are non-violent. Respect locals. We are proud to stand. No masks. No weapons (or what could be considered weapons). All campers <u>must</u> get an orientation. Direct action training is required for all taking action. No children in potentially dangerous situations. We keep each other accountable to these principles. This is a <u>ceremony</u>. Act accordingly. Property damage does not get us closer to our goal.

I saw the small school resource center and library being used. I saw water ceremony being conducted. I saw community in action with good intention.

The Dakota Access Pipeline protest camp is gone now, but the controversy has not ended. Construction of the pipeline continued. But court challenges by the Standing Rock tribe had success in 2020, casting doubt on the pipeline's long-term viability, though appeals will take years and do not have a certain outcome. Even though the pipeline has not been stopped or ripped out of the ground (yet), the unity and awareness raised by protesting against it remain. A different pipeline company, Enbridge, had to abandon the Sandpiper Pipeline in Minnesota because protests caused incredibly expensive delays. Protesters don't get everything they ask for, but they do engineer change. Frederick Douglass once said prophetic words about the importance of protesting injustice and making change: "Power concedes nothing without a demand."[68]

Do Indians face racial profiling from law enforcement?

Racial profiling does still happen.[69] Whites can be sure that the color of their skin was not a factor in being pulled over for speeding, but someone who is identifiably Native, especially one with tribal license plates, never knows for sure. Beltrami County (Minnesota) and the Red Lake Reservation have had disagreements about exercising each other's arrest warrants, and the Beltrami County sheriff's office intentionally profiled Indians at times, pulling over cars with Red Lake plates to see if the subjects of the warrants were in the vehicles, using only the racial profile (tribal license plate) to decide whom to pull over and investigate. That problem is being more effectively addressed by the sheriff's office now.

The Bureau of Justice Statistics reports that Natives are incarcerated at a rate 38 percent higher than the national average.[70] In 19 states, Native Americans are incarcerated at a rate higher than any other racial group. In Minnesota, Indians make up 1 percent of the state population and 17 percent of the state's prison population. In Alaska, Natives are 38 percent of the prison population but only 15 percent of the overall population. Native Hawaiians are 24 percent of the state population but 39 percent of the prison population. Indian youth are 1 percent of the U.S. youth population but make up 70 percent of the youth incarcerated in the U.S. federal prison system, because of discrimination in the system and the unique jurisdiction issues on reservations.

Native men are incarcerated four times as often as White men, and Native women are incarcerated at a rate six times that of White women. The system investigates, charges, tries, convicts, and incarcerates Indians at rates much higher than those of the general population. There are some great people working in law enforcement today who are trying to change this situation, but clearly much more needs to be done. Most Indians are policed by non-Native people. That's a problem only when race becomes a factor in how citizens are treated by law enforcement. Since race is a factor in many Indian cases, racial profiling continues to be a problem.

I am a college professor, and in my small town of Bemidji, I have been on the front cover of the local newspaper at least a couple times every year with some sort of good news. People respect me. I am friends with our chief of police and the county sheriff. But I have still been pulled over by the cops about 40 times in my life. Twice this past year I was pulled over for not wearing a seatbelt in broad daylight while I was wearing a seatbelt. I told the cop this each time, and each time he said, "Well, you're wearing it *now*." Once I had a cop unholster his weapon when he approached me for a routine traffic stop while I had kids in the car, again in broad daylight. When my blond-haired, blue-eyed wife and I first started dating, we got a flat tire and a cop pulled up behind us on the side of the road. He offered no help but did ask for my license, registration, and insurance card. The cop kept asking my wife, "Ma'am, are you okay?" He kept asking me who owned the car. I said that I did. I had given him the registration card. He didn't believe me and asked me to spell my name even though it was on the registration card and the driver's license in his hand. He made me open the trunk and scattered our belongings in the ditch while he searched it. Then he handed me my license and, having found no drugs and since I wasn't speeding, just said, "Have a nice day." My wife was freaked out. I had to ask, "Are you sure you want to date me? This won't be the only time this happens." I am 100 percent sure that I would not have these experiences if I looked White instead of Native.

What do Natives think about the Black Lives Matter movement?

Black lives do matter. I support the message that Black lives matter and the effort to raise awareness of the many ways in which they have not mattered as much as they should throughout history. I realize that saying "Black lives matter" is upsetting to some people, but only because they hear words that are not in the slogan. It doesn't say that Black lives matter *more* than other lives. It doesn't say that *only* Black lives matter. The facts are clear. Black lives matter. They matter just as much as anyone else's. But throughout history and in the present moment, the data say that Black lives have not been treated with value equal to that of other lives, so we all need a little reminder. That's healthy, and it doesn't take anything away from anyone else. An analogy can help here. If someone's house catches on fire and they call the fire department, they should not hear, "Don't tell me that your house matters. All houses matter." This house is on fire. And we all need to answer the call.

I do struggle with finding the right way to talk about the value of my life and all Native lives in the context of Black Lives Matter. A lot of Natives have the same feeling. I don't want to get lost in the "Oppression Olympics" or competing victimization by saying my people have suffered worse than someone else. All that does is take vital energy away from fighting oppression in all its forms. We have to work together and hold one another up. At the same time, the data does say that Native Americans are some of the most likely to be killed by police on a per capita basis. The life expectancy for a Native male in the Northern Plains and Great Lakes is 54.7 years (and they tell us to save for retirement). I want attention brought to these issues in a way that does not detract from the important message in the Black Lives Matter movement. My son Robert, who is Black and Native and looks Black, gets racially profiled based on his Black looks, but also has a very Native consciousness about who he is. He, and other multiracial Natives who are Black that I have spoken to, all say that we need to draw attention to the diminished humanity and lower level of safety experienced by all people of color, and that we should expand our calls for justice to include them without muzzling Black pain or the attention we all need to pay to that.

Natives have often experienced invisibility and marginalization. We struggle to get enough oxygen to breathe attention on the issues that affect our lives. It's death by apathy. And I don't have a perfect answer. But I do racial equity work in mixed company all the time, and I know from experience that when we advocate for one another, instead of alone, we do our most effective work. James Rattling Leaf is pulling together people from all racial backgrounds in Rapid City, South Dakota, to tackle race relations there. I regularly attend the National Summit for Courageous Conversation, and the Indigenous Affinity Group there is doing vital bridge-building racial equity work across the country and in New Zealand and Australia. That's the way forward.

How are Natives building bridges with other groups to fight racism?

On May 25, 2020, George Floyd (a Black man) was murdered by Minneapolis police officer Derek Chauvin, who kneeled on Floyd's neck for almost nine minutes while Floyd was handcuffed and pleading for his life. The entire event was caught on camera and shared across the country. Minneapolis erupted in protest. Floyd was killed in a neighborhood with high Native residency, and the Indigenous people of Minnesota protested in large numbers in passionate solidarity with the Black community. The Native response was more than solidarity too. Natives, like Blacks, get killed by the police at a disproportionate rate. We all saw George Floyd's life given so little regard by Chauvin as evidence that all of our lives have very little meaning to him and many other police officers. For many Natives, their protest was not simply to show sympathy or solidarity with Blacks, but a response to the permanent assault on Black and brown bodies.

Social justice work takes many forms. Sometimes it is the steady, persistent efforts of educators, tribal leaders, community organizers, and environmental activists to develop educational resources and engage in numerous conversations from local to international. Sometimes it is effort to change policy. Sometimes it is leading change inside organizations or training team members from the outside. But it is situational response too, like we saw when George Floyd was murdered.

Sometimes the situations bring people from many groups together. Natives have long led a fight to pressure schools and professional sports teams to do away with racist mascots. And taking on the NFL regarding mascots was a natural segue to combating other racial issues there, such as the NFL's treatment of Colin Kaepernick. Many Native people have lifted their voices and efforts around these and other racial issues. Racism dehumanizes all of us and the remedy to it benefits all of us.

What do Natives think about social activism in Latinx and other non-White communities?

The Latinx world is changing fast. In America, although some people think Latinx means brown people, the reality is very different. Many Latinx people are Black, many brown, and many White. Many have Indigenous blood in their veins too. Increasingly, those who do are trying to explore that part of their identities and even build bridges with other Indigenous people and communities. I think there is a lot to be gained by everyone as we build those connections and deepen the explorations. We can learn from one another and realize the power of collective action for social justice. I feel much as I do about the BLM movement in the Black community. We need to support one another's causes and support the ideals of justice and healing wherever they take us.

Do Natives in Canada, South America, and the United States ever work together or communicate about shared struggles?

We do work together, although there is always room to grow. In education, social activism, petitions to the United Nations, and politics, tribes and Indigenous people across North and South America often try to raise awareness about one another's struggles and find ways for collective action. Advocacy around missing and murdered Indigenous women in the United States and Canada crosses the border continuously. Many tribes in many countries have adopted and advocated for the United Nations Declaration on the Rights of Indigenous Peoples. That declaration has in turn been adopted by many non-Indigenous institutions and creates a great accountability statement that is influencing strategy and action in many places.

There are challenges to this kind of work. Much of the Native population has limited financial resources for travel to support other groups and to network in person. Academics and educators do have international conferences on Indigenous topics that bring many people together. But many tribal politicians have to respond so often to immediate concerns at home that it is a challenge for them to build bridges everywhere else. In Canada, a structure in the councils of First Nations enables greater ease of collective political action, but that hasn't always crossed the border. Language barriers can be significant. Some tribes are trying to work cooperatively with oil companies, pipeline companies, and

Oren Lyons (Haudenosaunee), acclaimed activist for Indigenous and environmental rights, addressing the United Nations.

mining companies, and most others see such efforts as a betrayal of core Indigenous values. Some who value economic partnerships with such companies don't want to upset their business partnerships to advocate for tribes in the Amazon being run over by the very same companies.

There is a lot of agreement between tribal people and their governments, which is why there is movement toward collective action and advocacy, but building collective effort can be complex and even contested. Social media has really changed the way people get information and advocate. That has helped span geographic distance and language barriers better than ever before, and it will only grow from here.

What happened at the confrontation at the Lincoln Memorial in 2019 and why does it matter?

On January 18, 2019, there was a confrontation near the Lincoln Memorial in Washington, D.C. Multiple groups were in the capital at the time for different purposes. Nathan Phillips, an Omaha Indian, was there for the Indigenous People March to raise attention about a variety of issues affecting Native Americans. While the Indigenous People March was passing the Lincoln Memorial, it encountered a number of students from Covington Catholic High School in Kentucky, who were in town for the March for Life to protest abortion rights. A confrontation ensued when the students, wearing "Make America Great Again" hats, began shouting "Trump 2020" and "Build the Wall." They also performed a mock Māori haka dance. Phillips and other Native American marchers felt they were being ridiculed. Tensions increased as the high school kids approached the Indigenous marchers. Some accounts claim the high schoolers blocked the marchers from moving forward. Photographs and video shorts went viral, some getting millions of views. News coverage exploded. Some of it was one-sided and distorted important details about the confrontation. Covington closed the school temporarily until their security concerns were addressed. There were defamation lawsuits brought by some of the high school students, which were settled out of court.

I always felt that Covington High School did their students a great disservice. If they wanted to encourage their kids to advocate on an issue like abortion which they were passionate about, they should have kept them focused on that and well chaperoned during both their protest and everything else they did in Washington. They put their charges in a potentially dangerous situation that hurt their own reputation and exacerbated racial tensions across the country. It was all easily avoidable with careful planning and proper supervision. Young people are the future leaders of this country. They can develop their own opinions and help lead us forward. They do not deserve to be manipulated by school officials (which is what the staff at Covington did by placing them in a racially charged environment without supervision) or put in unnecessarily dangerous situations.

Why is there so much concern about mascots?

Not all Indians find the use of Indians or Indian imagery by sports teams offensive, but many do. They view non-Native people dressed as Indians, doing a "tomahawk chop," or singing fake Indian songs as a mockery of their culture and history. Those opposed to the use of Indians as mascots usually point out that most people would not tolerate White sports fans dressed up in fake Afros with painted blackface singing mock African songs for a sports team using a stereotype of Black people as a mascot. The protest against using non-Native racial groups as mascots has led to the practice being abandoned in most places. But similar caricatures of Indians in other places have often been defended by school officials and community members, even officially celebrated as part of the sports culture at the schools.

Fans often inject racism to sport culture when their opponents have a Native mascot.

These mascots are on a spectrum of offensiveness. *Redskins* is worse than *Indians*, which is worse than *Chiefs*, which is worse than *Blackhawks*. But for many Natives all these team names are still offensive or at least invite people to be offensive, to caricature them and mock their culture. Redskins in particular has been a sore spot. Native Americans are not actually red. And the name Redskins is likely a reference not to skin pigmentation so much as to the bounties placed on Native people, paid by the presentation of scalps, leaving the killed Indians with red "skins." States like Minnesota and Arizona had long-standing bounties on Native Americans in the 1800s.

The two biggest defenses of Indian mascots are pretty weak. The first is the claim that "we are honoring Native Americans." If all Native Americans felt honored, then that argument would bear some weight, but most do not feel honored. I don't feel honored. And even if a home team truly believes it is honoring Indians through its mascot, opposing teams caricature and abuse each other's mascots in the name of team spirit. Other teams in a conference with a team that has a Native mascot will most definitely *not* be honoring Native Americans. Many high school sporting events have seen opposing fans bring signs saying things like "Hey, Indians, Get Ready to Leave in a Trail of Tears, Round Two." These kinds of statements are really painful for a lot of Native Americans. Sometimes opposing fans even hang Indians in effigy, and, as a result, many Natives feel unsafe in addition to disrespected in such settings. And these are schools that usually have mission statements with language about an inclusive learning environment and education. There is no positive purpose served with something divisive rather than inclusive and something so harmful to real education. And at schools, we have so many real battles to fight. Mascots are controversial at best. Why spend energy and resources protecting a controversial mascot when we could spend it educating?

Non-Native people also justify the practice by pointing to Indians who use Indian mascots for teams, such as the Red Lake Warriors. The difference is that the Indians at Red Lake are the descendants of warriors, so their use of that image or name is not a mockery. However, I never miss a chance to encourage Red Lake and other Native schools to change their mascots to something more benign, so that they do not confuse others about appropriate mascots, or invite their opponents to engage in racial ridicule.

Country music legend Gretchen Wilson has a song called "Redneck Woman," which is a celebration anthem

for the term. Does that mean I can call every White woman I meet "redneck woman"? Could that offend someone? Yes. Does that mean I can tell those offended that they have no right to be offended, because Gretchen Wilson loves that label? No. We have to listen to and respect people from the group to whom we might be causing offense, especially when those feelings are widespread. Furthermore, even though this particular form of racism happens to be directed at Native Americans, everyone is swallowing a spoonful of the racism every time we see a Native mascot, and that spoonful dehumanizes all of us, regardless of our race or cultural background.

The data is also very clear. Two tribes have sanctioned use of tribal mascots. The Florida Seminole gave permission for the use of their tribe's name to the Florida State

University team. The Meskwaki gave permission for use of one of their chiefs' names to the Chicago Blackhawks hockey team. But over one hundred tribes have passed resolutions repudiating the use of Native mascots and imagery. The National Congress of American Indians, which represents all federally recognized tribes in political advocacy at the national level, has passed a resolution to the same effect. The overwhelming majority of Natives want Indian mascots gone from professional sports and school teams. The bottom line is that if any mascot is truly offensive to a large percentage of the population, that mascot should go. Stick to lions, tigers, and bears. Human beings will never feel dishonored by them.

America started a racial reckoning after the murder of George Floyd in May 2020. Major corporate sponsors for the Washington Redskins threatened to pull their support for the team unless the owner promised to change the mascot. The team agreed to make a change, although it remains to be seen if they will do away with the name but keep a Native mascot. Clearly, they were responding to economic pressure, not a desire to lead the sport to the right side of history. But a win is a win, and even if that organization had to be dragged kicking and screaming into the light, more change like this is coming. It is heartening to see so many middle and high school students at the front of advocacy to change the mascots. I think those voices are some of the most effective in engineering change. They give me hope.

Why is there such a fuss about non-Native people wearing Indian costumes for Halloween?

The fuss is about cultural appropriation and respect. Non-Native people playing Indian takes tribal clothing and paint out of their appropriate cultural context. Even Natives usually wear eagle feathers and war paint only for specific activities, like powwows, and then there are cultural rules about who can use those things. The Halloween costumes are not designed to honor or respect Natives; they are designed to have fun, get candy, or look sexy. As a result, their use often upsets many Native people.

Whereas changing mascots requires systemic changes for professional sports teams and schools, the Halloween costumes really just involve individual choice. That should make it easier for people to do the right thing. But sometimes it makes it harder because being politically incorrect is often seen as a special American right. Nobody likes being told what to do. And people get defensive when they are told that what they are doing is offensive. Most Natives probably look at someone in a Native-inspired Halloween costume and think "What an idiot," and then they laugh at the "idiot." They are less likely to want to start a fight over it. Others do get hurt feelings. And almost all feel like the person in the costume is out of touch with reality and cannot see or care about the Native people in their world. Otherwise they'd take care not to willfully offend them.

How come the Johnny Depp cologne commercial made so many Natives so mad?

A cologne and perfume company named Dior produced a fragrance in the 1960s called Sauvage, which is the French spelling of *savage*. In 2019, Johnny Depp, who is not Native American but has played Native American characters in movies like *The Lone Ranger*, was paid to represent the fragrance in a rebranded advertising campaign. The advertisements called the fragrance "an authentic journey deep into the Native American soul." It featured Depp playing a guitar riff composed by a famous Native American guitarist from the Shawnee tribe named Link Wray. A beautiful Native woman follows Depp at a distance (attracted by his scent), and a male fancy dancer is dancing in the background.

Many Native Americans thought the ad was offensive because they saw it as a coded way of calling Indians savages and felt it sexualized their racial identity. Many were also upset that Depp was the super-Indian in the ad, as if to say that White men are better at being Native than the Natives. Dior received a lot of negative attention and eventually pulled the advertisements and deleted social media posts of Depp's association with the fragrance. But many Natives believe it was all an intentional ploy—the company knew it would offend people, and planned to do damage control after intentionally causing offense, ultimately feeling it was all worth it. Because after a few years nobody will remember the controversy, but they will remember the company name and its fragrances all the better.

Why is there such a fuss about public art, statues, and place names now?

There has always been a fuss. The difference is that now you and others are listening. And Native Americans and other minorities are getting better at making their feelings known. Social media and changes in social activism transform our world every day.

The tension concerning public art, statues, and place names really involves two positive public goods—freedom of speech and respect. Ideally, we should have few limitations on freedom of speech and nobody should have to suffer disrespect. We have the freedom to call everyone names, but we shouldn't exercise the freedom of speech just to be jerks, because that hurts people. However, not everyone agrees about what is respectful.

My heroes are not your heroes. Father Junípero Serra was founder and architect of the Spanish mission system in California, which enslaved whole tribes like the Chumash, killed thousands of Natives, forced their conversion to Christianity, and engaged in genocide against California's Natives. He is hated by many Native Americans. He was elevated to sainthood by the Catholic Church in 2015. Afterward, a couple of the statues honoring Serra were vandalized. When Natives asked and petitioned for the statues to be removed, they were ignored. The controversy is not just about what happened in history; it's also about which people deserve to have primacy of place in the public, especially when funded by taxpayer dollars.

Across America there are many statues of Christopher Columbus, Confederate generals, and historic figures who did horrible things. There are cities, towns, and streets named after them. I want my children to learn about and deeply understand these important figures in history. I don't want them to worship these guys. But from the Alamo to Washington, D.C., and everywhere else, we often have to swallow a spoonful of racism to go into public places, even our government buildings. The art and commemorations are often one-sided and invite hero worship rather than deep understanding. I believe a lot of those statues and art pieces would do well in museums, where we can study them. For the very public spaces, like city parks and government buildings, I think it's wise to put figures who cause less controversy and invite more unity. I realize that 100 years from now people will have different ideas about who should be publicly celebrated. And that's okay. Our public places should reflect the values of the public. And our institutions of learning and museums can be places where we strive to understand all historic figures, regardless of their character.

In 2016, I sat on a committee to decide what to do with art in the Minnesota state capitol building. Some of the art was offensive to Native Americans, and I suggested that we move offensive pieces from the capitol to a venue that would let us learn from rather than just celebrate them. I said that freedom of speech should not run over inclusive and respectful political space.

I told the committee that people do not come to the capitol just to learn about art from the 1800s. They come there to participate in their government. Minnesota's tribal leaders come there for the signing of bills and meetings with legislators. And they do so often with background art that is erroneous and insulting, such as Father Hennepin's "discovery" of the Falls of St. Anthony. That painting shows Hennepin holding a cross high above the Indians, with a bare-breasted Native woman running in the foreground. Hennepin was a Dakota captive at the time, so the power dynamics were not what's portrayed, and the depiction evokes a paternalistic Great White Father shining light on the savages. Some Natives are offended by the inaccuracy, the paternalistic message, or the nakedness of the Dakota woman.

Having an offensive backdrop for our politics is a problem. Only half of our voters turn out for elections. Our government is not representative in terms of class, race, or gender. We cannot afford to reinforce the perception that the government is made by White people, for the benefit of White people, and everyone else is window dressing, a spoil of war, or less. We need to make special efforts to be truly inclusive. There is no opportunity to provide context when a painting like this hangs behind the governor at a press conference. It is both unwise and just plain rude to expect Natives to endure racism every time they interact with their government.

We have many grade school children who tour the capitol. When they get a tour, they don't always remember what they

Father Hennepin Discovering the Falls of St. Anthony, Stephen A. Douglas Volk, 1905.

read or what the tour guide tells them. But they remember what they see. Big beautiful Greco-Roman arches and décor—and pictures of half-naked Indians, Indians attacking White people, and Indians dying in battle, many way off the mark.

A great number of Natives, including tribal leaders elected by the majority of their tribal citizens, say some of the art is offensive. We cannot tell them that they don't get to make that determination. We need to build bridges, not drive people apart.

Moving art is not censorship, which is defined as the "suppression or prohibition of art, film, or writing." We do not need to destroy, prohibit, or suppress art from the public sphere, just exhibit it in a different place.

Many other places in America wrestle with artistic symbols, and there is precedent for rearranging public space to show respect for all of our citizens. In the South, statues of Confederate generals have been moved out of public parks in New Orleans and the Confederate battle flag has been removed from prominent display on state capitol grounds. All people need to rearrange their houses from time to time as families change and grow and their needs evolve. There is nothing wrong with rearranging the furniture in our shared political homes to make everyone in the family feel more welcome and respected.

This is what many of our citizens want. It's not political correctness, it's just right. Capitol art is an important symbol about who we are and what we value. Symbols matter. A wedding ring is just a symbol, but it says something profound. I urged the committee on art in the Minnesota capitol not to keep our capitol building married to our racist past.

In the end, I lost most of those battles. Some paintings were moved elsewhere in the building. More context was provided. Tribal leaders were frustrated. But some things did change. More space was opened for new art. Many members of the art community were listening, and their politicians were too.

In Hawaii, most of the town and street names have been changed to Hawaiian words at the request and with the guidance of the Native Hawaiian community. Minnesota changed Lake Calhoun (named after a southern slaveholder) to its original Dakota name, Bde Maka Ska, after lots of political fighting. And these are just a few of many similar efforts to create respectful visibility for Natives and their history. Many battles are lost. Resistance is real and significant and tied up with the fear that many Whites have that they, after erasing so many tribes, languages, and cultures, will somehow experience their own erasure. Those fears are unfounded, but they are really there and deeply held by some. Over time, I believe we will build more bridges, create greater understanding, and create a more inclusive world. Martin Luther King Jr. said, "The arc of the moral universe is long, but it bends towards justice."[71]

Why is there so much advocacy about missing and murdered Indigenous women?

Human trafficking is a real problem in the United States, Canada, and around the world. People who get trafficked are less likely to be kidnapped by strangers than they are to be pressured by family members to do things they don't want to do. For example, an aunt or an uncle will ask their niece to have sex with a drug dealer so they can get drugs to feed their own addictions. They are coerced or forced to cooperate in situations like these. Patterns develop and some people lose all freedom to choose where they live and what they do. Once involved, they are moved to other parts of the country, where they are isolated from family members who might help them. Trafficking is a terrible form of violence and exploitation. It happens to many people from many groups in America, but poor people are especially vulnerable because their choices are more limited and substance abuse is more prevalent in those communities.

And Native Americans are more likely to be poor than most other Americans.

Tribal people have additional risks that other populations do not as well. Tribal governments and their police departments have very limited authority over non-tribal members. If a drug dealer or human trafficker is not Native and moves to a reservation, it is very hard for tribal police to put an end to their illegal activities. The laws are really messed up and inconsistent. On some reservations, major crimes like murder, rape, and arson cannot be policed by tribal law enforcement. They have to be referred to the federal government. That means the Federal Bureau of Investigation has to investigate. Often the FBI is so busy fighting terrorism and addressing other serious issues that they don't devote enough resources to investigating major crimes on reservations.

Elsewhere, as discussed earlier, the FBI does not investigate major crimes because state laws are in effect on the reservations. That usually means county sheriff departments and city police departments do the investigating. Poor funding for such agencies, racial bias, and jurisdictional issues combine to produce disappointing results. Again, tribes are left without enough power or resources to put an end to the problems. And tribal people suffer tremendously. Some sheriff departments and tribes have worked out compacts to share authority and to police things like gang activity and human trafficking. But some non-Native law enforcement agencies have refused to work with tribes.

A law was passed in the 1990s called the Violence Against Women Act, which was designed to increase the authority of tribes to police non-tribal members in crimes of violence against women (rape and sexual assault), which should have helped reduce some of the higher risk faced by Native women for being trafficked. But the legislation is weak because the protections go away unless it is regularly reauthorized. That was the strongest protection advocates could get out of Congress at the time it was passed. Often Republican legislators do not want to pass the reauthorizations because they don't want to strengthen tribal sovereignty. The end result is that Native American women are the most likely group of people in America to be trafficked.

Tribes and tribal people are not going to sit on the sidelines and wait for someone to protect them. Many organizations and tribal governments are working on more law enforcement compacts, pressuring American lawmakers about the Violence Against Women Act, and trying to raise public awareness to advance the safety of Native women.

Does being Native make you worry about your safety or the safety of your family?

Definitely. I have five sons. I worry all the time that if one gets pulled over by the police and has to reach in the glove compartment to find an insurance card, the officer might shoot him. I have all our insurance cards clipped to the visor right in front of the driver so that is less likely to happen. But I'm always afraid. I have four daughters. I worry about them being raped or sexually assaulted. They are smart and careful. But the data say that I will likely not be able to protect them all. I worry about myself and all my kids if anyone ever stays out late at night, because they might get caught behind a bar or in an alley by someone who doesn't like the way they look. I worry every time I use my Ojibwe language in public because some Americans think any language other than English is foreign and they might try to call immigration services or even assault us. This has happened to many brown people in America. I worry about our safety in Native spaces too. The daycare facility I used to take my kids to was once shot up in the middle of the night. Again, the life expectancy for a Native American man in my part of America is 54.7 years. I think White Americans don't have all the same worries at the same intensity that I do. And in addition to being less safe, feeling less safe is not healthy either. For many Natives that contributes to higher blood pressure, anxiety, and depression. I actually feel pretty healthy and happy in spite of all this, but it is *in spite of* being less safe because I'm Native. It really shouldn't be that way.

PERSPECTIVES

COMING TO TERMS AND FUTURE DIRECTIONS

Nothing can stop an Indian who knows who he or she is.

–Margaret Treuer in *Ojibwe in Minnesota*

Indigenous people today are seeking to transcend the history of pain and loss that began with the coming of Europeans into our world.

–Taiaiake Alfred

Why are Indians so often imagined rather than understood?

Part of the story is simple math. Natives are a very small percentage of the global population and even a small percentage of the U.S. and Canadian populations. In some places, one is likely to run into an Indian. But for many people, direct contact with an Indian is rare, and a deep conversation with one even more so. The situation is very different for many other racial groups. Black, Asian, and Latinx people are more numerous and more visible to most people.

However, there is more to the story than the math. Part of the reason for this lack of understanding about Indians has to do with who controls the story. The number of well-educated Black, Asian, and Latinx people in the United States and Canada is growing and they are starting to penetrate positions of economic, political, and educational power. Surely there are not enough. But their numbers still greatly outpace Native representation. Very few Indians have PhDs and write books. The civil rights movement, for example, brought a great deal of attention to America's unfair treatment of Black citizens. Since then, there have been successful efforts to weave strands into the curriculum about Black history and Black heroes. But there has never been a comparable effort to weave Native heroes into curricula on a systemwide basis. With so few Indians in the world, and so few of them in positions of economic, political, and educational power, prevailing assumptions about Indians often go unchallenged, or the challenges are not effective. Indians proliferate as mascots for sports teams when no other racial group in the country is similarly denigrated or mocked. When it comes to Indians, Americans are left to their imaginings.

For Natives who do pursue higher education, there is an understandable urge to return to their home communities and serve their own people. Tribal governments and tribal colleges are eager to hire their own. As a result, Indians do their part to maintain their isolation, even if their actions are not intended to isolate. And that also allows people to imagine, rather than to understand through personal experience.

As a White person, I don't feel privileged. So what do Indians mean by that term?

Most White Americans are reluctant to say that they are privileged, even though many may feel and say that people of color in this country are sometimes underprivileged. However, if others around us are less privileged than we are, our status is defined as one of greater privilege. Peggy McIntosh, author of *White Privilege: Unpacking the Invisible Knapsack*; Robin DiAngelo; Tim Wise; Ta-Nehisi Coates; James Baldwin; and others have done a lot of good writing on this subject.

There are many ways in which White Americans are privileged. A number of those privileges are ones that everybody should enjoy. They include relatively benign things like being able to walk into a store and purchase Band-Aids that more or less match the color of one's skin. Or walking into a barbershop or beauty salon knowing that you will find someone who knows how to cut your hair. These are simple, basic privileges that make life easier for Whites than for others but are usually taken for granted.

White privileges extend to more serious things, too. A White person who is pulled over by the police can assume that the color of his or her skin was not a factor in being detained, but people of color can never be entirely sure. And people with reservation license plates often wonder if it was a factor.[72] Whites also never have to wonder if the color of their skin was part of the process (conscious or not) in banking decisions or loan approvals, but Indians often feel that it is, and historically it has been.[73] White-passing Natives can benefit from White privilege too when dealing with cops or shopping. But being White-passing doesn't eliminate racism for them. As soon as someone's racial identity is known (from a checkbox on a form to an identifiable last name or a tribal license plate) that identity can be and often is used to discriminate.

Whites are never asked to speak for all White people. Everyone knows there is a diversity of opinion among Whites on any subject, and nobody could speak for all members of their race, but Indians are often asked to speak for or represent their entire race. This happens to young people all the time. A White student is not asked in class what life is like for White people, but a Native student often gets such a question. This can be embarrassing and uncomfortable.

These are among the types of differential treatments and attitudes that create White privilege.

Of course, many things—such as economics, gender, and race—affect every person's advantages and disadvantages. We are affected by these and many other things 100 percent of the time. But we are affected by our race specifically every time we get pulled over by the cops and every time we are not. If you are White you might not feel the impact the same way a person of color will because you are less likely to be pulled over. The extra benefit of a doubt you receive every time you are not pulled over is a racial impact—it just happens to be a positive one for you.

My wife and I see this all the time. She has blond hair and blue eyes. I am brown-skinned with dark hair and dark eyes. Sometimes gender overwhelms our experience. We go out to eat often. About 85 percent of the time the waiter or waitress gives me the bill. About 15 percent of the time the bill goes in the middle of the table. They never give it to her. Both male and female waitstaff assume that I—because I am a man—have the money and make the money decisions. That's sexist.

And every morning both of us like to go for a run, although we don't usually run together because I'm an early riser and my wife is not. But we live in a rural area. When my wife is running and a car pulls over (to make a call on a cell phone perhaps), she gets scared. Could this be a stalker? A sexual predator? Should she turn back now? Run into the woods? She is less safe than I am because she is a woman. And she always feels less safe than I do because she is a woman. So I experience a privilege just because of being born a man. I am safer and I feel safer. That's a male privilege. But when my wife and I drive cars it's the other way around. I've been pulled over forty times, and often in clearly racial circumstances. I have had cops pull guns on me twice when I was unarmed. My wife has never had an experience like that and never worries that she will. That's because she's White. She experiences racial privilege. And we live in the same house, in the same state, in the same county, in the same country. When it comes to isms—classism, sexism, racism—it's not either one thing or another, it's one thing *and* another. We are all affected by classism, sexism, and racism all the time. Some of the impacts are positive and some are negative. But the barriers are not fairly distributed. Some people have many more disadvantages than others. Seeing that is critical to becoming an agent for positive change.

What do you think about the #MeToo movement and its impact on Sherman Alexie's career?

Sexism affects every human all the time, the same way racism does. We are either privileged by our sex or disadvantaged. And for all of human history, men have received unearned advantages because of the way political, economic, and social power has been distributed. Women have been fighting for more power and better treatment for a long time. And they have won some key battles. In America, they gained the right to vote in 1920. Women now occupy 17 percent of the world's congresses, senates, and other elected political positions, and that number will likely continue to grow. In many other areas, women are gaining freedoms and empowerment, but that fight is far from over. In America, Canada, Europe, and other places the #MeToo movement has been one front where women have recently been pushing for greater fairness. Most women are sexually harassed sometime in their lives, and many are sexually assaulted. It's hard for women to get justice when they are mistreated because the legal standard of "innocent until proven guilty" has been conveniently used as the social standard by men accused of sexual harassment and sexual assault. In other words, when men are accused of sexual harassment or sexual assault, they have often said that they are innocent, denied any wrongdoing, and forced women to prove them wrong.

#MeToo is pushing for a different standard, one that says you go to jail when proven guilty beyond reasonable doubt, but that when a woman says she was harassed or assaulted, she must be believed and supported. We should believe and support women who are victimized, instead of ignore and deny bad conduct by men. And when a serial harasser or assaulter has been exposed, other victims have stepped up, been brave, faced the pushback, and said, "me too." The goal is to fight for accountability and generate social pressure and other consequences for men who do not respect women.

#MeToo has had some success. Many men have had to face greater accountability, and even legal action, because of their behavior. The pressure is starting have impact, but we have a long way to go. We still have presidents and other powerful people accused of sexual misconduct who have not been removed from their offices or experienced consequences. But some have.

One such person is Sherman Alexie. He is a Coeur d'Alene Indian and one of the most successful Indigenous authors of all time. In 2018, Litsa Dremousis revealed a consensual affair with Alexie but also claimed that he used his influence in the writing and publishing world to promise promotion to other women if they would have sex with him. Alexie was never charged with any crime, but he experienced painful fallout from the accusations. The Institute of American Indian Arts renamed a scholarship that had been named after him. His work was dropped by numerous schools where it had been regularly assigned. The American Library Association had just given Alexie the Carnegie Medal, and to spare public humiliation for both, Alexie returned the award and the ALA gave it to someone else. They also rescinded a 2008 award for Best Young Adult Book. Since then, Alexie's career has taken a major step backward.

I think Sherman Alexie is a very talented writer and produced literature that was not just authentic and entertaining, but sometimes profound. His talent makes his actions all the more painful. No matter how good a writer he is and no matter how beautiful his work and contributions to the world, these things do not excuse and cannot erase the pain he caused to others. I don't judge anyone, but we owe it to all women to empower them and their humanity and to believe the victims of sexual misconduct. And we owe it to the Native world to center people and voices that will represent us all with dignity and respect.

Why don't tribes solve their own problems?

Tribes are doing more than most people think to address the problems in their communities, as I hope you'll understand if you've made it this far in the book. They have education, work, health, and poverty programs. They are developing infrastructure and working with state and local governments in spite of the fact that their sovereignty does not require them to do so. Not all tribes have the same resources to work with, so they do not develop or heal at the same rate. Some of the tribal efforts have been heroic and truly made positive changes. But problems are so deep and pervasive that it will take years of consistent intervention to really make things better. There is improvement on many fronts, though surely more work needs to be done. But the rest of society should join that effort as well, and not just because of historical injustices. Natives are part of the country too.

All these problems are not my fault. Why should I be asked to atone for the sins of my ancestors?

I once had a conversation with a woman at Princeton University who opposed affirmative action. Her great-great-grandparents were southern plantation slave owners and extremely wealthy. Even after the Civil War, the family held on to tremendous wealth and passed it on through generations. I asked this woman, who had attended the most prestigious private high school in the country and now was enrolled in one of the best and most expensive universities in the world, how she felt about the fact that her opportunities were purchased with wealth built on the backs of others in slavery. I told her that the direct descendants of the enslaved people her great-great-grandparents had owned had the exact opposite experience. Even if they were just as bright and just as deserving of the opportunities and privileges she enjoyed, they were denied access to private schools and universities because of discrimination, financial status, and other barriers. Those same barriers likely applied to other areas of advancement as well. How fair was that? I did not believe that she should jump off a bridge to make things right, but I had a hard time reconciling her opposition to affirmative action with her personal history.

On a larger though less obvious level, this is the issue with atonement for the sins of one's ancestors. White people have consistently enjoyed privileges (educational, financial, social, political) that Indians and other people of color have been denied. The world is not a fair place. The past cannot be changed, but there are many things in the present that are also not just that we can do something about. While it is not right to hold individuals entirely responsible for the sins of their ancestors, it is fair to expect our society to remedy the current effects of historical trauma and injustice and inequity. German and Swiss banks had to make reparations to the families of Holocaust victims for the gold fillings extracted from the teeth in their dead bodies and minted into coin. The German government had to make formal apologies for the Final Solution and mandate instruction about the Holocaust in its school systems. All of that makes perfect sense. Canada's Truth and Reconciliation Commission started a conversation about restorative justice there, but here in America, we have yet to get to meaningful formal apologies, much less required instruction about genocidal policies toward Indians.

Guilt for Whites and anger for Indians are neither healthy nor positive emotions. They are natural responses, but they won't fix anything. The critical challenge of all the troubling history in our country is to turn guilt and anger into positive action. We all need to come to terms with our collective past.

Is there anything wrong with saying that some of my best friends are Indians?

Yes. Some of your best friends might be Indians, but touting that sounds like you are using your friends to tell the world, "See, I'm not racist." It sounds like an effort to hide personal guilt or insecurity about race. So, be friends with Indians, but don't use your friendships as a badge or public statement about race.

Is there something wrong with saying that my great-grandmother was a Cherokee princess?

Yes. A large number of White and Black Americans have Native ancestry, and Cherokee are one of the groups widely represented in the gene pool. But the Cherokee did not have kings, queens, princes, or princesses. And saying that "my great-grandmother was a Cherokee princess" makes a profound statement about identity. If your great-grandmother was Cherokee, then one of your grandparents was too, and one of your parents, and in actuality you are Cherokee as well. Someone who truly identifies with his or her Native ancestry will say, "I am Cherokee." Everyone understands by that statement that at least some of that person's ancestors were, too.

Claims that "my great-grandmother was a Cherokee princess" usually come from some level of ignorance about Cherokee history and culture, no matter how well intended the statement. To many Indians, it also sounds a lot like claims that "some of my best friends are Indians." To them, such a statement speaks less to one's personal identity and more to one's sense of guilt (or ignorance). It sounds like another way of saying, "See, I'm not racist," rather than like a proud statement about heritage. Those who have investigated their heritage would say, "I'm Cherokee," "I am Cherokee and Black," or "I am Cherokee and White," and know that princesses had nothing to do with it.

I might have some Indian ancestry. How do I find out?

A lot of people do have Native ancestry. There has been a very high rate of adoption and foster care in Native communities, in part carried out by missionary organizations and others as one of the assimilation initiatives that dominated American Indian policy for decades. Lots of Indians also married outside of their communities, and their descendants were absorbed into the general population after a couple of generations. And there are large groups of Métis and other mixed Indian-European groups. Some Métis have been absorbed into the general population in Canada and the United States, some into tribal populations at Turtle Mountain and other places, and some maintained distinct communities. The diversity of experiences makes tracking ancestry complicated.

The best way to begin to find out if you have Native ancestry is to exhaust your personal information and archives. Talk to relatives. Once you can show a connection to a specific Indigenous tribe or community, ask that group. Many tribes keep extensive genealogical records for purposes of tribal enrollment and sometimes separate databases for specific land settlements or lawsuits. Those places do not often have large staffs to help with generic questions like "Am I Indian?" But if you have the names of specific Indians from those specific communities, they can usually help. Check online, as most tribes keep websites and some have moved some records online. Other places to look include the Mormon church database, which is quite large, Ancestry.com, other research institutions and archives, and your school library.

Are DNA tests changing how people connect to tribes?

Yes and no. Many tribes honor paternity tests when there is a request for tribal enrollment and a question about who the father is. Some will honor an affidavit (sworn statement) about paternity if a blood test is not possible. But I am not aware of any tribe that will take someone's Ancestry.com report and enroll them in a tribe. Services like Ancestry are kind of like the Wikipedias of bloodlines. They often get it right, but not 100 percent of the time, and sometimes they get it really wrong. The potential is there, however, for people to use such services to learn who their relatives are, connect with those relatives, and then narrow records searches (birth certificates, adoption records, and so forth) to connect to their families and tribes of origin. Tribal enrollment is evolving in many places too, so the criteria for enrollment may change for many tribes in the future.

What do Natives think about Elizabeth Warren's Native ancestry?

Senator Elizabeth Warren of Massachusetts does have Cherokee ancestry. And I think anyone who has Native ancestry can and should be able to claim it and learn about that part of their history and identity. Warren received a lot of criticism because she didn't use her ancestry to explore her own identity on her own. To her credit, she didn't use it to advance her academic or professional career either. But she did try to use it to advance her political career. She claimed her Cherokee roots when she thought doing so would give her a political advantage. She was playing identity politics, not trying to connect. If she had tried to connect first, she likely would not have received the same reaction. In the end, the Cherokee tribe issued a formal letter that did not challenge her Cherokee descent, but did make it clear that she was not an enrolled member of the tribe and that they felt she was being opportunistic instead of genuine about her Indigenous identity. Politically it made her seem disingenuous or even a little dishonest.

Why is that picture *End of the Trail* so popular in Indian country?

I have often wondered the same thing myself. The picture, which itself is based off of a sculpture, shows a half-naked, feathered Indian slumped over his horse, as if defeated and emotionally devastated. I never identified with that image or message. But the artwork became extremely popular in America in the early 1970s.

Dee Brown's famous book *Bury My Heart at Wounded Knee* (1970) was one of the first published histories that was truly sympathetic to Indians. It covered the most famous stories of Indian military defeat and massacre in the American West. That book, and the statements it quoted from *Black Elk Speaks* (which included the oral history of Black Elk's experience at the Wounded Knee Massacre in 1890), grabbed the attention and inspired the empathy of many Americans. Indians were fading into the sunset. And the image from *End of the Trail* seemed to capture the popular sentiment well. So it went up on posters and postcards across the country. Why Indians like it so much is still confusing to me. I think

The original *End of the Trail* sculpture, 1915, by James Earle Fraser.

Indians were desperate to find something Native for their walls, and this image was readily available.

How do Canadian First Nations people feel about the Truth and Reconciliation Commission findings?

There are mixed feelings about the Truth and Reconciliation Commission (TRC). The Canadian government began a truth and reconciliation process about its treatment of Canadian First Nations people in 2007 and concluded the

A march during the closing events of the Truth and Reconciliation Commission, Ottawa, 2015.

TRC in 2015. The final conclusion of the government was that they had engaged in cultural genocide. A Canadian First Nations citizen and judge named Murray Sinclair chaired the commission, and he is well respected across Canada, having recently been elected to the Canadian Parliament as a senator. The TRC findings were agreeable to most Canadians. But the reconciling has been a lot more clunky.

There is no way to fully repair all of the historical injustices in Canada. Hundreds of Canadian First Nations don't even have safe, potable water because mining and other environmental degradations have poisoned their water supplies. Health issues for Canadian First Nations people remain horribly inequitable and inadequately addressed. Poverty, displacement of tribal populations for hydroelectric projects, and many other major issues pervade the experience and daily lives of Indigenous Canadians. The TRC allocated significant funding as reparation to victims of physical and sexual abuse in the schools run by the Canadian government for First Nations children. Thousands of victims testified and received compensation, but many felt the process reopened old wounds and needed more sensitive attention to the mental health and healing needs of the victims. More money is likely to be allocated for Indigenous language revitalization in Canada, and that move has been welcomed by First Nations governments and language activists.

All told, a lot of education has happened in Canada. Awareness of historical injustices is higher now than it was before the TRC, but the political and economic power dynamics in Canada still keep First Nations people at an obvious and persistent disadvantage. Restorative justice has begun, but it needs to continue and deepen to have lasting effect.

What do you think about land acknowledgments?

There has been a movement, supported by the findings of the Canadian Truth and Reconciliation Commission and many Indigenous activists in many countries, to have governments and organizations acknowledge the original and current Indigenous peoples of the land. Land acknowledgments vary because they focus on the local Indigenous people. Here is an example of a land acknowledgment that I developed for the National Summit for Courageous Conversation when it was held in Louisiana in 2019:

> *Welcome to the current and ancestral homeland of the Caddo, Natchez, Atakapa, Houma, Tunica, Chitimacha, and Choctaw peoples. These tribes have called Louisiana home for tens of thousands of years. Nobody asked their permission to come here, settle here, or build a new civilization on top of theirs. Their entire population endured generations of genocide and enslavement in the French, British, Spanish, and American colonies built here. And still they endure.*

I support land acknowledgments because they address invisibility and marginalization of Indigenous people. The real trick is to make sure we don't stop there. Acknowledgment is a first step, not the end of the journey. We need to work toward equity, inclusion, and empowerment of Native people in everything we do.

Regarding casinos and treaty rights, I'm not racist, but it doesn't seem fair to me. What's wrong with that line of thinking?

Any benefit that a tribe or tribal member gains from casinos or treaty rights pales in comparison to privileges White people enjoy every day in the form of economic, educational, and political opportunity. In a couple of Indian communities, casinos have provided a truly outsize benefit for tribal members, but those are the exceptions, not the rule, for 99 percent of the tribal population in America. In addition to the fairness barometer, treaty rights and Indian law are so deeply embedded in the American legal system that changing the status of tribes as nations or canceling their treaty rights would involve changing the U.S. Constitution and the treaties that gave America to non-Native people. The financial and political cost of that change would overwhelm any benefit gained by tribes or their members. Tribal benefits and sovereign status are part of the price America paid for the land.

I'm not racist, but it all happened in the past. Why can't Indians just move on?

Historical trauma is a complicated subject. It's kind of like this. Someone was hitting the Indian in the head with a hammer for decades, and it did a lot of damage. Now the government says that it is done hitting the Indian in the head with a hammer. But there is still all this damage, which takes a very long time to repair. And the government is not interested in making repairs—it all happened in the past. So Indians are left to heal themselves. Language and culture loss, many health issues, substance abuse, the educational opportunity gap, lack of economic opportunity, and many other problems in Indian country can be directly attributed to specific government policies. It's easy to push people into a pit, but it can be very hard for them to climb back out.

Another way to look at it is this. If a husband cheats on his wife but then decides he wants to reconcile and make the relationship work, he cannot say, "It all happened in the past. Just forget about it." Making peace has to start with him saying, "Hey, I did you wrong. I am sorry. And it will never happen again." Then there is a chance that they can make the relationship work. That is a fair analogy to what happened with the U.S. and Canadian governments and Natives. Instead of cheating in a marriage, the U.S. government used genocidal warfare, residential boarding schools, suppression of religious freedom, and a host of other pernicious policies against Indians. But the government has never even said that it was wrong, much less apologized or tried to make things right. And every time the government comes up with a new English-only law, or ignores the 50 percent unemployment rate in some Indian communities, or tries to renege on or renegotiate a promised treaty right, Indians see it as another hammer blow to an ancient wound. The historical baggage and the ongoing damage make it very difficult for Indians to move on, discard anger, forgive, or heal. And the fact that most Americans have no understanding of this dynamic makes the struggle all the more frustrating.

Why do Indian people often seem angry?

People in pain are rarely happy, and Indians are in pain. Chronic unemployment and poverty, pervasive substance abuse, and lack of economic and political power plague many Native communities. The situation would be bad enough if it were just bad luck or circumstance, but we know that a lot of the problems in Indian country can be traced to specific government actions. The U.S. and Canadian governments carried out a systematic effort to politically and economically disempower Indians and to destroy their lives and cultures. That makes people angry.

And many of the most harmful policies are not so ancient. Circular 1665, which was used to actively suppress tribal religions, was in effect until 1933, within the living memory of some tribal elders today. Religious persecution of Natives persisted long after that, even after the American Indian Religious Freedom Act of 1978. Most of the Native grandparent generation carry vivid memories and emotional scars from their experiences at residential boarding schools. Anger from such experiences does not fade overnight. And on top of it all, most American people do not understand Indians or their experiences very well. The curricula in most schools still give candy-coated versions of Christopher Columbus and Thanksgiving, when Indians know the history was far different. Being imagined and misunderstood breeds anger, too.

Anger is not a healthy emotion. Many Native people challenge themselves and others to convert that understandable feeling into positive action, but there is not always much help from the outside. Curriculum reform is slow and often resisted. Politicians are more likely to pass a bill requiring that English be declared the official language than to support tribal language and culture revitalization. All of that serves to stir up the hornet's nest. It's an uphill battle.

How are social media and smartphones affecting life in Indian country?

Indian country is connected and online like the rest of the world. There are exceptions, of course, but most tribal people and communities get a lot of their information and run a lot of their lives online. I do. This has transformed communication, governance, and social activism.

Some tribes, like the Citizen Potawatomi Nation, run all tribal council meetings online, and they are open to tribal members all over the world. Some attend the meetings from foreign countries. The Seminole run numerous multinational businesses like the Hard Rock Cafe enterprise online. Protesters at Standing Rock livestreamed police actions and instances of private security firms using attack dogs on unarmed protesters. This widely accessible documentation

deeply affected public opinion. I shared earlier in this book how a company selling Squaw Bread was overwhelmed by social media response and had to change the name of its product. Navajo, Chickasaw, and Ojibwe have developed Rosetta Stone applications for their languages that anyone can use on their phones anywhere on planet earth. Some tribes have electronic dictionaries that are both visual and voice—you can read and listen to the words you look up.

The new technology has connected everyone and created greater ease of access to information. But it has disconnected us at the same time. We watch Netflix and Hulu and play Xbox games like everyone else. That means less time being in the woods and participating in other traditional Native activities. We are changing all the time. Some of those changes are fantastic and others are troubling. Personally, I find social media, smartphones, and other new technologies fun and empowering. They enhance my standard of living and help me connect with my language, culture, and community. But I am intentional about balancing them with a healthy mix of direct human experience and time in the woods.

What are some good books to read about Indians?

Many great books, documentary videos, and websites about Native Americans have been produced in recent years, and I've listed some suggestions for further reading at the back of this book. There are several things to remember as you read. Writers of all races and genders have points of view, so you have to be alert and understand that when you see it. You can't judge the accuracy or authenticity of a book by the race of its author. Indian writers can get it wrong; non-Indian writers can get it wrong. Both can get it beautifully right. And it may sound odd to say this, but also keep in mind that even the most authentic works of fiction are not history.

What do Natives think about books by non-Natives that have Native content?

This can be tricky terrain. I believe in free speech. And I also think that everyone of every group should be empowered to join and contribute to conversations about race, culture, and the Native experience. Anyone who lives in the Americas is living on Native American land. We all have connection to that land now, so acknowledging and connecting the Indigenous human history and current relationship with the land to our contemporary experience makes perfect sense to me. Furthermore, when it comes to things like music, art, and dance, we have so many languages and musical traditions speaking to one another through the art form, it is really hard to say which group owns it. And a big fight about such things can lead to calling one another out rather than calling one another in to meaningful communication. We need more meaningful communication.

At the same time that I see and feel these things, there are dimensions of the Native experience and the White experience that sometimes make non-Natives claiming voice on Native subjects problematic. First of all, Native people have had a really persistent and painful experience with marginalization and invisibility. When non-Native folks suck up all the oxygen, it adds to that negative experience and often triggers a negative response from Natives. How would you feel if an outsider started speaking on behalf of your church, community, ethnic group, language community, or race? Now there are numerous Native authors, academics, politicians, and actors. If their work, words, stories, and voices are not being centered, people want to ask why. If there isn't a really compelling answer to that question, you can run into real resistance or criticism. Also, White people tend to speak first, speak the most, take charge, and try to rescue people they perceive as weak, like minorities. This feels really patronizing. Even when intentions are good, the impact can be alienating.

Listen to Catholics about what it means to be Catholic. Listen to Black people about the Black experience. Listen to Indians about the Native experience. When you do these things, you get authenticity and provide empowerment where it belongs. When you are creating books, music, and art, it is okay to be influenced by and to speak to the influences from people outside your racial and cultural group. If those influences are Indigenous, acknowledge and empower them. And if you are thinking about creating, writing, or speaking in controversial or "gray" areas, I recommend connecting with some authentic Native voices who can provide an honest sounding board to you. That approach offers the best chance for your work to have the reception and impact you are striving for.

Are there any good Indian movies?

I like some of the old spaghetti westerns because the Navajo extras they hired spent the entire time talking smack about the actors in the Diné language. With proper translation, it's incredibly entertaining. Hollywood has a really hard time getting away from creating a White character who is better than the Indian at being Indian, like Kevin Costner in *Dances with Wolves.* A lot of Indians loved that movie, by the way, simply because the Indians didn't all die and there were many Native actors in it. Hollywood also often has a White guy like Johnny Depp play the Native part, as happened in *The Lone Ranger.* I find that unnecessary and really frustrating. We have come a long way from *Peter Pan* or *Pocahontas.*

Both of those movies did a great deal of stereotyping about Natives, from exaggerating features (big noses and reddish skins) to making Native women romantic or sexual objects (like the characters Tiger Lily and Pocahontas). Many Indians favor independent films like *Dance Me Outside, Powwow Highway,* and *Smoke Signals.* And there is new work happening all the time. I believe Hollywood is evolving in good ways. At the time of this writing, we are developing one of my books, *The Assassination of Hole in the Day,* into a movie. But movies are entertainment, and if you want genuine understanding, the list of documentaries and published works in the back of this book is a better place to look.

Have you ever been the object of direct racial discrimination?

My experiences are like those of many other Indians, but the pain at the time was all my own. In first grade, I had long hair, and my teacher dressed me up like a girl, complete with barrettes and makeup. She and everyone else in class had a good laugh at my expense. It was completely humiliating. When I was in seventh grade, I sat in shop class with three non-Native kids who were horribly, deliberately racist. They spent the entire class saying that Indians were all drunks and I would be a drunk too, that Indians were a disgrace and shouldn't be allowed to live in America, that Indians were all on welfare and sucking the country dry, that Indians were responsible for all the crime in the area, and that tribal governments designed license plates with numbers that were hard for cops to read so Indian criminals could escape. I told them they were wrong, but they insisted that their parents told them these things were true and I was wrong because I was a dumb Indian. I confronted one of the kids before school, telling him it had to stop. He pounded my lips onto my braces, and the comments and snickers continued for the rest of the quarter. Usually racism is subtle, but these encounters with its overt forms left some very deep scars.

I have also experienced forms of racism so common they are clichés. As a teenager and as an adult, I have sometimes been followed around stores by clerks who apparently thought I was likely to shoplift because I am identifiably Native. A couple of times while shopping, the clerk at the checkout have asked me to present my EBT card (the current form of food stamps), apparently assuming that all Indians pay for their groceries that way.

You're a testament to your race. How did you turn out so good?

Be careful. For one thing, I'm really not that good. But more important, stereotyping is highly problematic, and you can never judge an entire race by the actions of one person. A statement like the one in this question suggests a negative stereotype—that a good Indian is not typical. Indians are diverse and complicated. Not all White people are the same, and not all Whites have the same beliefs. It's the same for Indians.

How can I learn more?

In addition to consulting the list of resources in the back of this book, I encourage all of you (young and old) to open your minds and hearts. Seek out Indians for answers about Indians. Attend a powwow. Go to a tribal language table. Volunteer for your area race relations task force. Connect with Native people and organizations on social media. I'm on Instagram, Twitter, LinkedIn, Facebook, and Snapchat. Find me anytime. It amazes me how many of the books and resources about Indians had no input from Indians. Tribes and tribal people are getting better at reaching out and developing more resources online and in print. Seek out those things, and don't be discouraged. There are still a lot of Indians who are understandably angry about a lot of things, and they can be discouraging to others, even those engaged in a genuine quest for understanding and a desire to help. But it is only through the combined efforts of a great many Native and non-Native people that we will make it easier for Indians to be understood rather than imagined.

CONCLUSION

FINDING WAYS TO MAKE A DIFFERENCE

If you have come to help me, you are wasting your time. But if you have come because your liberation is tied up with mine, then let us work together.

—Lilla Watson

We ought to recognize that our greatest battle is not with one another but with our pain, our problems, and our flaws. To be hurt, yet forgive. To do wrong, but forgive yourself. To depart from this world leaving only love. This is the reason you walk.

—Wab Kinew

Sometimes the brambled racial borderland of my youth seems as impenetrable as it ever was. Indians continue to be imagined more than they are understood. Public and political backlash against Indian casinos and treaty rights is still obvious. Indians are still often used as mascots for sports teams, with broad resistance to change or a lack of understanding of the impact of that resistance on Native people. Problems persist in Indian country, and with the types of drugs and ease of access in the modern world, things like substance abuse seem even worse.

But looks can be deceiving. A few years ago I brought my van to Kenny's Clark Station in Bemidji, Minnesota, to get new tires. I have known the owners, the Merschmans, most of my life, and I like to support family businesses in our area. They have always been kind and respectful to me, and they know how to fix cars. Paying for new tires is a painful experience for a penny-pincher like me, but I was amazed when I settled my bill to hear owner Alan Merschman tell me, "Miigwech. Giga-waabamin miinawaa." My White mechanic spoke to me in the Ojibwe language. My language. This had never happened to me before. And it would not have been possible just a few years earlier. Something was changing in the borderland.

The town of Bemidji, in northern Minnesota, is among the three largest Indian reservations in the state. About a third of the population there is Native, but about half of the shopping population is Native. The Natives from the nearby reservations usually shop in Bemidji because that's where the stores are. Bemidji was not always a friendly place for Indians, though. In 1967, local resort owner and Beltrami County Commissioner Robert Kohl gave a live radio broadcast on KBUN in which he went on a racist rant, declaring that Indians were all drunks and leeches on the government. Kohl said that Indians "are so low on the human scale that it is doubtful they will ever climb upward . . . Perhaps we should have let nature take her course, let disease and malnutrition disrupt the reproductive process and weed out those at the very bottom of the heap."[74] The fact that Indians did half of the shopping in Bemidji and had none of the jobs was hard enough, but this was intolerable.

Red Lake Tribal Chairman Roger Jourdain led a boycott of Bemidji area businesses, soon joined by the people on the Leech Lake and White Earth reservations. The Bemidji Area Chamber of Commerce tried to apologize on Robert Kohl's behalf, but the boycott continued until Kohl himself apologized. Realizing the importance of his Native patrons, Joseph Lueken, owner of the local grocery chain, instituted an affirmative action employment policy after the boycott as well.[75]

The boycott was a big step forward in my community, but the Indian and non-Indian worlds still rarely interacted unless they had to. When interactions were unavoidable, they were often negative. Indians had to deal with non-Native police, lawyers, judges, teachers, and bankers. They often perceived their treatment to be racially biased. Some of that perception was based on a misplaced assumption that all non-Native people in positions of educational, political, and financial power were prejudiced against Indians (because so many of them had been in the past). But some of that perception was accurate. Independent studies of law enforcement in Bemidji have indicated a real issue with racial profiling in particular.[76]

Many White educators, bankers, and lawyers had negative attitudes about Indians, but many more wanted to get along with Native Americans. However, they were so terrified of offending angry Indians that they found it safer not to teach about them or take perceived risks by doing business with them.

How did we get from that dynamic to Alan Merschman engaging me in my tribal language with no outside pressure or formal training? Enter Michael Meuers, Rachelle Houle, and Noemi Ayelsworth. Together, these three non-Native people envisioned and carried out an ambitious initiative as part of Bemidji's antiracism organization, Shared Vision. Michael Meuers was the primary advocate for tribal language proliferation in Bemidji. He wanted welcome signs for local businesses and informational signs about bathrooms to be presented bilingually in the local tribal language (Ojibwe) and in English. When you travel to Hawaii, everyone knows what *aloha* means, and everyone in northern Minnesota should know what *boozhoo* means. Local heritage and language are part of what makes every place special. The idea of bilingual signage was also to present non-Native store owners with a safe way to reach out to Indian communities around Bemidji. Rachelle Houle joined him, going to door to door to convince area businesses to post their signs bilingually. Noemi Ayelsworth, owner of the Cabin Coffee House at the time, was the first businessperson to post bilingual signs and join the effort.

Soon, along with Eugene Stillday, a tribal elder and fluent speaker from Ponemah on the Red Lake Reservation, I joined a list of resource people to translate phrases, words, and signs. I worked with fellow staff at Bemidji State University to develop instructional materials available for free

Michael Meuers.

online. With no money, this grassroots effort soon convinced over 120 area businesses to put up bilingual signs, and the initiative continues to grow. The university, hospital, area schools, and regional events center all have bilingual signs, and Ojibwe language is proliferating throughout the community. Even the police cars in Bemidji have "to protect and serve"—"ganwenjigeng miinawaa naadamaageng"—printed on them in Ojibwe. It is now common to hear cashiers at Target engage tribal elders in Ojibwe. Alan Merschman is not alone. Indians feel welcomed in places where they never did before. Shop owners feel there is a safe way to reach out to Native clientele. Bilingual signage does not solve all the big problems. But it does enlarge the safe space in which we can talk about those big problems, and that's a huge start. And that start began through the advocacy of three non-Native people.

There are many ways to get involved. If you are not Native, there are many way to lean in to the efforts that tribal people have embarked on to improve their world. We need you. And trying to make a difference is not an act of charity for those less fortunate than you. It is something that elevates everyone's humanity and heals us all.

If you're Native, the best way to equip yourself as a change agent is to deepen your knowledge of yourself. Humans these days are often busy and stressed. If you find out what you are passionate about, work doesn't feel so much like work anymore. Find that passion and then figure out how it can intersect with a critical need for your tribe or community. Tribes have many kinds of jobs. They often have to hire non-Native people because there aren't enough tribal members or other Natives to fill those jobs. If you are inspired to be a teacher, nurse, community organizer, social worker, accountant, language speaker, writer, reporter, or web developer, your tribe will likely have work for you. If you need schooling to be credentialed to do that kind of work, go for it. It's worth the time and effort. If you want to help right now, there are many possibilities. Every tribe has a powwow committee that needs lots of volunteers. Social services and educational programs have many community outreach needs and opportunities. Social activism is always moving in Indian country. If you're passionate about environmental issues, you can volunteer to circulate petitions for legal action or help develop informational brochures or websites. Each tribe has its own cultural landscape; find out what's going on for your tribe. Often there are opportunities to participate, and frequently there are ways to help. Whether there is a sweat lodge ceremony, powwow, or other kind of ceremony, organizers may need help getting firewood, mowing grass, setting up, and cleaning up. These kinds of volunteer efforts can put you in touch with other culture-minded folks from your community, and the connections grow and often lead people to deeper explorations of their culture.

Sometimes the first person from your tribe you talk to isn't the right person to tell you who you should be in touch with. Stay patient and persistent. Native people are as busy as everyone else. If you're connected to your community, talk to family members and seek their advice. If you're not

Madeline Treuer and Jim Mitchell developing stories in the Ojibwe language for publication.

connected, don't despair. Read the tribal website listings for jobs and community events, go to events, talk to people. Once you get your foot in the door, things will develop a life of their own. Usually you will have better luck by contacting the office that runs programs you're passionate about. The tribal chair is probably scheduled for months in advance. But the Tribal Historic Preservation Office can let you know what's going on in their world. Most tribes have tribal newspapers and message boards too, covering everything from volunteer opportunities to jobs and cultural events. Most Natives, whether they grew up on a reservation or not, want to learn more about their culture. You're not alone.

The grassroots language revitalization effort in Hawaii that I mentioned increased the number of fluent speakers from 500 to around 23,000, and a few thousand of those speakers are White. Most were working in schools with Native Hawaiians and picked up the language as part of the effort to preserve and revitalize Native culture and language. Their involvement has been welcomed. In economic development, political networking and advocacy, education, health care, and many other fields, there are roles for Native and non-Native people. Indians are a tiny percentage of the population in this country, but in Minnesota and many other places they make up 20 percent of the homeless population. We need help with everything from education to grant writing and advocacy. If you are not part of the solution, you might be part of the problem. Teachers too afraid to teach about Indians are likely perpetuating stereotypes of Indians or erroneous versions of the Christopher Columbus story, alienating Native Americans without even realizing they are doing it.

It can be very frustrating for non-Native people to know how best to reach out to Indians or to help address the problems in Indian country. Most human beings are terrified of offending others or being accused of racism. Sometimes it seems safer and easier not to teach about Indians, not to learn more and more deeply about them, and not to advocate for change. But we have to be brave if we want to make the world a better place. So don't imagine Indians, understand them. Keep asking questions, reading, listening, and advocating for change. Don't tolerate stereotypes; don't be afraid to ask everything you wanted to know about Indians. And if you're Native, learn as much as you can about yourself and give meaningful responses to those questions rather than angry rebukes. It really does make a difference. In the words of my White mechanic, Alan Merschman, "Miigwech. Giga-waabamin miinawaa."[77]

RECOMMENDED READING

Tribal Language and Culture

Broker, Ignatia. *Night Flying Woman: An Ojibway Narrative.* St. Paul: Minnesota Historical Society Press, 1983.

Johnston, Basil. *Ojibway Heritage.* Lincoln: University of Nebraska Press, 1990.

Kegg, Maude. *Portage Lake: Memories of an Ojibwe Childhood.* Minneapolis: University of Minnesota Press, 1993.

Treuer, Anton. *The Language Warrior's Manifesto: How to Keep Our Languages Alive No Matter the Odds.* St. Paul: Minnesota Historical Society Press, 2020.

Early History

Blackhawk, Ned. *Violence over the Land: Indians and Empires in the Early American West.* Cambridge, MA: Harvard University Press, 2006.

Brown, Dee. *Bury My Heart at Wounded Knee: An Indian History of the American West.* New York: Holt, Rinehart & Winston, 1970.

Copway, George. *The Traditional History and Characteristic Sketches of the Ojibway Nation.* London: Charles Gilpin, 1850. Reprinted in the United States as *Indian Life and Indian History by an Indian Author: Embracing the Traditions of the North American Indians Regarding Themselves, Particularly of That Most Important of All the Tribes, the Ojibways.* Boston: Albert Cosby and Company, 1858.

Cronon, William. *Changes in the Land: Indians, Colonists, and the Ecology of New England.* Rev. ed. New York: Hill and Wang, 2003.

Josephy, Alvin, Jr. *500 Nations: An Illustrated History of North American Indians.* New York: Gramercy Books, 2002.

Koning, Hans. *Columbus: His Enterprise; Exploding the Myth.* New York: Monthly Review Press, 1991.

Kugel, Rebecca. *To Be the Main Leaders of Our People: A History of Minnesota Ojibwe Politics, 1825–1898.* East Lansing: Michigan State University Press, 1998.

Mann, Charles. *1491: New Revelations of the Americas Before Columbus.* New York: Knopf, 2005.

Meyer, Melissa. *The White Earth Tragedy: Ethnicity and Dispossession at a Minnesota Anishinaabe Reservation.* Lincoln: University of Nebraska Press, 1994.

Miller, Cary. *Ogimaag: Anishinaabeg Leadership, 1760–1845.* Lincoln: University of Nebraska Press, 2010.

Rethinking Columbus. Milwaukee, WI: Rethinking Schools, 1991.

Tanner, Helen Hornbeck, ed. *Atlas of Great Lakes Indian History.* Norman: University of Oklahoma Press, 1987.

Treuer, Anton. *The Assassination of Hole in the Day.* St. Paul: Borealis Books, 2010.

——. *Warrior Nation: A History of the Red Lake Ojibwe.* St. Paul: Minnesota Historical Society Press, 2015.

Warren, William W. *History of the Ojibway People.* St. Paul: Minnesota Historical Society Press, 1984. Originally published as *History of the Ojibways Based Upon Traditions and Oral Statements* (1885).

Legal History

Duthu, N. Bruce. *American Indians and the Law.* London: Viking, 2008.

Getches, David H., and Charles F. Wilkinson. *Cases and Materials on Federal Indian Law.* 2nd ed. St. Paul: West Publishing, 1986.

Wilkins, David. *American Indian Sovereignty and the U.S. Supreme Court: The Masking of Justice.* Austin: University of Texas Press, 1997.

Contemporary History and Government Indian Policy

Adams, David Wallace. *Education for Extinction: American Indians and the Boarding School Experience, 1875–1928.* Lawrence: University Press of Kansas, 1995.

Child, Brenda. *Boarding School Seasons: American Indian Families, 1900–1940.* Lincoln: University of Nebraska Press, 1998.

Dunbar-Ortiz, Roxanne. *An Indigenous Peoples' History of the United States*. Boston: Beacon Press, 2014.
Fixico, Donald L. *Termination and Relocation: Federal Indian Policy, 1945–1960*. Albuquerque: University of New Mexico Press, 1986.
Graves, Kathy David, and Elizabeth Ebbott. *Indians in Minnesota*. Minneapolis: University of Minnesota Press, 2006.
Hoxie, Frederick. *A Final Promise: The Campaign to Assimilate the Indians, 1880–1920*. Lincoln: University of Nebraska Press, 2001.
Olson, James, and Raymond Wilson. *Native Americans in the Twentieth Century*. Provo, Utah: Brigham Young University Press, 1984.
Prucha, Francis Paul. *The Great Father: The United States Government and the American Indian*. Lincoln: University of Nebraska Press, 1986.
Russell, Steve. *Sequoyah Rising: Problems in Post-Colonial Tribal Governance*. Durham, NC: Carolina Academic Press, 2010.
Treuer, Anton. *Ojibwe in Minnesota*. St. Paul: Minnesota Historical Society Press, 2010.

Perspectives and Philosophy

Alfred, Taiaiake. *Peace, Power, Righteousness: An Indigenous Manifesto*. Don Mills, Ontario: Oxford University Press, 2009.
Berkhofer, Robert Jr. *The White Man's Indian: Images of the American Indian, from Columbus to the Present*. New York: Vintage Books, 1978.
Deloria, Philip. *Playing Indian*. New Haven, CT: Yale University Press, 1998.
Deloria, Vine Jr. *Custer Died for Your Sins: An Indian Manifesto*. New York: Macmillan, 1969.
——. *Red Earth, White Lies: Native Americans and the Myth of Scientific Fact*. New York: Scribner, 1995.
Lyons, Scott. *X-Marks: Native Signatures of Assent*. Minneapolis: University of Minnesota Press, 2010.
Neihardt, John G. *Black Elk Speaks: Being the Life Story of a Holy Man of the Oglala Sioux*. Lincoln: University of Nebraska Press, 1979.
Russell, Steve. *Sequoyah Rising: Problems in Post-Colonial Tribal Governance*. Durham, NC: Carolina Academic Press, 2010.
Weatherford, Jack. *Native Roots: How the Indians Enriched America*. New York: Crown, 1991.

Literature

Alexie, Sherman. *Reservation Blues.* New York: Atlantic Monthly, 1995.
Erdrich, Louise. *Tracks.* New York: Henry Holt, 1988.
Momaday, N. Scott. *House Made of Dawn.* New York: Harper & Row, 1968.
Orange, Tommy. *There There.* New York: Alfred A. Knopf, 2018.
Silko, Leslie Marmon. *Ceremony.* New York: Penguin, 2006.

Books for Young Readers

Dimaline, Cherie. *The Marrow Thieves.* Toronto: Dancing Cat, 2017.
Gansworth, Eric. *Give Me Some Truth.* New York, Scholastic, 2018.
Gonzalez, Xelena, and Adriana Garcia. *All Around Us.* El Paso: Cinco Puntos Press, 2017.
Little Badger, Darcie. *Elatsoe.* New York: Levine Querido, 2020.
Mailhot, Terese. *Heart Berries.* Berkeley: Counterpoint, 2018.
Maillard, Kevin Noble, and Juana Martinez-Neal. *Fry Bread.* New York: Roaring Brook, 2019.
Sorell, Traci. *We Are Grateful: Otsaliheliga.* Watertown, MA: Charlesbridge, 2018.
Staples, Dennis. *This Town Sleeps.* Berkeley: Counterpoint Press, 2020.
Wagamese, Richard. *Indian Horse.* Toronto: Douglas McIntyre, 2012.
Welch, James. *Winter in the Blood.* New York: Penguin, 1974.

Video Documentaries

The Dakota Conflict (1993)
Dodging Bullets (2018)
First Speakers: Restoring the Ojibwe Language (2010)
500 Nations (1995)
Geronimo and the Apache Resistance (2007)
Incident at Oglala: The Leonard Peltier Story (1992)
Lighting the 7th Fire (1995)
Waasa Inaabidaa: We Look in All Directions (2002)
We Shall Remain (2009)
Woodlands: Story of the Mille Lacs Ojibwe (1994)

NOTES

1. "Becoming Visible: A Landscape Analysis of State Efforts to Provide Native American Education for All," IllumiNative, 2019.
2. There are no such references in Columbus's journals or letters. David Wilton did a good job exposing the untruth of this assertion in *Word Myths: Debunking Linguistic Urban Legends* (New York: Oxford University Press, 2004).
3. Sherman Alexie, reading, Schwartz Books, Milwaukee, WI, March 1993.
4. Ives Goddard, letter to the editor, *News from Indian Country*, mid-April 1997.
5. National Congress of American Indians Policy Research Center, "Policy Insights Brief: Statistics on Violence Against Native Women," February 2013.
6. Centers for Disease Control and Prevention, "National Intimate Partner and Sexual Violence Survey," 2010 Summary Report. Atlanta, Georgia: November 2011.
7. The Forest County Potawatomi (Wisconsin) and the Citizen Potawatomi Nation (Kansas) prefer *Potawatomi* to other spellings. Billy Daniels, Forest County Potawatomi elder, affirmed this spelling when I interviewed him. The Ho-Chunk Nation of Wisconsin prefers *Ho-Chunk* to the commonly used term *Winnebago*. The Assiniboine of Fort Belknap prefer *Assiniboine* to its numerous alternate spellings. The Menominee of Wisconsin prefer *Menominee* to the published alternatives. The Grand Traverse Band (Michigan) and Oklahoma Band of Ottawa (Oklahoma) both prefer *Ottawa* to the other versions of their name. These spellings are listed on each tribe's respective website and official tribal correspondence.
8. Charles C. Mann, 1491: *New Revelations of the Americas before Columbus*. New York: Knopf, 2005.
9. James Adovasio with Jake Page, *The First Americans: In Pursuit of Archaeology's Greatest Mystery* (New York: Random House, 2002); N. Guidon and G. Delibrias, "Carbon-14 Dates Point to Man in the Americas 32,000 Years Ago," *Nature* 321 (1986), 769–71; Robson

Bonnichsen and Karen L. Turnmire, *Clovis: Origins and Adaptations* (Corvallis: Oregon State University Press, 1991); Mary C. Stiner, "Modern Human Origins—Faunal Perspectives," *Annual Review of Anthropology* 22 (1993), 55–82; David Hurst Thomas, *Exploring Ancient Native America: An Archaeological Guide* (New York: Macmillan, 1994); David S. Whitley and Ronald I. Dorn, "New Perspectives on the Clovis vs. Pre-Clovis Controversy," *American Antiquity* 58, no. 4 (1993), 626–47; John Noble Wilford, "Support for Early Date of Arrival in America," *New York Times*, February 1, 1994; Charles C. Mann, *1491: New Revelations of the Americas Before Columbus* (New York: Knopf, 2005). Other sites under current excavation and investigation that challenge the Clovis First Theory include Channel Islands (California), Leech Lake (Walker, Minnesota), Big Eddy (Missouri), Page-Ladson (Jefferson County, Florida), Mud Lake and Schaefer-Hebior Mammoth (Kenosha County, Wisconsin), Paisley Caves (Oregon), Cactus Hill (Virginia), Tlapacoya, Lake Chalco (Mexico), Pedra Furada, Serra da Capivara National Park (Brazil), Lagoa Santa (Minas Gerais, Brazil), Cueva Fell and Pali Aike Crater (Patagonia), and Taima Taima (Venezuela).

10. Christopher Klein, "New Study Refutes Theory of How Humans Populated North America," *History*, updated August 29, 2018; Brian Handwerk, "Ancient DNA Reveals Complex Story of Human Migration Between Siberia and North America," *Smithsonian*, June 5, 2019.
11. George Catlin, *Letters and Notes on the Manners, Customs, and Conditions of North American Indians,* 2 vols. (New York: Dover Publications, 1973), 1: 238–40; Frances Densmore, *Chippewa Customs,* reprint ed. (St. Paul: Minnesota Historical Society Press, 1979), 135; George W. Featherstonhaugh, *A Canoe Voyage up the Minnay Sotor: With an Account of the Lead and Copper Deposits in Wisconsin; of the Gold Region in the Cherokee Country; and Sketches of Popular Manners* (St. Paul: Minnesota Historical Society Press, 2003), 1: 362–63; Basil Johnston, *Ojibway Ceremonies*, bison book ed. (Lincoln: University of Nebraska Press, 1990), 75–76; Edmund Jefferson Danziger Jr., *The Chippewas of Lake Superior* (Norman: University of Oklahoma Press, 1979), 24–25; Henry Lewis, *The Valley of the Mississippi Illustrated,* trans. A. Hermina Poatgieter (St. Paul: Minnesota Historical Society Press, 1967), 173–75; Samuel W. Pond, *The Dakota or Sioux in Minnesota: as They Were in 1834* (St. Paul: Minnesota Historical Society Press, 1986), 130–31; Henry H. Sibley, "Memoir of Jean Nicollet," *Collections of the Minnesota Historical Society* 1 (1902): 224; James H. Howard, *The Plains-Ojibwa or Bungi: Hunters and Warriors of the Northern Prairies, with Special Reference to the Turtle Mountain Band* (Lincoln: J&L Reprints Co, 1977), 104; Mary Eastman, *Dahcotah; or Life and Legends of the Sioux around Fort Snelling* (Minneapolis: Ross and Haines, 1962), xx.

12. Frederic Baraga, *Chippewa Indians, as Recorded by Rev. Frederick Baraga in 1847* (New York: Studia Slovenica, 1976), 45.
13. Reuben Gold Thwaites, ed., *The Jesuit Relations and Allied Documents,* 73 vols. (New York: Pageant Book Company, 1959), 59: 129, 310; Catlin, *Letters and Notes,* 2: 214–15.
14. Interviews, Earl Otchingwanigan (Nyholm), 1992; Mary Roberts, 1988, 1989; Archie Mosay, 1993; Dora Ammann, 1994; Thomas J. Stillday, 1995; Anna Gibbs, 1998. See also Erwin F. Mittelholtz and Rose Graves, *Historical Review of the Red Lake Indian Reservation: Centennial Souvenir Commemorating a Century of Progress, 1858–1958* (Bemidji, MN: Council of the Red Lake Band of Chippewa Indians and the Beltrami County Historical Society, 1957), 136; Martha Coleman Bray ed., *The Journals of Joseph N. Nicollet: A Scientist on the Mississippi Headwaters with Notes on Indian Life, 1836–37,* trans. André Fertey (St. Paul: Minnesota Historical Society Press, 1970), 165, 199–211; Walter Williams, *The Spirit and the Flesh: Sexual Diversity in American Indian Culture* (Boston: Beacon Press, 1992), 67–68, 110, 167–68; Alexander Henry and David Thompson, *New Light on the Early History of the Greater Northwest,* ed. Elliott Coues (New York: Harper, 1897), 1: 163–65; Louise Phelps Kellogg, *Early Narratives of the Northwest, 1634–1699* (New York: Charles Scribner's Sons, 1917), 244n; Vernon W. Kinietz, *Chippewa Village: The Story of Katikitegon* (Bloomfield Hills, MI: Cranbrook Press, 1947), 155; Peter Grant, "The Saulteux Indians about 1804," in *Les Bourgeois de la Compagnie du Nord-Ouest,* ed. L. R. Masson (Quebec City: Imprimerie, 1890), 2: 357; Catlin, *Letters and Notes,* 2: 214–15; Thwaites, *The Jesuit Relations and Allied Documents*, 59: 129, 310; Edwin James, ed., *A Narrative of the Captivity and Adventures of John Tanner: During Thirty Years Residence among the Indians in the Interior of North America* (London: Carvill, 1830; reprint, Minneapolis: Ross and Haines, 1956), 105–6; Densmore, *Chippewa Customs,* 87–89; John Parker, ed., *The Journals of Jonathan Carver and Related Documents*, bicentennial ed. (St. Paul: Minnesota Historical Society Press, 1976), 108–10; William W. Warren, *History of the Ojibway People*, reprint ed. (St. Paul: Minnesota Historical Society Press, 1984), 264; Pond, *The Dakota or Sioux in Minnesota,* 93–96, 124. An excellent secondary account is discussed in Rebecca Kugel, *To Be the Main Leaders of Our People: A History of Minnesota Ojibwe Politics* (East Lansing: Michigan State University Press, 1998), 71–73, 92n.
15. Interview, Mary Roberts, 1988.
16. I prefer the term *educational opportunity gap* over *achievement gap* but want to avoid confusion here.
17. Christopher Columbus, *The Four Voyages: Being His Own Log-Book, Letters and Dispatches with Connecting Narratives*, trans. J.M. Cohen (New York: Penguin, 1992).

18. Bartolomé de Las Casas, *History of the Indies* (1552), as cited in Alvin Josephy, Jr., *500 Nations* (New York: Pimlico, 2005).
19. Bartolomé de Las Casas, *History of the Indies* (1552), as cited in Alvin Josephy, Jr., *500 Nations* (New York: Pimlico, 2005), 114.
20. The state of Wisconsin passed Act 31, which mandates that all certified K–12 educators take a class on Indian history or culture, but the requirement is easily satisfied with a weekend workshop. Some public officials have also stated apologies, but here too the efforts have been small, scattershot, and largely unsupported by either the government or the general population.
21. The Minnesota state seal has a very similar image: a White farmer plowing the land as a symbol of progress, with an Indian riding into the sunset. The caption, in French, reads: "L'Étoile du Nord (The Star of the North)."
22. The Powhatan were a confederacy of thirty Algonquian tribes in Virginia in the sixteenth and seventeenth centuries. The term *Powhatan* has been used to refer to the largest tribe in the confederacy, the people of all tribes from the confederacy, the principal village in the confederacy, and its primary chief. Confederacy nations include the Powhatans, Arrohatecks, Appamattucks, Pamunkey, Mattaponis, Chiskiacks, Kecoughtans, Youghtanunds, Rappahannocks, Moraughtacunds, Weyanoaks, Paspaheghs, Quiyoughcohannocks, and Nansemonds.
23. Anton Treuer, *Ojibwe in Minnesota* (St. Paul: Minnesota Historical Society Press, 2010), 35; Jill St. Germain, *Indian Treaty-Making Policy in the United States and Canada, 1867–1877* (Lincoln: University of Nebraska Press, 2001). The decision to end treaty making with Indian tribes in 1871 was possible only when Indian nations could be treated as subjects of American policy rather than as independent nations.
24. *Merriam-Webster*, s.v. "genocide," accessed [2011].
25. Article 2, Convention on the Prevention and Punishment of the Crime of Genocide, United Nations, December 9, 1948. Text available at http://www.hrweb.org/legal/genocide.html.
26. Lord Jefferey Amherst, Commander of British North America Forces to Colonel Henry Bouquet, July 16, 1763. The letter was authenticated by Francis Parkman, and discussion of it is available at http://www.straightdope.com/columns/read/1088/did-whites-ever-give-native-americans-blankets-infected-with-smallpox.
27. "Alexander Ramsey," Alexander Ramsey House, https://www.mnhs.org/ramseyhouse/learn/alexander-ramsey.
28. Alexandra Pierce, "Shattered Hearts(Summary Report): The Commercial Sexual Exploitation of American Indian Women and Girls in Minnesota" report compiled for Minnesota Indian Women's Resource Center (August 2009): 11.

29. Jared Diamond, *Guns, Germs, and Steel: The Fates of Human Societies* (New York: Norton, 1999); Daniel Quinn, *Ishmael* (New York: Bantam, 1992).
30. Andrés Reséndez, *The Other Slavery: The Uncovered Story of Indian Enslavement in America* (Boston: Houghton Mifflin Harcourt, 2016); Alan Gallay, ed., *Indian Slavery in Colonial America* (Lincoln: University of Nebraska Press, 2009).
31. Philip Sheridan in 1874, as cited in Gilbert King, "Where the Buffalo No Longer Roam," *Smithsonian,* July 17, 2012.
32. Richard Dodge, as cited in J. Weston Phippen, "'Kill Every Buffalo You Can! Every Buffalo Dead Is an Indian Gone,'" *Atlantic,* May 13, 2016.
33. Interview, Billy Daniels, Potawatomi elder, 1996.
34. Interview, Thomas Stillday, 2006.
35. Leila Salazar-López, "Amazon Fires Ignite Global Movement to Protect the Planet," TEDxBerkeley, February 2020.
36. William T. Hagan, *Quanah Parker, Comanche Chief* (Norman: University of Oklahoma Press, 1993).
37. "State Urges Denial of New Trial Bid in Sweat Lodge Case," *Bemidji Pioneer,* July 26, 2011, 12.
38. For a copy of the Code of Indian Offenses, see http://tribal-law.blogspot.com/2008/02/code-of-indian-offenses.html.
39. There are a few scattered references to *powwow* as old as the late nineteenth century, but they are actually references to ceremonial Big Drum dances rather than to powwows as they are performed and understood today. Modern powwow culture emerged around World War II, and its current contest configurations developed in the 1970s.
40. Mii o'ow gidinwewininaan. Mii ow memadweyaashkaagin zaaga'iganiin miinawaa sa go gaye minweweyaandagaasing miinawaa sa go gaye minwewebagaasing ani-dagwaaging. Mii o'ow enitaagoziwaad bineshiinyag nagamotaadiwaad megwayaak miinawaa go ma'iinganag waawoonowaad, naawewidamowaad. Mii ow gidinwewininaan wendinigeyang bimaadiziwin, gikenindizoyang anishinaabewiyang, gidinwewininaan gechitwaawendaagwak gaa-ina'oonigooyang gimanidoominaan.
41. The Oneida case was dismissed by the Second Circuit Court of Appeals in May 2011 but is being appealed to the U.S. Supreme Court. Caitlin Traynor, "Oneida Indian Nation Appeals Land Claim Dismissal," *Oneida Daily Dispatch,* May 24, 2011.
42. Wendy Wang, "Interracial Marriage: Who Is 'Marrying Out?'" Pew Research Center, June 12, 2015.
43. Ada Deer as cited in Treuer, *Ojibwe in Minnesota,* 48.
44. The total number of terminated tribal governments is 109, including California Rancherías and Oregon tribal communities covered

in blanket termination policies and individual termination acts from 1953 to 1964. There are additional Native groups like the Lumbee that seek official federal recognition but lack a treaty-based government-to-government history with the United States since most are in the East, where they had relations with the British but lost most of their land before the American government came into existence.

45. Jeffery T. Ulmer and Mindy S. Bradley, "Punishment in Indian Country: Ironies of Federal Punishment of Native Americans," *Justice Quarterly* 35, no. 5: 751–81.
46. Public Law 280, Act of August 15, 1953, ch. 505, 67 Stat. 588. For background on and legal challenges to Public Law 280, see Kevin K. Washburn, "The Legacy of *Bryan v. Itasca County*: How an Erroneous $147 County Tax Notice Helped Bring Tribes $200 Billion in Indian Gaming Revenue" *Minnesota Law Review,* January 16, 2012; Harvard Public Law Working Paper No. 07-14, Minnesota Legal Studies Research Paper No. 07-37.
47. Bryan v. Itasca County, 426 U.S. 373 (1976). In *State of Minnesota v. Stone* and *State of Minnesota v. Jackson,* the Minnesota Supreme Court ruled that the state could not regulate most traffic laws on reservations for Indian defendants.
48. Information on AIM activism is taken from Paul Smith and Robert Warrior, *Like a Hurricane: The Indian Movement from Alcatraz to Wounded Knee* (New York: New Press, 1996).
49. Information on these AIM activities is taken primarily from "Concerned Indian Americans," charter statement; interview, Clyde Bellecourt, 1994; Russell Means, *Where White Men Fear to Tread: The Autobiography of Russell Means* (New York: St. Martin's Press, 1995).
50. All of the statistics on adoption and foster care of Native children, including the Minnesota-specific figures, are taken from expert testimony on the bill Public Law 95–608 (Indian Child Welfare Act), 9–10, 336–37. Information on impacts of the act and caseload numbers is taken from Kathy David Graves and Elizabeth Ebbott, *Indians in Minnesota,* 5th ed. (Minneapolis: University of Minnesota Press, 2006) 227, 238.
51. Graves and Ebbott, *Indians in Minnesota,* 91.
52. James Dao, "In California, Indian Tribes with Casino Money Cast Off Members," *New York Times,* December 12, 2011. Michigan and other states have seen many tribal members removed from the rolls in recent years as well. Disenrollment usually has less to do with blood quantum than with political infighting or per capita payments.
53. David L. Beaulieu, "Curly Hair and Big Feet: Physical Anthropology and the Implementation of Land Allotment on the White Earth

Chippewa Reservation," *American Indian Quarterly*, 8, no. 4 (Fall 1984): 281–314; William W. Folwell, *A History of Minnesota* rev. ed., (St. Paul: Minnesota Historical Society Press, 1956), 291–93; Anton Treuer, *The Assassination of Hole in the Day* (St. Paul: Minnesota Historical Society Press, 2010) 198–200.

54. White Earth has unsuccessfully tried to change the criteria for enrollment. Without support from the Bureau of Indian Affairs and the Minnesota Chippewa Tribe, it might never be able to do so.
55. "Death of a Tribe: Strict Standards May Doom Salish Kootenai," *Spokesman Review*, May 27, 1997; "Flathead Reservation Keeps Blood Quantum," *Indian Country Today*, January 24, 2003.
56. It is a mutually beneficial proposition. More people would be eligible for help from the tribes, yes, but expanding tribal membership would also give the tribes larger pools of voters, tribal political leaders, advocates, and educators. Waning membership means waning political power. Italy and Japan, for example, have declined in military and diplomatic position in the world in part because of lower birth rates relative to those of other countries.
57. Diane Wilson's *Beloved Child: A Dakota Way of Life* (St. Paul: Borealis Books, 2011) provides some great anecdotal examples of this dynamic.
58. Interview, Sean Fahrlander, September 2009. Fahrlander placed the emphasis on *land*, to clarify that he was serving his people and his place, not the U.S. flag. He also added, "Things were so bad on the reservation that what we were going to was no worse than what we were coming from."
59. Graves and Ebbott, *Indians in Minnesota*, 95. This data is for the enrolled tribal population. The number of self-identified Indians living on a reservation is much smaller.
60. Seminole Tribe of Florida v. Butterworth, 657 F.2d 310 (U.S. Court of Appeals, Fifth Circuit 1981).
61. *Woodlands: The Story of the Mille Lacs Ojibwe*, oral history video documentary (Onamia, MN: Mille Lacs Band of Ojibwe, 1994); interviews, Melvin Eagle, 2008; James Clark, 2002; Luella Seelye, 2009; David Wallace Adams, *Education for Extinction: American Indians and the Boarding School Experience, 1875–1928* (Lawrence: University Press of Kansas, 1995); Tim Giago, *Children Left Behind: Dark Legacy of Indian Mission Boarding Schools* (Santa Fe, NM: Clear Light Publishing, 2006); Brenda Child, *Boarding School Seasons: American Indian Families, 1900–1940* (Lincoln: University of Nebraska Press, 1998); James Olson and Raymond Wilson, *Native Americans in the Twentieth Century* (Urbana: University of Illinois Press, 1986); Frederick Hoxie, *A Final Promise: The Campaign to Assimilate the Indians, 1880–1920* (Lincoln: University of Nebraska Press, 2001); Graves and Ebbott, *Indians in Minnesota*, 16–17, 192–93; Colin Calloway, *First Peoples: A Documentary*

Survey of American Indian History, 2nd ed. (Boston: Bedford/St. Martin's, 2004), 335–96; Janet Chute, *The Legacy of Shingwaukonse: A Century of Native Leadership* (Toronto: University of Toronto Press, 1998).

62. Captain Richard Henry Pratt, as cited in Charla Bear, "American Indian Boarding Schools Haunt Many," National Public Radio (May 12, 2008).
63. Commissioner of Indian Affairs William A. Jones, speech to Congress, 1899.
64. The Canadian government issued a formal apology for residential boarding school abuses and a procedure for reparations to those who were abused. The testimonies and reports from that process give us a clear indication of the patterns and molestation rates in Canada. See also Lewis Merriam, *The Problem of Indian Administration: Report of a Survey Made at the Request of Honorable Hubert Work, Secretary of the Interior, and Submitted to Him, February 28, 1928* (Baltimore: Johns Hopkins University Press, 1928), better known as the Merriam Report.
65. All statistics about the health conditions and death rates at the residential schools are taken from the Merriam Report.
66. Michael Krauss, "Status of Native American Language Endangerment," in Gina Cantoni, ed., *Stabilizing Indigenous Languages* (Flagstaff: Northern Arizona University, 1996), 17.
67. Cinnamon Janzer, "States Move to Add Native American History to Curriculum," *US News & World Report,* November 29, 2019.
68. Frederick Douglass, "West India Emancipation," Speech at Canandaigua, New York, August 3, 1857.
69. Graves and Ebbott, *Indians in Minnesota,* 284–85; *Minnesota Statewide Racial Profiling Report: Beltrami County Sheriff's Department,* report to Minnesota State Legislature by the Institute on Race and Poverty, September 23, 2003; Chris Williams, "In Minnesota, Claims of Racial Profiling Indians," *News from Indian Country,* 2002.
70. Lawrence Greenfield and Steven Smith, "American Indians and Crime," U.S. Department of Justice, Bureau of Justice Statistics, 1999; Leah Sakala, "Breaking Down Mass Incarceration in the 2010 Census: State-by-State Incarceration Rates by Race/Ethnicity," Prison Policy Initiative, May 28, 2014; Jake Flanagan, "Native Americans Are the Unseen Victims of a Broken US Justice System," *Quartz,* April 27, 2015; Lakota People's Law Project, "Native Lives Matter," February 2015; Graves and Ebbott, *Indians in Minnesota,* 284–85; *Minnesota Statewide Racial Profiling Report,*; Williams, "In Minnesota, Claims of Racial Profiling Indians."
71. Martin Luther King Jr., Selma to Montgomery March, 1965, based on King's paraphrase of a sermon by Theodore Parker in 1853.

72. Some studies have proven that it is for many Indians. *Minnesota Statewide Racial Profiling Report;* Williams, "In Minnesota, Claims of Racial Profiling Indians."
73. For Indians living on trust property owned by the tribe, there is an additional obstacle to obtaining loans for housing because the property cannot be mortgaged to a bank, another issue that Whites have the privilege of never having to worry about.
74. Chuck Haga, "A Long Year at Red Lake: From Condemnation to Compassion During a Crisis," *Minneapolis Star Tribune,* March 14, 2006.
75. Interview, Thomas Stillday, 2006; Haga, "Long Year at Red Lake."
76. *Minnesota Statewide Racial Profiling Report;* Williams, "In Minnesota, Claims of Racial Profiling Indians."
77. "Thank you. I'll see you again."

PHOTO CREDITS

p, 18, 86, 94, 113, 117, 120–121, 124, 133, 141, 155 (right), 164, 170–171, 186, 221, 225, 233, 281, 346, 349: courtesy of the author
p. 38: photo by John H. Fouch, ca. 1877, courtesy of Dr. James Brust
p. 96, 114, 140, 264, 297: Shutterstock.com; p. 44, Everett Collection / Shutterstock.com; p. 188–189, Victorian Traditions / Shutterstock .com; p. 246–247, Felix Mizioznikov / Shutterstock.com; p. 295, miker / Shutterstock.com
p. 48: Lifetime Learning Systems, Inc.
p. 49: engraving by Theodore de Bry, University of Houston Libraries
p. 54: *American history*, by Marcius Willson
p. 57: painting by Simon van de Passe, National Portrait Gallery
p. 59, 76: National Archives
p. 61, top: painting by John Mix Stanley, Granger Collection
p. 61, bottom: painting attributed to Owen Staples, Toronto Library
p. 65: painting by John Gast, Autry Museum of the American West
p. 66: *New York Times*
p. 78–79: Burton Historical Collection, Detroit Public Library
p. 90: Wisconsin Historical Society Library
p. 102–103: Pax Ahimsa Gethen
p. 138: photo by Warren K. Leffler, Library of Congress, U.S. News & World Report Magazine Collection, LC-U9- 36362A-21A; p. 204: photo by J. A. Anderson, Library of Congress, LC-USZ62-102187; p. 211 (top right): Library of Congress, LC-USZ62-101459; p. 264 (top): Library of Congress, LC-USZC4-4961
p. 142 (top): Alexander Jonesi
p. 142 (bottom): NABI Foundation, PO Box 25606, Phoenix, AZ 85002-5606, www.NABIFoundation.org, 501 (c) (3) Non-profit Corporation
p. 152–153 (left and middle), p. 154–155: Nedahness Greene
p. 195: Indianz.com
p. 209: SPUTNIK / Alamy Stock Photo
p. 210–211 (bottom): National Guardian Photographs, NYU Libraries
p. 211 (top): DC Public Library, Washingtoniana Division
p. 231: U.S. Army Signal Corps
p. 243: John Lloyd

p. 257: National Anthropological Archives, Smithsonian Institute NAA_73383; Photo Lot 81-12 06815700
p. 258–259 (bottom): http://www.texasbeyondhistory.net/forts/images/carlisle.html *Frontier Forts*
p. 259 (top): Beinecke Rare Book & Manuscript Library, Yale University
p. 260: Keith Stokes
p. 269: Courtesy of Ke Kula ʻO Nāwahīokalaniʻōpuʻu
p. 273, 274–275, 276–277: Josué Rivas
p. 290: United Nations Photo Library
p. 293: @rrrrrrrachh
p. 302: Minnesota Historical Society
p. 325: *End of the Trail.* James Earle Fraser, 1915, plaster. National Cowboy & Western Heritage Museum. 1968.01.01
p. 326: Ben Powless
p. 333: Chickasaw Nation and Rosetta Stone

ACKNOWLEDGMENTS

This book was originally published by the Minnesota Historical Society Press, and developing it into its current form would not have been possible without the gracious permission and support of Josh Leventhal and Ann Regan and the fine editorial scrutiny of Cary Miller, Ann Regan, and Shannon Pennefeather, all of whom helped me refine my ideas and presentation at MHS. My work grew in new directions and evolved in presentation through the attention and support of Nick Thomas at Levine Querido. My time devoted to this project was in part enabled by support from the American Philosophical Society, the Bush Leadership Fellows Program, and the John Simon Guggenheim Foundation.

Thank you to Michael Meuers for suggesting the title for this book and the lecture series that inspired it and for his leadership in promoting bilingual signage in Bemidji along with Rachelle Houle and Noemi Ayelsworth. Thanks also to Rose Jones, whose advocacy helped make the development of free online Ojibwe resource material a reality. Thank you to those who shared the podium with me for some of the "Everything You Ever Wanted to Know" events, including Donald Day, Benjamin Burgess, Renee Gurneau, and Minnie Oakgrove. I am also deeply indebted to Rose Tainter, Thelma Nayquonabe, Monique Paulson, Lisa LaRonge, Lisa Clemens, Alex Decoteau, Cathy Begay, and Michelle Haskins for assistance with cultural information. Thank you to Andrew Wickert for fact-checking the section on Clovis. Thanks to Jill Doerfler for feedback on enrollment. Miigwech to Gerald Auginaush and Michael Meuers for help with pictures.

I received lots of support while writing this book and traveling on the lecture series that inspired it. Special thanks to Alfred Bush; Thomas Stillday; Anna Gibbs; Eugene Stillday; Archie Mosay; Dora Ammann; Brooke Ammann; Sean Fahrlander; Keller Paap; Lisa LaRonge; Rick and Penny Kagigebi; Isadore Toulouse; Daniel and Gail Jones; Dennis Jones; Dustin Burnette; Charles Grolla; James Hardy; Adrian Liberty; Henry Flocken; Diane Amour; Donna Beckstrom; Donovan Sather; Jordyn Flaada; Chato Gonzalez; Melissa Boyd; Paul and Betty Day; Donald and Priscilla Day; Benjamin and Tahnee Burgess; Collette Dahlke; Stephanie Hendricks; Thomas Goldtooth; Ted Waukey; Leon Valliere; Linda Wade; Irene Benjamin; Skip and Babette Sandman; Leonard and Mary Moose; Michael and Krysten Sullivan; Mark Pero; John Patrick; John Daniel; Michael, Midge, Frank, and Mark Montano; Jim Barta; Dick Hanson; Faith Hensrud; and Nancy Erickson.

I have a large and incredible family that has been my greatest strength in all that I do. I am especially indebted to my parents, Robert and Margaret Treuer; my siblings, Smith, Paul, Derek, Megan, Micah, and David Treuer; and their spouses. My children have been forced to share me with the rest of the world because of my ceremonial obligations and academic work. Their generosity always amazes me. Thank you to Jordan, Robert, Madeline, Caleb, Isaac, Elias, Evan, Mia, and Luella. My wife, Blair Treuer, really deserves to have her name on the cover of every book I write because she gives so much to the effort. I could never say thank you enough to show my real appreciation.

INDEX

A Tribe Called Red, 143
Aboriginal (as word), 13
abortion, 123, 291
Acoma people, 113
Act 31, Wisconsin, 359n
adoption and foster care, 68, 213–216
affirmative action, 318–319, 344
Afghanistan, War in, 231, 233
Africa, 43–44, 68, 75, 292
agricultural age, 36, 69–71
Akwesasne Freedom School for Mohawk, 270
Alamo, 300
Alaska, 31, 55; Alaska Natives and Alaska Native corporations, 184–185, 283
Albuquerque, New Mexico, 149
Alcatraz takeover, 210
alcohol and substance abuse, 7, 40, 179, 223–227, 236, 238, 304, 330–331, 343
Aleut language, 163
Alexie, Sherman, 15, 315–317
Alfred, Taiaiake, 309
Algonquian people, 34, 89, 125, 359n; languages of, 17, 24, 89
allotment, 181, 183, 187–192, 194, 196, 198
American Indian (as term), 14
American Indian Movement, 14, 138, 203, 210–213; AIM Legal Rights Center, 212; AIM Patrol, 212; American Indian Opportunities Industrialization Center, 212; burning of Custer courthouse, 212
American Indian Religious Freedom Act, 138–141, 331
American Library Association, 317
American Progress, 65
American Revolution, 72
Amherst, Jefferey, 67
Amish people, 92, 177
Anasazi people, 118
Ancestry.com, 322–323
anger, 6, 329–332, 339, 345, 351
Anishinaabe (as word), 20
antiracism, 345
Apache people, 67, 197, 234
apple (as word), 262
Apsáalooke (Crow) people, 38, 95; language of, 163
Arapaho people, 77
archaeology, 29–33, 34
architecture, 118–119
Arctic, 34, 68
Arizona, 32, 66, 113, 137, 143, 164, 237, 293
Armenia, 76
art and artists, 76, 98, 114–115, 148, 334–337; Institute of American Indian Arts, 317. *See also* beadwork; kachinas
Asia, 34, 43, 45, 68–69
Asian people, 198, 311
Assassination of Hole in the Day, The 337

Assembly of First Nations, 194
assimilation, 40, 70, 73, 100, 109, 116, 166, 172, 181, 187, 200, 219, 226–227, 238, 242, 262, 265, 321
Assiniboine of Fort Belknap, 21, 356n
Association on American Indian Affairs, 213
Atakapa people, 328
Auginaush, Joseph, 190–191
Auschwitz, 51
Australia, tribal peoples in, 101, 220, 286
Austria, 51
authenticity, 87, 97–98, 137, 298, 334–336
Ayelsworth, Noemi, 345–346
Aztec Empire, 22, 29, 118

Bad Boy, Damien, 139–140
Bagone-giizhig (Hole in the Day), 37, 126, 271
Bahamas, 46
Baldwin, James, 312
Balsam Lake, Wisconsin, 120
bands, 21, 23–24 90; *band* (as word), 23
banks and banking, 105, 249, 313, 344–345, 364n
Baptist church, 74, 109
Baraga, Frederic, 26
baseball, 141
basketball, 77, 142–143
baté (as word), 38
Battle of Brownstown, 63
Battle of Fallen Timbers, 62
Battle of Point Pleasant, 62
Battle of the Thames, 63
beadwork, 77, 86, 98, 147, 149–151
beavers and fur trade, 99
Bellefontaine, Ohio, 62
Beltrami County, Minnesota, 282, 344
Bemidji Area Chamber of Commerce, 344
Bemidji State University, 167, 346
Bemidji, 1, 25–26, 141, 284, 343–347
bilingualism and bilingual signage, 345–347
bin Laden, Osama, 234–235
birch bark, 168
birth rate, 143–144
Bismarck, North Dakota, 278–279
bison, 77–80, 99, 236
Black Elk, 324; *Black Elk Speaks*, 324
Black Lives Matter, 276, 285–288
Black people, 17, 52, 198, 262–263, 285–288, 292, 311, 320, 321, 336; Black Natives, 15, 80–81, 214, 223, 286, 321
Blackfeet people, 24, 42, 197; Blackfeet Nation, 24; Blackfeet Indian Reservation, 24
Blackhawks (as mascot name), 293, 296
blankets, 136, 280; blanket dances, 159; smallpox blankets, 67
blood quantum, 42, 216–222
blueberries, 99, 124, 130
Bois Forte Reservation (Minnesota), 207–208
borderland, 1-7, 343
bounties, 34–35, 78, 293
boycotts, 344
boys, 89–90, 128, 132–134
brave (as word), 17; "brave" competitions at powwows, 157
Brock, Isaac, 63
Brown, Dee, 324
Brown, Kirby, 137
buffalo. *See* bison
Bureau of Indian Affairs, 20, 182, 193, 194, 207, 230, 257; takeover of by AIM, 211–212
Bureau of Indian Education, 265
Bury My Heart at Wounded Knee, 324
Bush, George H. W., 52–53

Caddo people, 328
California Rancherías, 360-361n

California v. Cabazon Band of Mission Indians, 248
California, 18, 67, 76, 105, 206, 218, 248, 299–300
Canada, 22, 24, 33, 63, 79–80, 93, 141, 163–165, 172, 199, 214, 216, 220, 221, 225, 229, 289, 304, 311, 316, 322; Canadian government, 13–14, 19, 40–43, 68, 86, 177–182, 187, 194, 237, 243, 246, 259, 261, 320, 326–328, 330, 331
Canary Islands, 45
Cannonball River, 273, 278
Cape of Good Hope, 43–44
Caribbean, 14, 29
caribou, 102
Carlisle Indian Industrial School, 257–262
Carnegie Medal, 317
Carter, Hodding, 255
casinos, 9, 97, 177, 217–218, 224, 237–238, 245–254, 268, 329, 343
Catawba people, 201
Catholic Church and Catholics, 48, 71–75, 92, 108–109, 116, 291, 299, 336. *See also* Christianity and Christians
catnip tea, 125
cedar, 131
ceremonies, 4, 6–7, 25, 35, 39, 76, 83, 87, 90–91, 96–98, 104, 106, 110–116, 122, 136–137, 139, 147, 151, 156–159, 166, 179, 221, 223, 225, 232, 281–282, 348; coming of age, 88, 104, 128–134; drum, 111, 136–137, 147, 151, 158–159, 199; longhouse, 87, 90; naming, 126–127, 150. *See also* drums and drumming; powwows; religion and spirituality; sweat lodges
cession, land, 165, 185, 189, 190
Chaco Canyon, 118
Chauvin, Derek, 287
checks and balances, 193, 229
Cherokee Freedmen, 80–81
Cherokee people, 80–81, 181, 183, 320–321, 323–324; Cherokee language, 163, 169
"Cherokee princess" claims, 320–321
Cheyenne people, 77
Chicago Blackhawks, 293, 295–296
Chicago, 30, 198
Chickasaw people, 183; Chickasaw language, 333
Chief Buffalo, 90
Chief Joseph, 271
Chief Massasoit, 56
Children in Need of Protection or Services (CHIPS) petition, 215
children, 2, 37, 40, 57, 62, 65, 67, 68, 75, 80, 85–86, 88, 96, 110, 115, 122–127, 134, 143–144, 163, 175, 184, 191, 209, 213–216, 221–222, 255–270, 279, 281, 327. *See also* boys; girls; infants
Chile, 31, 33
China, 32, 43
Chippewa (as word), 19–20. *See also* Ojibwe
Chitimacha people, 231, 328
Choctaw people, 183, 328
Christianity and Christians, 32, 48, 69–75, 98, 108–112, 115–116, 135, 141, 172, 248, 257–258, 321. *See also* Catholic Church and Catholics; mission schools; mission system; missionaries
Chukchi people, 33
Chumash people, 76, 299
Circular 1665, 139, 331
circumference of globe, knowledge of, 45
civil rights movement, 263, 311
Civil War, 57, 59–60, 76, 318
clans, 89–91
Clark, James, 136

clothing, 6, 37, 39, 77, 93, 97-98
100, 136, 170, 257, 261, 297
clouded title, 190-192
Clovis First Theory, 31-32
Coates, Ta-Nehisi, 312
Cobell v. Salazar, 192
Cochiti Pueblo people, 89, 110
Code of Indian Offenses, 139
Cody, William "Buffalo Bill", 78-79
Coeur d'Alene, 317
College of Menominee Nation, 101
colleges and universities, 141-142, 200, 265, 267-268, 270, 312, 318-320
Collier, John, 261
colonization and colonialism, 22-23, 36, 40-41, 44, 54, 67, 70-73, 76, 110, 165-166, 230, 328
Columbian Exchange, 54-55
Columbus, Christopher, 9, 11, 14-15, 29-30, 33-34, 43-56, 72, 75, 111, 263, 300, 332, 350
Comanche people, 4, 77, 111
community, 24, 91, 104-106, 108, 116, 134-135, 149, 157, 173, 184, 199, 216-223, 226-230, 282
Comstock, William, 79
concentration camps, 51, 180
Confederacy, 60, 300, 303
Connecticut, 245
Cook, George, 203
Coquille people, 201
cornmeal, 112
corporate governance model, 193-194, 229
costumes, 297-298
cottonwood, 115
courts, 41-42, 140, 191-192, 206, 209, 214, 248, 282; Courts of Indian Offenses, 205; Minnesota Supreme Court, 361n; U.S. Court of Claims; 191-192. *See also* tribal courts
COVID-19, 227-228
Covington Catholic High School, 291-293
cowry shell, 151
cradleboards, 123-125
Crazy Horse, 77-78
Creator, 112, 115-116, 161. *See also* Great Spirit
Cree people, 17, 23; Cree language, 17, 163, 168
Creek (Muscogee) people, 183
Crow Dog, 203-205
Crow Dog, Leonard, 203
Curtis Act, 183

da Gama, Vasco, 43
Dachau, 51
Dakota Access Pipeline and protests at, 103, 273-282
Dakota people, 16, 20, 21, 32, 67, 89, 126, 147-148, 158, 233, 245, 301; Dakota language, 21, 163, 165, 303; Dakota War of 1862, 67; Spirit Lake, 32
dance arbor, 148-149, 151
Dance Me Outside, 337
Dances with Wolves, 3, 87, 336
dances, 89, 94, 106, 114, 116, 139, 145, 156-159, 164, 335; Big Drum, 360n, blanket, 159; fancy dance, 150, 153, 298; fancy shawl, 151, 154; grass, 148, 150, 152-153, 158; jingle dress and jingle dress healing songs, 148, 151, 153-154; men's traditional, 149, 152; scalp, 35, 148; Sun Dance, 87, 137; wacipi, 147; war, 147, 148-149; women's traditional, 151, 154. *See also* ceremonies; drums and drumming; powwows; regalia; religion and spirituality
Daniels, Billy, 356n
Dawes Act, 183, 187, 189
de Bry, Theodore, 49
de Champlain, Samuel, 34
de Las Casas, Bartolomé, 29-30, 48, 50, 53, 74
Deer, Ada, 201

Deloria Jr., Vine, 2, 11
Democrats, 107, 237, 251
Denver, 198
Depp, Johnny, 298–299, 336
diabetes, 96
DiAngelo, Robin, 312
Dias, Bartolomeu, 43
Diné people (Navajo), 21, 23, 85, 227–228, 231, 259, 336; Diné language (Navajo), 93, 163–164, 333, 336
Dior, 298–299
discovery (as word), 43, 50
disease and illness, 29, 67, 75, 258, 260, 344
Doctrine of Discovery, 51, 68–73, 108
Dodge, Richard, 77
dog soldier, 147–149
Dominican Republic. *See* Española
dreams, 126, 150, 151
Dremousis, Litsa, 317
drums and drumming, 111, 136–137, 147, 150–151, 158–159, 199, 360n. *See also* ceremonies; dances; powwows; religion and spirituality
Dutch people, 41, 75, 182

Eagle Bear, Barrett, 4–5
Eagle, Melvin, 96–97
East Coast, 29–30, 105
East Lake, Minnesota, 119–120
education and schools, 2, 4, 15–16, 40, 50, 52, 108–109, 141, 164, 167, 173, 180, 194–196, 199, 234, 238, 244, 249, 250–251, 253, 254, 255–270, 279, 282, 287–289, 292–297, 311, 312, 318–320, 327, 329–330, 345, 348, 350, 359n; curriculum in schools, 8–9, 48, 50, 53–55, 226, 263, 269, 301–302, 311, 331–332. *See also* residential boarding schools; tribal languages
Egypt, 32
elders, 33, 134, 171–172
Enbridge, 282
End of the Trail, 324–326
Energy Transfer Partners, 278–279
England and English people, 23, 26, 29, 32, 40–41, 44, 56–58, 60–63, 67, 68, 71–72, 74, 75, 104, 181, 182, 328
English language, 17, 24–25, 156, 163–164, 166, 167, 169–171, 257, 262, 265, 267, 307, 330, 332, 345
enrollment, 20, 42, 81, 173, 180, 183–184, 186, 192, 198–199, 214, 216–222, 241, 244–245, 260, 267, 322–324; disenrollment, 218, 362n. *See also* blood quantum; lineal descent
enslaved people and slavery, 46–47, 52, 57, 72, 75–76, 80–81, 118, 299, 303, 318–319, 328
environmental and ecological stewardship, 98–104, 195, 273–282, 287, 290, 327, 348
Episcopal church, 73–74, 109
Eratosthenes, 45
Erdrich, Louise, 84
Española, 29, 46–49
eugenics, 218
Europeans, 20–22, 26, 29–30, 34–36, 39–40, 75–80, 87, 99, 106, 118–119, 121, 147, 163, 168, 185, 309, 322
Every Student Succeeds, 266–267
Ex Parte Crow Dog, 203–205

Falls of St. Anthony, 301–302
farming, 37, 54, 56, 69, 99, 130, 199, 250, 280, 359n
fasting, 88–89, 115, 126, 132, 137, 150
Father Hennepin, 301–302; *Father Hennepin Discovering the Falls of St. Anthony*, 302
Father Junípero Serra, 299

FBI, 202–210, 305
feasts, 106, 127, 130, 134
feathers, 4, 91, 111, 111, 147, 149–150, 324; eagle feathers, 147, 150, 232, 297
Ferris, Jean Leon Gerome, 264
Fertile Crescent, 69–70
First Nations and First Nations people, 13–14, 40–43, 163–165, 177–182, 187, 199, 216, 220, 243, 246–247, 259, 289, 326–328; Canadian Aboriginal Festival, 148; Canadian Citizenship Act, 181–182; Constitution Act, 194; *First Nations* (as term), 13; sovereignty, 178
First Thanksgiving, The, 264
fishing, 36, 41, 69, 92, 96, 101, 101–104, 130, 132, 184, 185–187, 199, 201, 222, 236, 250, 278. *See also* treaties
Flagstaff, Arizona, 113
Flathead Reservation (Montana), 219
Florida, 238, 245, 248; Florida State University, 295–296
Floyd, George 287, 296
fluency rates, 163–165
food, 37, 54, 68–70, 77, 96, 99, 104–105, 123, 130–131, 134–136, 151, 280
football, 143, 288, 293, 296
forestry, 99, 101, 200
"49" songs, 156. *See also* music and musicians
four directions, 76, 125
Fox people, 67
France and French people, 17, 21, 34, 41–42, 44, 61, 71–72, 74, 75, 91, 156, 182, 328
Fraser, James Earle, 325
fraud, land, 190–192, 218. *See also* clouded title
freedom of speech, 299–301, 334
Freire, Paulo, 271
French and Indian War, 34, 67
frontier age, 41
fry bread, 95–96
funerary beliefs and practices, 85, 92, 105, 109, 124, 135, 164, 179, 253

garbage, 98–100
Gast, John, 65
Gathering of Nations, 149
gathering, 37, 69, 94, 101, 185, 199
gender 36–40, 106–108, 147–148, 151, 158–159, 314
genocide, 30, 32, 42, 52, 55–56, 62, 64–68, 72, 73, 299, 320, 327–328, 330
Georgetown, 26
German Americans, 92–95
Germanic languages, 25, 95, 163, 169
Germany, 27, 51, 95
Geronimo (code name), 234
Gibbs, Anna, 84, 164
gifts, 88, 97, 114, 127, 136, 151, 159, 161, 222
girls, 90, 128–134
giveaways, 139, 157, 159
Goddard, Ives, 17
gold, 45–47, 319
Goodman, Amy, 280
Grand Traverse Band (Michigan), 356n
grants, 182, 194, 202, 244, 350
Graves, Peter, 207
Great Lakes Indians and region, 3, 26, 30, 34–35, 60–63, 68, 74, 76, 80, 87, 99, 110, 111, 118, 122, 129, 141, 150–151, 286; Great Lakes Inter-Tribal Council, 196
Great Spirit, 33, 88, 123. *See also* Creator
Greece, 32; Greek language, 25, 169–170
Guacanagari, 46
Guatemala, 119
Gulf War, 232–233

hair, 75, 85–86, 120, 171, 218–219, 257, 313–314, 337
Haiti. *See* Española
Halloween, 297–298
Hamilton, Ontario, 148
Hard Rock Café, 247, 332
Harrison, William Henry, 63
harvest, 3, 56, 68–69, 94, 99, 103–104, 114, 130, 132, 200, 221–222, 236, 250
Haskell Indian Nations University, 260
Haskell Institute, United States Indian Industrial Training School, 260
Haudenosaunee (Iroquois) people, 34, 87, 90, 290. *See also* Mohawk; Oneida; Onondaga; Seneca
Havasupai, 163
Hawaiian people, 164, 283; Hawaiian language, 109, 163, 269–270, 303, 345, 350
Heart of the Earth Survival School, 212–213
Hebrew language, 167–168
heredity and ancestry, 91–92, 95, 216, 320–324. *See also* blood quantum; enrollment; lineal descent
high-stakes bingo, 248
historical trauma, 100, 226, 242, 262, 319, 329–332
Hitler, Adolf, 27, 76–77
Ho-Chunk (Winnebago), 21, 54, 112, 126, 142; *Winnebago* (as word), 21
hockey, 141, 296
hogans, 87, 227
Holocaust, 51–52, 319–320
homelessness, 68, 350
homesteads, 105, 187
homosexuality, 38, 107–108
Hopi people, 32, 113–114, 128; Hopi language, 163
Houle, Rachelle, 345–346
Houma people, 328
Hrdlička, Aleš, 218
Hudson Bay, 69
Hull, William, 63
human origin in the Americas, 30–33
human trafficking, 304–306
humor, 95–96, 135, 169–171
hunting, 41, 69, 77–80, 92, 101–104, 132–134, 149, 151, 184–187, 199, 201, 250. *See also* treaties

Ice Age, 68–69
identity, 9, 38, 83–95, 97, 104–108, 182, 214, 219–223, 236–237, 269–270, 298, 313, 320–324
Illinois, 252
immigrants, 32, 198
Incident at Oglala, 209
India, 43, 45, 76
Indian (as word), 14–15
Indian agents, 139, 182, 193
"Indian cars," 97–98
Indian Child Welfare Act, 213–216
Indian Citizenship Act, 181
Indian Claims Commission, 191
Indian Gaming Regulatory Act, 248
Indian names, 88, 126–128; namesakes, 88, 127, 129–130, 232; naming ceremonies, 126–128, 150
Indian Reorganization Act, 193, 194–197, 200, 206
Indian Self-Determination and Education Assistance Act, 194
"Indian time," 83, 96–97
Indiana, 62
Indigenous (as word), 14
Indigenous People March, 291
Indigenous Peoples' Day, 55–56
infants, 85, 123–126, 213
interracial Natives, 15, 80–81, 90–91, 158, 214, 223, 286
interracial relationships, 120–122, 198

intertribal (as word), 158
Inuit (Eskimo) people, 13, 33, 68, 181, 243, 259; Inuit language, 163, 165
Inupiat people, 33
involuntary sterilization, 68
Iraq War, 233
Iroquoian languages, 89. *See also* Haudenosaunee (Iroquois) people
Islam, 44, 70–72, 112, 115–116
Isleta people, 113

Jamestown, 57
Japan, 69, 104
Jenks, Albert, 218
Jones, Nancy, 117–118
Jourdain, Gordon, 161
Jourdain, Roger, 344
Judaism, 70, 112, 115–116, 135, 141
jurisdiction, 2, 177–178, 183, 186–187, 192, 202–208, 235, 241–245, 283, 305

kachinas, 113–115
Kaepernick, Colin, 288
Kansas, 63, 109, 260, 356n
Kenny's Clark Station, 343
Kentucky, 62, 291
Kinew, Wab, 341
King Philip's War, 56–57
kinnickinnick, 112. *See also* tobacco
kivas, 110
Klamath people, 201
Koenig, Bronson, 142
Kohl, Robert, 344
Kootenai people, 219
Korean War, 232

Lac La Croix First Nation (Ontario), 161, 164
lacrosse, 60, 141
Laguna people, 113
Lake Bemidji, 26
Lake Calhoun, 303
Lakota people, 21, 21, 23, 67, 77, 126, 203, 236; Lakota language, 21, 163; land claims, 192
land-bridge theory, 30–31
land; acknowledgments, 328–329; claims cases, 23, 191–192; conceptions of ownership, 185, fraud, 190–192, 218; speculators, 188; trusts, 105, 187–189, 192, 197, 201, 241. *See also* allotment; cession; relocation; surplus
Language Warrior's Manifesto, The, 166
Latin language, 25, 44, 54, 169
Latinx people, 263, 288, 311
latitude and longitude, 45
Leech Lake Reservation (Minnesota), 1, 148, 197–198, 220–221, 253, 344
LGBTQ people, 38–40, 106–108. *See also baté*; homosexuality; *two-spirit*
life expectancy, 286
Lincoln Memorial confrontation, 291–292
lineal descent, 217, 321–322
Lone Ranger, The, 298, 336
Longest Walk protest, 138
Louisiana Purchase, 72
Louisiana, 328
Lueken, Joseph, 344
Lumbee people, 182, 361n
Lutheran church, 72
Lyons, Oren, 175, 290
Lyons, Scott, 175

MacArthur, Douglas, 231
Mahnomen, Minnesota, 139
Maine, 55
Major Crimes Act, 196, 205–208, 305–306
Makah, 101–104, 222
Manifest Destiny, 65
Manitoba, 134

Manitoulin Island, 165
maple, 87, 125; maple syrup processing, 3, 221
March for Life, 292
marijuana legalization, 235–237
marriage, 36–37, 40, 80–81, 90–91, 119–122, 198, 321–322
Marshall Trilogy, 178
Marx, Karl, 68
mascots, 9, 288, 292–297, 312, 343
Massachusett language, 17, 24, 147. *See also* Algonquian people
Massasoit, 56
Mayan people, 118; Mayan languages, 164, 168
McCain, John, 237
McIntosh, Peggy, 312
Mdwakantonwan Dakota (Minnesota), 245
Meadowcroft Rockshelter, Pennsylvania, 31
medicine, 4, 54, 75, 85, 88–89, 96, 111, 113, 131, 137, 141, 164; fake medicine men, 136–137
Mediterranean, 43
Menominee Nation, 21, 101, 158, 183, 189, 200–201, 207, 280
menstruation, 129–131
Merriam Report, 260–261
Merschman, Alan, 343, 345, 347, 351
Meskwaki people, 85, 126, 177, 296
Metacom (King Philip), 56–57
Methodists, 74, 109
Métis people, 13, 42, 165, 182, 243, 259, 322
#MeToo, 315–317
Meuers, Michael, 8, 345–346
Mexico, 30, 46, 108, 119, 163–164
Michigan, 60, 103, 123, 141
Michilimackinac, 60
Middle East, 36, 43, 69–70, 72
Midwest, 93, 95
Mille Lacs, 85, 96, 136, 171, 195, 220, 232–233, 249
Milwaukee, 14, 30, 48, 198–199
mining, 101, 188, 190, 290, 327
Minneapolis, 1, 198–199, 210, 212–213, 287
Minnesota, 1, 18, 23, 25, 26, 55, 67, 72, 83, 92, 102–103, 108, 119, 126, 139, 141, 143, 165, 189, 195–196, 198, 206–207, 212–216, 218, 220, 224, 241, 245, 248–249, 253, 282–283, 287, 293, 309, 343–347; Indian Family Preservation Act, 215; Minnesota Chippewa Tribe, 196–197; Minnesota Historical Society Press, 7; state capitol building, 300–304; state seal, 359n; Supreme Court, 361n
missing women, 289, 304–306
mission schools, 258. *See also* residential boarding schools
mission system, 76, 299
missionaries, 37, 73–75, 76, 108–111, 165, 168, 172, 181, 257. *See also* Catholic Church and Catholics; Christianity and Christians
Mississippi River, 25–26
Mitchell, Jim, 349
Mohawk people, 85, 181, 270; language, 17, 163, 270
Montana, 24, 143, 219
Monte Verde, Chile, 31
Moose, Leonard, 85, 125
Mormon church database, 322
morphemes, 169, 171
Mosay, Archie, 119–120
movies, 41, 87, 91–92, 298, 336–337
murders, 202–209, 287, 289, 296, 304–305
music and musicians, 114, 137, 143, 145, 147–148, 156–159, 269, 335–336

Nakota people and language, 21
Narragansett language, 24, 147
Natchez people, 328
nation (as word), 24. *See* sovereignty

National Congress of American Indians, 14, 195, 296
National Indian Education Association, 195
National Summit for Courageous Conversation, 286, 328
Native (as word), 14
Native American (as term), 14
Native American Basketball Invitational, 142
Native American Church, 109, 111, 112, 141
Native American Rights Fund, 14
Navajo. *See* Diné people
Nawahi school, 269
Nebraska, 54, 109, 206
Nelson Act, 196
Nevada, 245, 247, 251
New Jersey, 4, 6, 99, 252
New Mexico, 31, 66, 110, 143, 149
new world (as term), 45, 48, 50, 53
New York, 26, 30, 58, 105, 141, 192, 270
New Zealand, tribal peoples in, 220, 286
Ni'ihau (Hawaii), 164
Nigigoonsiminikaaning First Nation (Ontario), 117
niiyaw (as word), 122, 127
niiyawe'enh (as word), 127
9/11, 234
No Child Left Behind, 265-267
non-federally-recognized tribes, 42, 182-185, 200-201, 214, 267
North Carolina, 55, 182
North Dakota, 79, 273, 278-280
Northern Cree, 143

Oakland, 198
Obama, Barack, 279-280
Oceti Sakowin (Seven Council Fires), 21. *See also* Dakota; Lakota; Nakota; Sioux
offerings, 112, 113, 132, 134, 136
Office of Indian Affairs, 193-194, 205
official apology, 51-52, 319-320, 330, 344, 363n
Ojibwe people, 9, 22-23, 37, 40, 42, 72, 76, 85, 90, 96-97, 106, 117, 120-123, 125-127, 129-135, 145, 147-148, 151, 158, 164, 166, 186, 196, 210, 217, 221, 233, 236, 249, 252, 309; Chippewa, 19; Great Flood story, 69; Ojibwe language, 17, 19-21, 25, 92, 163, 168, 170-172, 265, 270, 307, 333, 343, 345, 347, 349
Oklahoma Band of Ottawa (Oklahoma), 356n
Oklahoma, 4, 63, 74, 80, 107, 109, 183, 237; Oklahoma Land Rush, 187-189
Old Northwest War, 62
Omaha people, 148, 291; Omaha Grass Dance Society, 150
Oneida, 16; land claims of, 192, 360n
Onondaga people, 181
Opechancanough, 57
Oregon, 23, 55, 206, 360-361n
Orman, Suze, 239
Osh-Tisch, 38
oshki-nitaagewin (as word), 132
Otchingwanigan, Earl, 123, 125
Ottawa people, 21, 60-61, 126, 356n; Ottawa language, 163
Ottawa, Canada, 30, 326

papal bulls (bulla), 71-72
papoose (as word), 17
Parker, Ely, 58-60
Parker, Quanah, 111
Patuxet people, 56
Pawnee people, 231
Peltier, Leonard, 209-210
Pennsylvania, 31, 92
Pequot people, 56, 245; Mashantucket Pequot, 148
per capita payments and entitlements, 249-251, 253-254

Peter Pan, 336–337
peyote, 109, 111, 139–141
philanthropy, 246
Phillips, Nathan, 291–292
Phoenicia, 32
Pilgrims, 56
Pima people, 231
Pine Ridge Indian Reservation, 209, 210–212
pipelines and oil, 101, 276–278, 289
Pipestone Singers, 143, 145
place names, 25–26; changing of, 16, 18, 299–304
Plains Indians and region, 3, 30, 35, 62, 74, 87, 89, 110, 141, 150, 286
Plymouth, 57
Pocahontas, 57–58; *Pocahontas* movie, 336–337
Poland, 51
policing and incarceration by non-Natives, 141, 177, 183, 202–203, 206–210, 212, 243, 280, 282–287, 305–307, 313–315, 332, 338, 344–345, 347
polygamy, 36–37, 119
Polynesians, 33, 51, 69
Ponemah, Minnesota, 92, 105, 346
Pontiac, 60–61
Poor Bear, Myrtle, 209
Pope, 71–73, 116
population numbers; growth rate of, 144, 219; percentage of general, 18, 41, 83, 101, 311, 350; pre-contact, 29–30, 46
Portugal, 43–44
positions of power, Natives in, 311
Potawatomi people, 21, 112, 126, 158, 222, 356n; Citizen Potawatomi Nation (Kansas), 332, 356n; Forest County Potawatomi, 90, 356n
poverty, 60, 68, 74, 97–98, 99–100, 167, 172, 179–180, 185, 212, 225–226, 232, 238, 242, 245–246, 249, 252, 260, 262, 268, 318, 327, 331
Powhatan Confederacy, 57–58, 359n
Powwow Highway, 337
powwows, 42, 87, 95, 98, 111, 143, 145–159, 172, 199, 232, 297, 339, 348, 360n; contest powwows, 148–149, 150, 156–157; *powwow* (as word), 24–25; "princess" and "brave" competitions, 157
Pratt, Richard Henry 257
prayer, 35, 116, 121, 127, 135, 151, 281
pregnancy and childbirth, 88, 122–127, 130, 143–144
primitive communism, 68
Princeton University, 3–4, 7, 318
Prophetstown, 62
Ptolemy, 45
public art and statues, 299–304
Public Law 280, 186, 196, 202, 205, 206–209, 243
Pueblo people, 32–33, 87, 89, 106, 110, 112, 113–116, 118, 128, 197, 217, 222; Tiwa and Tewa (Pueblo) languages, 163, 169
Puerto Rico, 253
Puritans, 57

Quincentenary Jubilee Commission, 52–53

racial ambassadorship, 5–10, 347–351
racism, 3, 17, 36, 59, 65, 199, 206, 212–216, 219–220, 222–223, 233–235, 260, 276, 282–284, 286–288, 292–296, 298, 300–301, 303, 305–307, 312–315, 318–321, 329–330, 337–338, 344–345, 350, 364n
Ramsey, Alexander, 67
Rapid City, South Dakota, 286
Ratcliffe, John, 57–58

Rattling Leaf, James, 286
Ray, James Arthur, 137
Red Cliff Ojibwe, 186
Red Cloud War, 77
Red Jacket, 58
Red Lake Reservation, 83, 92, 97, 105, 108, 164, 189, 207, 220, 282–283, 294, 344, 346; Red Lake Warriors, 294
"Redneck Woman", 294–295
Redskins, 293, 296; *redskin* (as word), 17
regalia, 114, 147–155
religion and spirituality, 32–33, 73–76, 83–89, 92–93, 95, 98–99, 105, 109–116, 122–141, 148, 151, 157, 225, 330–331. *See also* ceremonies; drums and drumming; sweat lodges
relocation, 54, 64, 67, 73, 80, 189, 192, 197–199
reparations, 51–52, 319, 327, 363n
Republicans, 107, 237, 251, 306
reservation (as word), 23–24
reserves (as word), 13
residential boarding schools, 2, 40, 68, 75–77, 86, 109, 165, 172, 257–262, 327, 330–331; sexual abuse in, 75, 259, 327, 363n
revitalization of traditional culture, languages, and religion, 9, 104, 109–110, 149, 165, 166–168, 172–173, 196, 225–227, 238, 263–265, 269–270, 327, 332, 350
Rice, Henry, 72
roach, 149–150
Roberts, Mary, 39–40, 134
Rolfe, John, 58
Rolfe, Thomas, 58
Romance languages, 163
Rosebud Indian Reservation, 203
Rosetta Stone, 333
Ross, Gyasi, 271
round Earth, knowledge of, 44–45
Russia and Russian people, 41, 67, 104, 182

sachem (as word), 58
sage, 111
Salazar-López, Leila, 83, 101
Salish people, 219, 236
Sami people, 101
San Francisco Peaks, 113
San Francisco, 30
Sandpiper Pipeline, 282
Sandy Lake (Minnesota), 195
Santee, Nebraska, 54
Sault Ste. Marie Ojibwe, 252
Sauvage, 298–299
scalping, 34–35, 66, 85, 147, 149, 293; scalp dance, 35, 149
scholarships and financial aid, 184, 192, 222, 267–268
Schoolcraft, Henry, 26
scientific method, 117–118
Section 87, Indian Act, 243
Sedona, Arizona, 137
Seelye, Eugene, 235
self-identified Indians, 198–199, 217, 219, 222
self-referential labels, 16, 19–21
Seminole people, 183, 238, 245, 247–248, 295, 332
Seminole Tribe of Florida v. Butterworth, 248
Seneca people, 58–60, 181
Sequoyah, 169
settlers and settlement, 27, 30, 57, 62–65, 183, 187–188, 193, 328
Seven Council Fires. *See* Oceti Sakowin
sexism, 313–314, 315–317
sexual assault and violence against women, 17, 205, 305–306, 316
sexual identity, 38–39, 107
Shared Vision, 345
Sharp, Fawn, 195
Shawnee people, 61–63, 298
Sheridan, Philip, 77
Sherman, William Tecumseh, 62

Siberia, 31
Siege of Detroit, 63
Siege of Fort Meigs, 63
Sinclair, Murray, 327
Sioux people and language, 21, 67; *Sioux* (as word), 21
Smith, John (Ojibwe elder), 76
Smith, John, 57–58
Smoke Signals, 337
smudging, 111, 131
snaring rabbits, 3, 132–133, 221
social activism, protests, and demonstrations, 7, 100–103, 138, 201, 210–213, 271–282, 291–306, 332, 348; cooperative action in, 276, 285–290
social media and technology, 18, 108, 164, 290, 299, 332–334, 339
social service agencies, 68, 213–216, 244, 251, 279, 348
soldiers, warriors, and veterans, 35, 58–63, 85; military traditions, 147–149, 232, 294; service in U.S. military, 59–60, 147–149, 181, 231–235
soul or spirit, 35, 113, 122–124, 126–127, 135,
South America, 29, 30, 33, 37, 69, 108, 163, 178, 220, 289
South Dakota, 55, 209, 212, 245, 247, 251, 279, 286
Southeast, 80
Southwest, 76, 87, 113–114, 118
sovereignty, 9, 13, 15, 22, 24, 40–43, 64, 104, 166, 177–183, 196, 200–201, 203, 206–208, 220, 237–238, 243, 246, 248, 306, 318, 329; *sovereignty* (as word), 177
Spain and Spanish people, 14–15, 21, 29–30, 41, 43–56, 67, 74–76, 110, 182, 299, 328
spelling, 19–22, 24–26
Spotted Tail, 203
squaw (as word), 17–19
St. Croix Ojibwe (Wisconsin), 217
Standing Rock Reservation, 103, 273–282, 332
status (as word), 216
stereotypes and myths, 3, 7, 30, 50, 56, 87, 91–92, 100, 143–144, 180, 224–226, 249, 268–269, 292, 301–302, 337–338, 350–351
Stillday, Eugene, 346
Stillday, Thomas, 83, 97
surplus, land, 187–188
swastika, 76–77
sweat lodges, 4, 88, 136–137, 139–141, 348
syllabics, 168–169

Tadoussac, 34
Taino (Arawak), 46–48
taxes, 167, 177–178, 183, 200–201, 241–245, 253
Tecumseh, 61–63
Tennessee, 140
Tenskwatawa, 62
termination, 182–183, 200–201, 207
Texas, 4
Thanksgiving, 10, 56–57, 224, 263–264, 332
Thomas X, 143
timber, 188, 190
tipis, 77, 87, 111
Tisquantum (Squanto), 56
tobacco, 88, 97, 112–113, 125, 127–128, 132, 134, 136, 141; dogwood, 113; red willow, 113
“tomahawk chop,” 292
Tonkawa people, 77
Torlino, Tom, 259
Toronto, 30, 148
totems. *See* clans
trade routes, 43
traditional (as word), 92–95; art, 76, 114–115; food, 96, 130; lifeways, 3, 41, 91–94, 101–104, 250; powwows, 148, 150–151, 157, 333; values, 38, 39, 73, 76, 97–100, 107, 127, 141, 147, 195,

traditional (as word) (*continued*) 224, 226, 249, 250. *See also* art and artists; ceremonies; music and musicians; religion and spirituality; revitalization of traditional culture, languages, and religion; tribal governments; tribal languages
"traditional fry bread taco," 95–96
Trail of Broken Treaties, 211–212
Trail of Tears, 80, 294
transgender identity and people, 38, 106–108
treaties, 23, 41, 58, 64, 72, 74, 147, 175, 177–180, 182, 184–187, 190, 193, 196, 201, 203, 211, 242, 329–330, 343; treaty period, 22–23, 37, 58, 64, 203; treaty rights, 177–178, 185–186, 329, 330, 343
Treuer family, 86, 94, 113, 124, 133, 221, 286, 309, 349
tribal courts, 183, 201–202, 206–208, 214–215, 229
tribal government(s), 19, 21–24, 41–42, 148–149, 168, 172, 175–197, 200–201, 216–220, 223–224, 228–230, 235–239, 241, 244, 248–250, 252–254, 312, 318; business operations, 177, 183, 200, 235–237, 249–250, 252–254, 268–269, 290, 332; collective efforts, 289–290; confederated tribal governments, 23, 195; chairs and leaders, 24, 168, 172, 185, 193-194, 202–203, 207, 228–230, 237–238, 242, 287, 301–303, 349; constitutions, 20, 23, 41, 193–194, 197, 229
tribal housing, 184, 198, 241, 250, 253
tribal languages, 91–93, 161–173, 177, 182, 217, 219–220, 226–227, 339, 350; academic achievement, 166–167; deeper meaning, 25–26, 169–172; destruction of, 15, 42, 73, 75, 93, 104, 163, 257–261; fluency rates, 41, 163–165; oral, 169; revitalization and schools, 93-95, 109, 167–168, 197, 213, 238, 265, 267, 269–270, 327, 330, 332–333, 350
tribal license plates, 243–244, 282–283, 313, 337
tribal police, 177, 201–209, 304–306
tribe (as word), 24
Trudell, John, 1
Trump, Donald, 280
Truth and Reconciliation Commission, 42, 320, 326, 328
Tunica people, 328
Turtle Mountain, 322
two-spirit (as term), 39, 107

U.S. Army, 61–63, 77–78, 148, 181, 231–235,
U.S. citizenship, 139, 180–181, 231, 236, 244
U.S. county government(s), 208, 214–216, 241–244, 282, 284, 305, 344
U.S. federal government, 20, 23, 40–42, 52, 58–60, 64, 68, 74, 77, 95, 105, 139, 141, 177, 180–195, 197–216, 218, 223, 228–230, 241, 244–245, 247, 248, 253–254, 260, 266, 283, 305, 330; commissioner of Indian Affairs, 60, 139, 258, 261; Congress, 64, 181, 187, 193, 201–203, 206, 306; Constitution, 42, 64, 72, 139, 186, 229, 242, 329; Court of Claims, 191–192; Department of Health, 68; Department of the Interior, 187, 194–195; Supreme Court, 72, 178, 183, 193, 203, 248
U.S. state government(s), 20, 139,

141, 166, 177–178, 181–182, 186, 192, 203–208, 214–215, 235, 241–245, 248, 251–253, 262–266, 279–280, 300–303, 305, 318
Union Army, 59–60
United Nations, 65, 268, 289–290; U.N. Declaration on the Rights of Indigenous Peoples, 289
University of Mary in Bismarck, 279
urban Indians, 105, 116, 197–200, 212, 213, 237
usufructuary rights, 185

Vicksburg, 60
Vietnam War, 232–233
Vikings, 33, 51
villages, 22–23
Violence Against Women Act, 305–306
Virginia, 57–58, 216
visions, 88, 115–116, 126, 158–159
Volk, Stephen A. Douglas, 302
voting in U.S. elections, 107, 181, 237, 301, 362n
Voting Rights Act, 181

Waadookodaading Ojibwe Language Institute, 166, 265, 270
Wahunsenacawh, 57–58
Wampanoag people, 56
War of 1812, 62–63
Warren, Elizabeth, 323–324
Washington, 23, 104
Washington, D.C., 291–292, 300
Washington, George, 26, 50
water, 25–26, 101, 104, 114, 130, 227, 278, 282, 327
Watson, Lilla, 341
ways of knowing, 33, 117–118
welfare, 194, 201, 244–245, 337
West Coast, 30
West Indies, 57
Western tribes, 151
whaling, 101–104
Whipple, Henry, 74
White Earth Reservation, 139, 190, 197, 218, 220, 344
White people, 1–8, 15, 17–18, 27, 35, 54, 56–57, 65, 79, 102, 111, 120, 122, 137, 169, 183, 187–194, 198, 205, 214, 222–224, 232–234, 262–263, 278–279, 282–284, 292, 295, 298, 301–304, 307, 321, 336, 338, 343, 345, 350–351; apathy; 329–331; fears, 304; guilt, 30, 320; privilege, 312–313, 315, 319, 329, 335, 364n
white pine, 125
wigwams, 7, 87, 129
wild rice, 3, 94, 96, 130, 221, 236, 250
Wilson, Gretchen, 294–295
Wilton, David, 356n
Wind, Nodin, 83
Wisconsin, 54, 90, 101, 103, 120, 125, 166, 189, 192, 196, 201, 206, 217, 245–246, 265, 270, 356n; state seal, 54
Wise, Tim, 312
World War I, 151, 181, 231–232
World War II, 231–232, 234–235, 261
Wounded Knee, South Dakota, 209; Occupation of, 210–212; Massacre at, 324
Wray, Link, 298

Yupik people, 33; Yupik language, 163

Zuni people, 113

SOME NOTES ON THIS BOOK'S PRODUCTION

The art for the jacket and case was created by Jana Schmieding (Lakota), who, when imagining a cover for this book, pulled from her own experience as an adolescent educator and teacher of young adult text. She combined the two-needle appliqué style and contemporary seed bead colors to portray a take on the traditional floral designs of the Ojibwe, the nation to which the author belongs. The text was set by Westchester Publishing Services in Danbury, CT, in ITC Legacy Serif, a hand-drawn revival of Nicolas Jenson's 15th-century types, designed by Ronald Arnholm in 1993. The display was set in Intro and Nexa Rust Sans, two approachable sans serifs. The book was printed on FSC™-certified 98gsm Yunshidai Ivory paper and bound in China.

Production was supervised by
Leslie Cohen and Freesia Blizard

Book jacket and case designed by
Rodrigo Corral Studio

Book interiors designed by Suet Chong

Edited by Nick Thomas

LEVINE QUERIDO